THE VALUE

MOTIVE

THE VALUE

MOTIVE

The Only Alternative
to the Profit Motive

Paul Kearns

BICENTENNIAL
1807
WILEY
2007
BICENTENNIAL

John Wiley & Sons, Ltd

Other Wiley Editorial Offices

John Wiley & Sons Inc., 111 River Street, Hoboken, NJ 07030, USA

Jossey-Bass, 989 Market Street, San Francisco, CA 94103-1741, USA

Wiley-VCH Verlag GmbH, Boschstr. 12, D-69469 Weinheim, Germany

John Wiley & Sons Australia Ltd, 42 McDougall Street, Milton, Queensland 4064,
Australia

John Wiley & Sons (Asia) Pte Ltd, 2 Clementi Loop #02-01, Jin Xing Distripark,
Singapore 129809

John Wiley & Sons Canada Ltd, 6045 Freemont Blvd, Mississauga, ONT, L5R 4J3,
Canada

Wiley also publishes its books in a variety of electronic formats. Some content that
appears in print may not be available in electronic books.

Library of Congress Cataloging-in-Publication Data

Kearns, Paul.
    The value motive : the only alternative to the profit motive / Paul Kearns.
        p.   cm.
    Includes bibliographical references and index.
    ISBN 978-0-470-05755-1(cloth : alk. paper)
    1. Management.   2. Leadership.   3. Value.   4. Organizational effectiveness.
    I. Title.
    HD31. K37 2007
    658.4'092—dc22
                                                                    2006036076

British Library Cataloguing in Publication Data

A catalogue record for this book is available from the British Library

ISBN 978-0-470-05755-1 (HB)

Typeset in 11.5/15pt Bembo by SNP Best-set Typesetter Ltd., Hong Kong
This book is printed on acid-free paper responsibly manufactured from sustainable forestry
in which at least two trees are planted for each one used for paper production.

CONTENTS

ABOUT THE AUTHOR   ix

PREFACE   xi

INTRODUCTION   xix

**1 PROFIT IS NOT A DIRTY WORD BUT VALUE
   IS MUCH CLEANER**   1

Is profit the best way to allocate scarce
   resources?   1
Profit can be a very emotive word   7
The Microsoft Paradox   11
Not-for-profit? Does that mean
   not-for-value?   17
Profit is an increasingly unpopular king   22

2 VALUE – A VERY SLIPPERY WORD INDEED — 29

Defining value — 29
A working definition of value — 34
Basic value — 37
Moving on to added value — 41
Private equity partners – value adders
    or asset strippers? — 44
The value motive already exists — 47
Value as a distillation process — 51
Declaring value in a public statement — 54
The value agenda — 62
A value statement for a commercial company — 63
A value statement for a public sector organization — 68
'Intangibles' confuse the issue of added value — 71

3 THIS POWERFUL MOTIVE FORCE WE CALL VALUE — 77

Harnessing the power of motive — 77
Value means output, not input — 80
Defining value as an economic system — 85
Does the capitalist system deliver the best value? — 88
When we say value we should really mean it — 92
A holistic value system for everyone — 96

4 VALUE HAS TO BE THE RAISON D'ÊTRE FOR EVERY TYPE OF ORGANIZATION — 101

All value is good — 101
Value is the raison d'être of all organizations — 103
Corporate social responsibility (CSR) and the 'triple'
    bottom line — 106
Social enterprise — 117
Is the public sector an obsolete construct? — 120

5 ORGANIZATIONAL PERFORMANCE MEASUREMENT HAS TO MEASURE VALUE   127

Turning human activity into value   127
The advent of the scorecard   130
The EFQM business excellence model   134
Agreeing value priorities using the 3 Box System   136
The gulf between performance measurement theory
    and practice   142
Activity, performance and added value measures   150
Taking a fresh perspective on the purpose of
    performance measurement   153
Measuring and managing 'intangibles'   156
E-valu-ation   161

6 VALUE IS ESSENTIALLY A PEOPLE THING   167

A fresh approach to people management   167
Measuring the value of people   171
Debunking the employee–customer–profit chain
    theory   176
Replacing performance management with value
    management   178
Managing value holistically   185
Valuing people 'intangibles'   187

7 THE PEOPLE MEASUREMENT 'BOX'   193

Only meaningful measures count   193
People measurement is a really serious matter   199
Does diversity add value?   205
Human capital management, a revolution in
    management thinking   210
People – are they personnel, human resources,
    assets or capital?   214
Human capital measures and indicators of value   216

8 **HOW THE VALUE MOTIVE COULD UPSTAGE THE PROFIT KING**   223

The value motive *is* leadership   223
The politician's definition of value   231
The first, second and third sectors have to
    become one   236
Value special cases and dead losses   241
Value management education   245
Auditing the value motive   249
A new management discipline – valuing the human
    contribution   252

INDEX   259

ABOUT THE AUTHOR

Paul Kearns started his career specializing in industrial relations management in 1978. He then moved into human resource management roles in engineering, construction and manufacturing businesses. His last corporate role in 1991 was sitting on the management team of an automotive business where he became acutely aware, for the first time, that managing value and managing profit were two entirely different objectives. He found, in particular, that managing the human aspects of organizations to create value had become probably the biggest management issue of modern times and one that had no easy solution and no single, coherent methodology. Since then he has been working in this field as a consultant, writer, teacher and business conference speaker. His writing has drawn a great deal of attention from both the business and academic worlds, although he has always regarded himself, first and foremost, as a pragmatic practitioner. As a consequence he regards his work as bridging the divide between academic theory and management practice. He teaches on MBA programmes and trains managers to understand the wealth creating opportunities presented by a more enlightened approach to people management. He has written eight books and is a regular, thought-provoking contributor to both academic and professional journals.

Paul was born in 1955 in Leicester (UK) and has a degree in economics and economic history. He is married to Nuala and they have three grown-up children.

Visit:

www.paulkearns.co.uk
www.TheNewburyIndex.com

email: info@paulkearns.co.uk

Other relevant books and essays by Paul Kearns include:

One Stop Guide – Human Capital Management (Reed Business Publishing, 2004).
HR Strategy: Business Focused, Individually Centred (Butterworth Heinemann, 2003).
Leadership Under the Microscope. (Defining and Measuring the Value of Leadership) (Leadership Trust, Ross-on-Wye, UK 2005).
Evaluating the ROI from Learning (CIPD, 2005).

PREFACE

As both a manager and consultant, with 30 years' working experience, I have never, ever come across an organization in which it was not easy to find many opportunities to create significantly more value (although Toyota came close). You might think, therefore, that I am always welcomed with open arms by the management teams I work with. On the contrary. If a management team is already 'hitting its targets' or 'keeping the city happy' or giving shareholders adequate returns then why should they put any more effort into unearthing and delivering such opportunities? The job of management is difficult enough already. So, this is the area I want to explore, the motivation, or lack of it, for producing extra value. But I also want to explore what trying to maximize value really means. What would any organization have to do to achieve this goal? Would it be that difficult or complicated to try to maximize value? Or would the pursuit of value actually simplify things? In fact it is the absence of simplicity and common sense in organizations that really intrigues me.

I have come across so many examples of organizations where common sense does not seem to prevail that every time I write an article or a book I have one overriding aim, to promote common sense as a guiding principle. I see change management initiatives where there is no clear focus, and no one knows how they are meant to add value; performance targets that no one is really committed to; management development and leadership programmes that have no business objectives. These, and many, many more examples of unfocused organizational activity, are all likely to fail because no one knew how to articulate what value they might add. Without articulating a common goal of maximum value the chances of achieving maximum value are negligible.

I have also tried to write a book that will be easy to read, even though, at times, some of the underlying philosophies and theories might appear very complex. My main purpose though is to construct a coherent case for a different type of organizational, motive force. What I have termed 'the value motive' is not only designed to complement and augment the profit motive but it also, potentially, is to become a universal, driving force behind all other types of organization.

I would hasten to add though that I, personally, have no problem with the profit motive. It has stood the test of time remarkably well and has proved itself, time and time again, to provide society with great wealth. In the absence of a better alternative I will remain a fully paid-up subscriber. I aim to make as much profit as I can out of my own business. The way I do that, with all of my commercial, profit-driven clients, is to try to help them make as much profit as they can out of theirs. Our combined desire to make profits benefits us both and should benefit their customers as well. Success breeds success and the profit motive, when employed to best effect, can produce a marvellous virtuous cycle. Unfortunately, the profit motive is not always automatically used to best effect and, in the worst cases, could be described as having a perverse or detrimental impact (environmental damage being one of the most obvious examples).

Regardless of the pros and cons of the profit motive there is the huge question of what drives my non-commercial clients who do not aim to make a profit? Therein lies an immediate problem. What motive force drives non-profit organizations? Altruism? Social justice? Where is the simple formula that tells us, and them, how well they are doing? The only language I know that can answer that question is the language of value – do they offer society the best possible value or not? That is an easy question to ask but a very difficult one to answer. Profit is calculated by way of reference to two variables in a simple equation, revenue and cost. However, this equation is increasingly being viewed as much too simplistic. Value can be expressed with equal simplicity but value is never simplistic, it is intrinsically holistic and complex. So we can express value, in its simplest terms, as the amount of output we get per input. How many patients get cured per £1000 invested? How many fresh water supplies are provided per £1000 donated? The two concepts are identical, in one sense, but using value as a motive force at both an individual and organizational level is much more powerful. This book will try to demonstrate just how powerful.

I already try to maximize value but that is certainly not the same as maximizing profit. I once asked a pharmaceutical company client of mine, who were certainly trying to maximize profit, what they were doing to bring down the costs of the clinical trials necessary to get new drugs to market? 'Nothing' came the reply. 'The most important thing is to get enough people on the clinical trials. The company has always been willing to throw money at it because it is so important.' But why, I persisted, can't the company do the same, effective, clinical trials but at a lower cost? That prompted just a shrug of the shoulders. A sort of 'why should we bother when we can make enough profit doing it this way?' That short conversation sums up why I think the search for value is so different to the search for profit. That complacency of 'if it ain't broke why would we stop to fix it?' That blinkered view of what the organization could achieve and the extra benefits it would bring.

That same employee, of the pharmaceutical company, or a member of their family, will one day be just another customer visiting a pharmacy who complains about the high cost of drugs and medicaments. Worse still, they might be asking their insurers or the state to provide the latest, life-saving drugs, which are deemed to be too expensive. As a consumer their view would be the same as mine but as someone who has to deliver that greater level of value, as an employee, I can fully understand why they would not want to go that extra mile. But then that is the whole point. Profit is a very one-sided view. Value addresses the profit and personal perspectives, and several others as well (e.g. the safety of the patients involved in the clinical trials) all at once.

If that doesn't test your own value motivation then maybe a different example will. Maximizing profit in a cigarette company means, inevitably, causing the premature death of many customers and placing a huge burden on healthcare services, not to mention the impact on the lives of the smoker's nearest and dearest. I do have a problem, therefore, with only looking at one side or just one part of a simplistic, incomplete equation and profit is certainly not the complete equation. Value is. This does not mean that I am suggesting those who love smoking should not continue to do so (even though I have never smoked myself). I follow the simple principle that I will fully support the choice of the individual, to do whatever they choose with their money and their lives, as long as it has no adverse effect on me. Nevertheless, the value motive could mean that tobacco companies do everything in their power to prevent people ever smoking (they already purport to run schemes to reduce under-age smoking) and help those who genuinely want to kick the habit. The value motive is certainly not about being mean-spirited or trying to stop mature adults doing something they enjoy. It is just about being clear what the ultimate objective is and then doing everything possible to achieve that objective.

Of course, I am well aware of, but profess to no expertise in, the vast amounts of literature going back as far as the 18th century and beyond, on the subjects of wealth, utility, value and the happiness of society. I would like to think this book will add further insights and clarity to that perpetual debate but it is certainly not just intended as another theoretical treatise. It is, first and foremost, a practical, business management book relevant to the needs of a manager working in the globalized economy of the 21st century. More precisely, it is a book on maximizing organizational effectiveness to create maximum value both for the organization and society, simultaneously. That sounds like a very grand ambition that might require a very sophisticated approach but in fact this book is designed to be just the opposite – a blinding flash of the obvious. Common sense taken to its logical conclusion.

However, the creation of maximum value does demand clear leadership and has to be at the heart of any organizational strategy; whether you work in the commercial sector or not. Moreover, value as the prime motive has far reaching implications for society at large. The value motive does everything the profit motive does but much, much more as well. It aims to reconcile the interests of shareholders, CEOs, citizens and government. It will be of interest to all sides of the political and socio-economic spectrum; the 'hard nosed' financial city analyst will see it as a means for improving investments while the 'ethical' reader will see it as a way of replacing the pure profit motive.

So what is the difference between these two motives and why might you find this management book of particular interest? Well, it takes a very simple and precise, yet powerful, definition of value and illustrates just how that can transform the way organizations and society work in harmony. Furthermore, the definition of value used here applies equally in any sector, profit or non-profit, commercial or public sector, charities and NGOs (non-governmental organizations).

Is there anything really new in this book though? In one sense, no. Most of the theories and concepts explored here are, by and large, already well accepted in economic and management thinking as having validity. However, this is not necessarily true of more recent concepts such as 'corporate social responsibility' and 'social enterprise'. If this book brings anything 'new' to these debates it is in reconciling the essential sense inherent in such concepts (e.g. why wouldn't we want our organizations to be socially responsible?) with the basic economic necessities of acquiring and allocating resources as well as we possibly can, while also matching organizational priorities with those of society at large.

Einstein once said that all he ever did was ask simple questions. If that was good enough for Einstein to turn the study of physics on its head then it should certainly be good enough for us lesser mortals who want to bring some fresh thinking to the subjects of economics and management. One key ingredient that is really supposed to make this book different is its ultimate focus on managing and capitalizing on the value of your people. After all, how can you get the best possible value out of your organization unless you aim to get the best possible value out of your people? Yet it is avowedly not a human resource management or 'people management' book and has no intention of being categorized as such. My own experience of working with human resource management professionals for over 25 years has convinced me, beyond any doubt, that they do not see their role as value maximization. In the worst cases, they even reduce value by producing overcomplicated bureaucracy and following an agenda that is driven by the motive of political correctness (e.g.

diversity, ageism). This does not mean that diversity cannot add value; far from it. Diversity that is focused on value creation should create enormous value. It is just that most diversity policies drawn up by HR people do not have value as their goal. Consequently, this should be viewed as a general management book that requires a new, critical perspective, of which the people element is just one, albeit major, component.

So, I have taken on the challenge of trying to say something meaningful and useful about one of the most difficult subjects in the world to pin down — value. What I think I have produced is a very simple book but with unlimited ambitions. I hope you enjoy it but, more importantly, I hope it helps you and your own organization add enormous value to mankind and to be confident and satisfied that you have done so.

Paul Kearns
September 2006

INTRODUCTION

This book has a single, very simple, message. Manage for maximum value. You may think that describes what you are already doing but 'maximize' means everyone in your organization has to be thinking 'maximization' as well. Even if you are the biggest company in your particular industry or market, and making the best profits, these are not necessarily indicators of maximum value. So what are? What does value really mean in management terms?

We all value things. The word value is inherently based on a personal perspective. Whether it is your shiny new car or your relationship with your partner or family, the whole concept of value is about your own, personal perceptions. It is also an intrinsically selfish word, you will be motivated to pursue the things you value. That is a truism. Joggers will still get up on a cold dark morning to run because they value the exercise and the endorphin rush so much. It is precisely because value is so selfish, by nature, that makes it an incredibly powerful motive force. You tend to spend most of your time, money and effort on the things *you* value (you wash and wax your car regularly; you take time to keep in touch with and visit family and friends). On occasions it will drive us to extreme behaviours (running into a burning house to save a child or even just an old family photograph) and this powerful force already helps to drive society (e.g. healthcare attracts huge resources because we all value it so highly).

Yet it is not always so easy to find common agreement on what society values. Without such common ground how can society keep moving forward, harmoniously? Take 'gas-guzzling' SUVs (sports utility vehicles) as just one example. What do we value more, the freedom to choose whatever mode of transport we like or the environment that may be damaged as a result? In a world with a growing population, and a mounting sense of injustice at glaring inequalities, these are increasingly the type of conflicting questions that are starting to bedevil modern democracies and the organizations that serve them. Note also how easy it is for us all to slip into an emotional reaction, using emotive terms such as 'gas guzzling', rather than a well-conceived and thoroughly considered response.

One possible solution might be to aim for a compromise that could please everyone: maybe an SUV that is no less fuel efficient or at least no more polluting than any other vehicle? The chances of that succeeding are small though. Just as a new vehicle is designed and manufactured to this specification the 'safety lobby' are dissatisfied with having such 'lethal' vehicles on the roads and the anti-congestion campaigners see them clogging up commuter routes on the 'school run'. Very quickly, the task of attempting to reconcile all of these very disparate views starts to look impossible.

Another possible answer might not be to redesign the vehicle but to try to convince everyone that some of these freedoms are part of a whole system of creating societal value. Drivers of

SUVs, for example, believe their choice of personal transport is their right and see it as the sort of reward they deserve for the hard work they do as a researcher on new life-saving drugs. Most of our choices in life come as a package. The disagreements we have on value may well stem from just being very selective about which bits of the package we don't like, rather than the package itself. So, those who complain about road congestion still drop their kids off at school, albeit in a smaller vehicle.

Of course, at the root of this debate, the total package, are the political and economic *systems* that we choose to run society; and let us not underestimate for one moment the full import of that word 'system'. We use systems to guide our behaviours (the traffic light system says 'STOP' on red). We adhere to these systems because they align with our values and principles (we all value safety and follow a principle that society is best served by rules rather than anarchy). In some countries traffic systems are ignored (e.g. pedestrian 'zebra' crossings do not seem to offer pedestrians protection because drivers do not regard them as mandatory) because, as with any system, the key ingredient in the system is the human element. The systems only work or fail because of the humans who choose to follow or ignore them.

In the 20th century we witnessed the birth of communism as an ideological and economic challenge to the capitalist system only to see it collapse in 1989. The market system, on which capitalism is based, then grew to become the pre-eminent philosophy behind our core economic system. At the heart of the market system is the goal of profit. Consequently, profit has become the main driver of society and has been shaping it accordingly. Unfortunately, though, not everyone believes that society is necessarily being shaped in a way that they like or support.

The other, main prerequisite for the market to work effectively is that there is genuine competition present. Otherwise the spectre of the unacceptable face of capitalism (e.g. profiteering, abuse of monopoly), that is always lurking in the background, soon reappears. Indeed, it is this apprehension about the workings of the market that provides part of the rationale behind not-for-profit organizations. It has also led to a variety of organizational concepts such as social enterprise, corporate social responsibility, diversity, business ethics and environmentalism; all of which are clamouring for an alternative to the purest (and purist) form of the profit motive.

This has now become one of the biggest challenges for the world economy and if any alternative is to be offered it has to at least match profit's two distinct advantages – its simplicity and coherence. You know where you are with profit, whereas the signals coming from all of the other schools of thought appear to be disjointed, even inconsistent and incoherent. They may all hold out what might appear to be a 'better view' of what society could be but such a view has to be translated into a demonstrably better system; in effect, the drivers who ignore zebra crossings will have to be convinced of the value of stopping.

Maybe one way out of this situation is to transform the profit motive into a very similar, but much more mutually beneficial, conceptual driver. A motive that would lend coherence to all of these other drivers towards a common goal of real, wide-ranging, individual and societal benefits. A motive that simultaneously enriches society materially and spiritually. That motive is *the value motive* and it needs, at last, to find its true and fullest voice and to be sung in unison.

CHAPTER 1

PROFIT IS NOT A DIRTY WORD BUT VALUE IS MUCH CLEANER

Summary Profit has done a great job but it is too simplistic, limited and narrow in scope to cope with the demands of modern economic and social systems.

IS PROFIT THE BEST WAY TO ALLOCATE SCARCE RESOURCES?

The profit motive has served society very well over the years, despite the fact that it has always had its detractors. Especially those who still subscribe to the view that it is easier to push a camel through the eye of a needle than it would be for a rich man to enter into the kingdom of heaven. Yet the profit motive still has a great deal going for it. First and foremost, no one invented it. It was and always will be an entirely innate, natural, automatic, human motive to try to get the greatest rewards for

one's efforts. If it is ever to be usurped, as the prime driver of
wealth, any contenders will have to be based on equally natural
motives; otherwise they are unlikely to be sustainable. Maybe
that partly explains the failure of communism and even cooperativism to replace capitalism. They may sound like laudable, even
attractive, alternative ways to run society but they have never
been as powerful as that most basic of human instincts, to profit
from one's own endeavours. Many of the world's greatest inventions have come about partly because of this desire. Would tele-
phones, televisions, computers, airplanes and life-saving drugs
have been invented if it were not for the rewards that profit brings
to the inventor?

Well, actually, yes they probably would have.

Profit is, after all, just one part of that highly complex equation we glibly call motivation. Donald Trump and Richard
Branson will always want to build the biggest golf courses or fly
tourists into space because of the challenge, the personal profile, fame and many other motivational factors. Equally, Mother
Teresa devoted her whole life to care for the sick because she was
motivated to do so. Some writers continue to write books (poets
particularly, it seems) without ever making any significant amounts
of money or achieving widespread recognition. So maybe one of
the key questions that we need to answer is how can we tap into
those other huge reservoirs of motivation, outside of the pure
profit motive, and convert them into something really valuable
(poetry that the vast majority of us want to read)? But before we
explore this subject in any depth let us first be clear about the
key role that profit has been playing for centuries in powering
economic systems.

To an economist, profit is a mechanism for the effective, some
would argue optimum, allocation of scarce resources. For example,
should wine drinkers be drinking the finest quality French wines
or should they be getting their wine from the new world growers
in countries like Chile? The only way to resolve this is to let the

consumer decide in an open market. If you want to drink the best French wines then you pay the price. If you are happy enough with a standard, Chilean merlot then you will save money. The market is a very unforgiving place though for producers who do not treat the customer as king. So are these resources being allocated effectively? Both the French and Chilean producers will have to make a profit (or at least break even) if they are to stay in business. The profit motive may be driving their respective business strategies (the French choosing a quality strategy, the Chileans price?) but a motive of value might produce a much 'better' allocation of resources. In 2005 and 2006 the European Commission spent hundreds of millions of euros turning French and Italian wines into petrol because they were unable to sell all of their produce, in a market where Australian and Chilean exports to Europe are now about 20 times higher than they were a decade ago. No objective observer, economist or not, would argue that turning wine into petrol is a good use of resources. But then this is a clear case of not letting the market do its job properly. Intervention by the EU is interference in the natural mechanism of the market because it places more importance on the livelihoods of European wine producers than it does on wine consumers. It could be viewed as a symptom of an institution that has failed to reconcile all aspects of its value to society.

In the absence of a clear definition of value at this point (for which see Chapter 2) this should at least start to provide some indication of one of the essential differences between profit and value, even though, at this stage, we are just restating conventional economic theory. You may still need some convincing, of course, that there are likely to be any new insights emanating from an analysis of how the market might work better with a different goal, that of value. After all, the discipline of economics has attempted, since the time of probably the most famous founding father of economic theory, Adam Smith, to explain how the enlightened self-interest of the entrepreneur, driven by profit, satisfies the needs of society through the 'invisible hand' of market forces. He summed this up very elegantly by saying:

> Every individual endeavours to employ his capital so that its produce may be of greatest value. He generally neither intends to promote the public interest, nor knows how much he is promoting it. He intends only his own security, only his own gain. And he is in this led by an invisible hand to promote an end, which has no part of his intention. By pursuing his own interest he frequently promotes that of society more effectually than when he really intends to promote it. (Adam Smith, *Wealth of Nations*, 1776)

Adam Smith's genius has always been well recognized in many quarters but his take on life was equally seen by others as just a selfish, capitalist's charter or an apologist's view of entrepreneurship. The fact that selfish interests can produce wider societal benefits does not, of course, rule out the possibility that some entrepreneurs' motives are as much, if not more, guided by societal benefits as they are by personal gain. In fact the history of capitalism is replete with instances of successful businesspeople that have had a strong, philanthropic streak. Unfortunately though making a profit and being philanthropic, simultaneously, tends to send what might appear to be conflicting signals about motives. Perhaps a more accurate and positive view of profit could be that voiced by the late industrialist and ex-Chairman of British Rail, Sir Peter Parker, when he said 'Profit is a measure of our service to the community.'

This was a very simple yet extremely profound description of profit and the likely motives that could lie behind it. The community will support the profit maker if it believes the profit maker is doing something in the interests of the community. The relationship between the profit maker and the community is intrinsically synergistic and symbiotic. Here was someone who could see the connection between running a profitable organization and yet, simultaneously, providing a much wider range of benefits to society than just pure profit. We will look later at how even the language of profit can make a discussion of economics highly emotive, especially when it has so many historical connotations of exploitation, greed and abuse of power. For now though, even if we accept that basic, conventional economic theory is sound we also have to acknowledge all of the provisos and limitations that come with the basic profit motive. In fact, the smooth running of any economic system is fraught with potential problems when:

- the entrepreneur sees that their own selfish interests are best served by *not* providing society with what is in its best interests (most obviously encountered in monopolistic situations);
- unfair competitive practices remove or exclude producers from the market or maintain artificially high prices (e.g. cartels);
- the 'interests' of the entrepreneur (or the organization) seem at odds with the perceived interests of society (e.g. citizens see an inherent conflict in the provision of healthcare by a commercial organization);
- the market price does not fully reflect the wider societal impact of the product/service (e.g. car manufacturers do not have to include in their prices the costs of recycling the cars at the end of their natural life);
- reconciling the interests of an increasingly vociferous and disparate group of stakeholders (e.g. environmentalists versus shareholders) requires a more flexible and adaptable market mechanism;
- it does not work at all well with the non-profit sectors (e.g. introducing quasi-markets into healthcare) and requires some fundamental rethinking if it is to be adapted.

All of the problems identified above are already well recognized and have taxed the minds of the greatest economic theorists for many years. Yet the theory is only part of the challenge. In practical terms, the theories have to be adapted if they are to provide a foundation for policies that will aim to achieve the optimum allocation of resources. In the UK the state-funded NHS (National Health Service), with its ethos of providing free healthcare at the point of need, provides us with a classic example of the sort of dilemma that can result from this type of thinking. Whatever success it managed to achieve in the past it has struggled to adapt and cope with a relentlessly growing demand for its services in a society that constantly wants to widen the definition of 'health'. However, rather than let the market decide, for obvious political reasons, economic theorists have had to develop a theory of quasi-markets to try to allocate health spending on a basis that will satisfy the demands of the majority of taxpayers. In effect, such a theory is trying to reconcile a whole range of self-interests from different groups with differing perspectives, including those individuals who have conflicting self-interests due to their dual perspectives as both taxpayer and consumer, without using a pure market system. Maybe what is really required though is to forget pure economics and market forces and, instead, find another way of reconciling such disparate views?

After all, using the profit motive to allocate healthcare is bound to rankle with those who do see profit as a dirty word. Profit, like religion (and some might think a not-too-distant cousin), can often have very admirable intentions but can equally, quite easily, become a travesty in the hands of the zealot or the bigot: it is, after all, determined by some very primal, human urges. There is nothing intrinsically wrong or evil about profit, per se; it can and has provided enormous benefits. It is so easy though for critics to attack the whole principle of the profit motive when it is occasionally misused or abused. Such critics seem to choose to ignore the fact that the guilty party in such cases is the unprincipled person who applies the tenets of the theory (maximize revenue, minimize costs) in a very narrow or cynical way, rather than the motive itself. We should not throw the baby out with the bath water. Separating out, and capitalizing on, the essential, most valuable ingredients of the market mechanism and profit, whilst also ensuring any transgressors are kept in check, will be the role of the value motive. One way to move towards a more enlightened approach might necessitate the removal of as much of the emotive element from the debate as we can. In order to do this maybe it is time we briefly revisited what profit actually means.

PROFIT CAN BE A VERY EMOTIVE WORD

If you look at dictionary definitions of profit they tend to be extremely simple. Typically, it is defined in accounting terminology as:

> the positive gain from an investment or business operation after subtracting for all expenses

or even more simply, albeit negatively, as:

> the opposite of loss
> (both from www.investorwords.com).

Profit definitions tend to relate immediately to a business context (as opposed to society at large), with all of the hard-nosed and exploitative connotations that sometimes go with the term. Profit is also described as a very black-and-white, positive–negative concept. You either make a profit or you do not, there is no happy medium or halfway house. Worse still, the same word is the root of profiteering, which means to make 'excessive' profits (although who decides whether profits are excessive or not is a moot point).

Yet the *Concise Oxford Dictionary*, in addition to the normal financial definition, puts a slightly different slant on the word:

profit *n.* & *v.* – *n.* an advantage or benefit.

This suggests a much more positive concept and the Latin roots of the word come from 'advancing', 'progress' and 'doing'. What better way to describe the role of profit in bringing about improvements in society? But even in this very short glimpse at what the word means it is very easy to see how subjective views ('excessive') slip into the discussion.

Now, if you are a business manager in a commercial organization, the profit motive may seem as natural and unquestionable as breathing. You probably believe it is a worthwhile, even worthy, goal. It is tangible, you can prove it by seeing how much money you bank each month. Of course, *how* you achieve a profit leads some people to question the ethics of making a profit (e.g. do you employ 'child' labour in developing countries?) and very quickly it becomes a very emotive subject again. We will look at the question of ethics later but first we need to explore why some people think profit is a dirty word because if they genuinely believe this it will get in the way of creating value. One of the big advantages that the word 'value' has over profit is simply that there is no reason why anyone should regard it as having a negative or pernicious meaning. So how can we remove profit's unhelpful baggage?

Well, perhaps we can stop using the word profit and start talking about surplus instead. A surplus occurs when your output is bigger than your input. This definition would have applied as much to the first subsistence farmer who managed to grow more wheat than his family needed as it would today to an investment banker who invests to make a return (a surplus over their investment and costs). Interestingly, the notion of the poor subsistence farmer, struggling against the elements, probably with minimal, rudimentary tools, immediately strikes us as a noble image. Whereas for some of us the picture of the investment banker, sitting in a palatial office in Wall Street or Canary Wharf, might be more closely associated with notions of asset-stripping or keeping 'greedy' shareholders happy. Moreover, by virtue of that impression, they may appear to be much less of a boon to society. It is incredibly difficult holding back our natural, emotional responses though. So, perhaps if we consider the banker as someone who lends money to farmers in developing countries, to increase their agricultural yield, it might seem to be a mental picture that is an ideal combination of both? Both sides win but then there is still the question of motives. What is the banker's motive, to help the farmer, to feed society or just to make money?

Now, just pause for a moment. The previous sentence hinted that the banker might have an ulterior, less ethically sound, motive and we are so used to hearing derogatory comments about bankers that we do not necessarily question it anymore. But what about the farmer's motives? There is no reason why the farmer's activities should inherently, automatically, be any more noble than the banker's. The loan might be to pay for dangerous pesticides, which the farmer may well use with a total disregard for the environment, the crops in adjoining fields or even the local population. You may well already have a very open-minded, balanced view of the relative positions of the banker and the farmer but did you consider how we could decide whether this investment was truly 'valuable' rather than just profitable? Do the motives of both parties matter as long as the farmer and the banker both get what they want from the deal?

One bank that has thought long and hard about these sorts of issues is the UK's Co-operative Bank plc; a business that stems directly from the co-operative movement of the 19th century, rather than a conventional, profit making, commercial banking operation. Here is its statement about its ethical policy:

> Business does not operate in a vacuum. Activities inevitably lead to a series of ecological and social impacts. Some industries, by

their very nature, have a huge and obvious impact on the environment and society, whilst the impact of others, such as the financial
services industry, is not always so immediately apparent. At the
bank, we recognise that our impact, through the provision
of finance and banking services to a wide variety of business customers, can be more far-reaching and profound than the direct
impact of our actual operations, so we have put measures in place
to ensure that this impact is managed. (www.co-operativebank.
co.uk – 15th June 2006)

All of this sounds very ethical so you may be encouraged to read
further on their website but you might be disappointed to find
that there appears to be no definitive statement or clear evidence,
anywhere, of whether this approach provides any more value to
society than some of its more profit-focused competitors. If so,
the reader is entitled to ask 'what makes this policy any more
ethical than any other banks'?' In fact, it could even be argued
that it is rather arrogant to declare that you have an 'ethical'
policy when there is no widely accepted set of criteria that
determine when an organization is acting ethically. If every
organization can define ethics for themselves it makes the term
meaningless.

What is required is a proper, clear statement of value, not just
profit figures or nice words: or even a combination of the two.
This value statement has to mean something to any external
observer as well as those direct stakeholders (e.g. board members,
trustees, shareholders, customers, employees). It would have to
say what the net result is after all inputs and outputs have been
taken into account. It is this 'net' result that helps us to distinguish between high and low value organizations, and the ones
whose policies genuinely add value as opposed to those who
simply declare their pretensions. It is so easy for the supposedly
ethical or philanthropic to be seen as contradictory. Worse
still, the goals of profit and societal value can so easily become
mutually exclusive.

THE MICROSOFT PARADOX

Trying to reconcile economic and wider societal goals is a huge issue but we might gain some insights if we consider what we will call the Microsoft Paradox. This could be defined as occurring where supposedly 'philanthropic' actions are not truly philanthropic. In other words, the philanthropist may think they are contributing something valuable to society but they are just re-allocating resources away from other, possibly equally important if not more important, philanthropic causes. Of course, those on the receiving end of the 'philanthropist's' benevolence will happily accept the donations but they could well be at the expense of other sections of society. Society as a whole may not gain any net benefit.

In order to explain this more fully, and simultaneously suggest why this apparent paradox should be attributed to Microsoft, we need to look at Microsoft's almost unique monopoly position. Bill Gates, one of the original founders of Microsoft, is the richest man in the world. Without a doubt, one of the key reasons why he has become so rich and powerful is that he is highly talented and spotted that the advent of personal computers would inevitably lead to something extremely rare – a global, natural monopoly in computer operating systems. Any businessperson worth their salt would give their eye teeth for a monopoly; they would probably also willingly give most other parts of their anatomy for a chance to gain such a natural, global monopoly. It gives the monopolist a licence to print huge amounts of money. It has to be said, though, that this did not just fall into Bill Gates' lap. He and his highly talented team had to work very hard and take some tough decisions in order to gain such a pre-eminent position in the computer market. Even most arch profit makers have to work hard. So, there is no intention here to detract, in any way, from their huge achievements and the world would have had a slower pace of development without a common operating system platform. Monopolies can generate significant benefits for society when managed for the greater good. But society will always be at the mercy of the monopolist's motives.

It is worth briefly digressing here to acknowledge an earlier point that many inventions would also have taken place without the profit motive driving the inventor. The world of information technology provides two perfect examples of this. One is the development of the Linux operating system invented by Linus Torvalds and another is the natural monopoly that could have been the invention of the internet, often attributed to Tim Berners-Lee, except that they both, for whatever reason, either did not choose to or were unable to make them into profit-maximizing monopolies. So what are the different motives of Bill Gates and Torvalds/Berners-Lee and does it matter from a 'value to society' perspective?

To add some further complexity to this question we have to acknowledge that Bill Gates is regarded as one of the biggest philanthropists the world has ever known. The Bill and Melinda Gates Foundation has amassed billions of dollars to sponsor charitable causes and research (and has now added Warren Buffett to its list of benefactors). This makes it appear that Microsoft, therefore, fits very well into the long tradition of profit-making but highly philanthropic organizations. Moreover, from a very selfish viewpoint, the recipients of donations from the Bill Gates Foundation could be forgiven for singing the praises of Microsoft and welcoming its largesse, regardless of how it came to obtain such huge funds. It appears therefore that profits, when used in this way, really do achieve the joint goals of economic and societal value.

There is an alternative viewpoint, however. Microsoft charges handsomely for its licences to use their Windows XP operating systems and Office suite of desktop products. Many of their customers include schools and colleges (non-profit-making organizations). The bill for such licences for a college could easily amount to a five-figure sum; money that the college, on a fixed and tight budget, could usefully use for many other competing needs (e.g.

books, teaching resources). So is it right that the college loses out and the extra profits made by Microsoft end up in the Gates' Foundation to be used for other purposes? Some might even argue that Microsoft's profits are not only excessive but immoral, in the sense that they have not been won through genuine competition but from an explicit strategy of Microsoft maintaining its monopoly wherever it can. This now becomes a question for society; who should decide how resources are to be allocated? If Microsoft continues to make monopolistically high profits it will enable Bill Gates to decide for us. But Bill Gates is not a democratically elected leader. Where customers have a genuine choice about software providers their choice of company could be described as a democratic choice. However, in a monopoly situation there is no one else to 'vote' for, so this is the land of the 'totalitarian' supplier and as such is not in society's best interests. This is an abuse of the profit motive. If Microsoft really wants to provide society with maximum value it needs to give its customers the best possible products and service at the lowest possible price. Then it can donate what it wants from its well-earned profits. So how does Microsoft fare when judged against these, more value-laden criteria?

Microsoft basically has three very big and profitable businesses; Windows was contributing $8 bn in 2004, Office $7.15 bn and 'server' software $1.3 bn. Windows and Office are still the main contributors to its profits but products such as the Xbox games console were not making money, despite revenues of $2.9 bn. Consequently, Microsoft is cross-subsidizing its forays into other more competitive product areas from its monopolistic products. That means the college that has to pay Microsoft's monopolistically high prices for Windows operating licences could be deemed to be cross-subsidizing computer games for students rather than educational resources. This does not look like the sort of value proposition that society should be seeking.

If this is not already regarded as a very serious matter, any views we may harbour about Microsoft's business practices are further coloured by the many instances where it has tried to stifle the sort of competition that could be giving better value to society. There have been numerous stories of Microsoft in court over unfair practices including in 2004 the EU's Competition Commission unanimously backing a watershed, antitrust ruling that found Microsoft guilty of abusing its software monopoly; resulting in sanctions and a fine amounting to hundreds of millions of dollars. This was a case involving Microsoft bundling its Media Player software with its Windows system in an attempt to keep companies like Real Player out of the market. Another case in 2004 involved a long running dispute with Sun Microsystems which eventually cost Microsoft $1.9 bn to settle. It would be hard for Microsoft to argue that overall, taking all the pluses and minuses into account, their motive is ultimately driven by providing the most value to society, even if the Gates Foundation does have some very laudable goals such as eradicating malaria.

The motives of organizational leaders therefore are not just important, they are the very essence of societal value. The fundamental motives that drive organizations drive the cultures and individual behaviours of those who work in them. In a recent article in the *Sunday Times* (18th June 2006), announcing that Bill Gates was stepping down as head of software architecture in the company, a Windows developer who had been with the company for five years, spoke about 'Deep in the bowels of Windows (the business unit) there remains the whiff of a bygone culture of belittlement and aggression. Windows can be a scary place to tell the truth.' The same article highlights the fact that Windows is a hugely complicated piece of software with '50m lines of code and 50 layers of interdependency'. So even in terms of developing its own products Microsoft does not seem to adhere to a philosophy or the practical principles of value. It certainly does not seem to be encouraging its own people to use their talents to deliver maximum value. Yet it is quite happy to do everything it can to maximize its profits. The real irony, what lies at the very root of the Microsoft Paradox, is that even by the sort of criteria we would use to judge any software development company Microsoft could be said to be performing very poorly, despite the wealth it has created for many of its shareholders.

The reason the profit motive fails when set against the value motive is because the value motive will actually produce better profits than the profit motive while simultaneously creating more value for society. Microsoft has obviously used much of its surpluses to support a huge research and development function (including the loss-making Xbox) but in reality it often wastes research funds, because of its strategy of maintaining monopolies, by reinventing something already invented quite satisfactorily elsewhere (as in the case of Internet Explorer trying to put Netscape out of business). But this huge effort in R&D has not stopped many other competitors from stealing a march on them. One only has to look at Skype for internet telephony, Google and MySpace among the many examples on offer. Is this because these organizations have unleashed, rather than stifled, their creative talents?

The real Microsoft Paradox is in Bill Gates trying to behave as a 'philanthropist' when his company's business practices are deemed, in law, to be anti-competitive and, in that sense, decidedly unphilanthropic. There is nothing wrong with an entrepreneur giving funds to charitable causes when those profits have been earned through competitive practices, it is the existence of genuine competition that makes such profits 'moral'. It is the ability of willing customers to choose between a range of products and providers, in a market based on fair competition, that makes capitalism inherently ethical and philanthropic. Whereas, distorting the market to produce excessive profits is inherently 'immoral' regardless of what genuinely good causes eventually benefit. Of course, anyone wanting to seek a cure for malaria will welcome the funds with open arms but they may be diverting resources away from equally important causes not sponsored by a wealthy monopolist.

The simple answer to resolving this paradox of course is simply to ensure that true and effective competition reigns. The Microsoft Paradox only pertains in monopolistic circumstances. There is no inherent contradiction or conflict between competitive capitalism and philanthropy. The organization is creating a surplus while satisfying society's needs. What it chooses to do with that surplus is up to the capitalist who has made it. One may criticize the good causes he or she chooses (e.g. the local dogs' home becomes a beneficiary in the will) but this could only amount to a different set of personal values. It would be difficult to challenge the capitalist's right to dispense with their own funds as they see fit whether we, personally, think animals should always come second to humans or not. There is no absolute in value that would ever resolve this particular argument.

Having said that, following Bill Gates' own insights, the world probably really only needs one effective internet browser and media player. If Microsoft produces the best at the lowest cost that is fine, but if they replicate the work already done by somebody else's research and development that is not the best allocation of scarce resources, it is a waste. This crime is then compounded by using a dominant market position to put competitors out of business, thereby possibly depriving the world of researchers and developers who are performing better than their own. If Bill Gates really wants his legacy to be the world's biggest philanthropist, rather than its richest inhabitant, he would be better advised to stop wasting money on R&D and give the money directly to a charity that will make better use of these valuable resources.

Microsoft was chosen to give this paradox a name because it is a perfect example of a complex issue. It was also chosen because it has attracted much criticism over the years for its business practices. This makes it an easy target and probably too easy a target. Any organization making huge profits, even if they are achieved through entirely legal and ethical means, will still be in danger of attracting criticism from those who just do not like the profit motive. Such critics seem to think there is something inherently more ethical about organizations that do not have profit as their goal. But is that true? Let us now move into an even more problematic area – how ethical and philanthropic are non-profit-making organizations? Do they add any value at all, or at least more than a commercial concern would?

NOT-FOR-PROFIT? DOES THAT MEAN NOT-FOR-VALUE?

Having defined profit earlier, if we are going to discuss the non-profit sectors we had better look for a clear definition as well before we go any further. Here is one definition of 'non-profit':

> 'non profit making = not commercially driven' (www.elook.org/dictionary)

This immediately indicates a clear distinction between organizations that work on a commercial basis and those that do not. For a little more detail we can also find a definition of 'not-for-profit':

> 'Not for profit – A non-profit organization includes a club, society or association organized and operated solely for social welfare, civic improvement, pleasure or recreation, or for any other purpose except for profit, no part of the income of which is payable to, or is otherwise available for the personal benefit of any proprietor, member or shareholder.' (www.communication.gc.ca)

This tries to spell out the differences between the two, except that if we remove the key word 'solely' the definition could apply equally well to profit organizations. Food companies provide 'welfare' needs; alcoholic drinks companies provide 'pleasure'; hotels and leisure centres provide recreation. So is there really any difference between profit and non-profit organizations? If you want to go for a swim you could choose to go to a municipal pool or a private leisure centre. Does the fact that one is run on a profit basis automatically mean that it will be managed differently? Are we to assume that one gives more societal benefit than the other (e.g. poorer children would not be able to swim if only the commercial pool was available)? This second definition seems to imply that there is something inherently wrong with trying to make a profit out of such services.

Maybe the clue is in the part that says 'no part of the income of which is payable to, or is otherwise available for the personal benefit of, any proprietor, member or shareholder'? We can only guess that this is suggesting any 'surplus' income should not end up in the hands of a shareholder, as would be the case with dividends in a publicly quoted, commercial concern. But does that denote any substantive difference between one type of organization and another? They both aim to serve customers and if either of them fails to satisfy customers they should cease to exist. Both are, in effect, 'operated solely' for that purpose. When viewed from this perspective the profit/non-profit dichotomy disappears in front of your very eyes.

The more you think about it the more you have to reach the conclusion that the whole concept of a 'not-for-profit' organization is very strange. When we looked at definitions of profit one described profit in the negative (i.e. not making a loss). It is always odd to hear something described negatively, in terms of what it does *not* do. How ridiculous if, say, a bank were to announce all of the things it was *not* intending to do. Can you imagine it declaring to its shareholders – 'our purpose is not-to-make-chocolate'? Following this warped logic, anyone of us could declare that we have just set up a not-for-profit organization by sitting down and watching television. Or we could put great effort into *not* producing a profit by sitting in a bar or on a beach all day. All of these non-activities would guarantee that we achieved our organizational objective – no profit.

Of course, in the process, we would not have produced any value either (sitting on a beach all day would hardly constitute value, even if it might satisfy one indolent individual's needs). The inherent contradictions exposed by this hypothetical scenario neatly directs us towards an obvious point, all organizations should be defined by what outputs they are meant to achieve (e.g. banking services, care for the elderly) and judged on what scarce resources they use up in achieving those outputs. In short, all organizations should be described as value organizations and should be able to declare, unequivocally, what value they add to society.

The cancer charity does not aim to make a profit but its value 'objective' is to care for or cure those who have cancer. However, it cannot escape the fact that it must create a surplus first. In fact all organizations have to be 'for-surplus', by definition, otherwise they would have no spare resources to work with. As soon as we describe them thus, using our surplus definition of profit, there is essentially no distinction to be made between profit and non-profit organizations. This is a statement of the obvious but no less worth pointing out for that. If not, consider what a change in definition to a 'not-for-surplus' charitable organization might look like? It would, at best, just cover its operating costs with no surplus left over to grow, develop, innovate or improve its offering to its customers. The cancer charity would have no funds left to actually fulfil its raison d'être of researching future cures and caring for the terminally ill. All of this can only come from a surplus created by the charity itself or by someone else who is willing to transfer their own surpluses to the charity for distribution.

The notion of creating a surplus to produce benefits is not alien to any of us but if we now apply this concept to, say, the main non-profit sectors, the public and government sectors, some of the implications are far-reaching, to say the least. Let us consider the local government authority that runs local libraries. Should the library be run to produce a surplus? We should not forget, of course, that the source of funds for this library will always be the surpluses already produced by the commercial sector (via the mechanism of taxation). The net 'value' of the library, whether its objectives are well defined or not, is probably to provide entertainment and educational opportunities for local citizens. This value statement might not have been challenged some years ago except that there is always competition for scarce resources and if the library is not well used then a serious question has to be asked about its continuing value; regardless of the broadly beneficial aim of providing a service for those who wouldn't otherwise be able to afford it.

If we believe such public services are valuable we are drawn to that interminable debate of whether the service (in this case libraries) should be run on a commercial basis or through public provision from taxes. However, if, as we have discussed above, there is no conceptual difference between non-profit and profit organizations this question suddenly becomes irrelevant. The only relevant argument is what does society value, and let us be crystal clear about that objective, and how can that be achieved at the minimum cost? This is the output per input argument of value that has little or no automatic interest in the mode of delivery chosen.

So, when we apply this thinking to the library, if one of the objectives is to maximize use of the library and this is measured in terms of books loaned, one simple measure of value is books loaned per £ spent on the library. Then all we have to ask is which type of organization is more likely to achieve this end – a commercial or non-commercial entity? Of course, we could equally use exactly the same approach to compare the value of two competing bookshops but in reality we would tend to judge the success of commercial bookshops simply by the amount of profit they make. It is worth just mentioning in passing though that municipal libraries loan books out at no cost to the borrower yet charge for the loan of videos and DVDs. This looks very inconsistent and this happens because they do not have a coherent statement of value that has been adapted to a changing world with the advent of video stores. Yet another example of what happens when different perspectives are not fully reconciled under the unified banner of value.

Now, just in case this line of reasoning still strikes you as nothing more than a statement of the obvious, let us take one other fresh perspective. Imagine if we referred to some organizations as 'not-for-value' instead of not-for-profit? This would suggest that, whatever they were doing, they were not intending to provide value for anyone. It would be difficult not to construe this as a very strange state of affairs. Perhaps the hospice has no patients or no one is borrowing books from the library and the head of the hospice/library still tries to justify their existence by declaring they are there to provide the service when someone needs it. This would sound inconceivable, an utterly preposterous proposition: organizations with a declared raison d'être but no customers. Why would anyone want to run an organization without being absolutely clear how it was intending to create some value for society?

Yet many such organizations have tried to do so (art galleries, museums, counselling services) and some still continue to exist (e.g. counselling services offered to people after disasters even though they do not want any counselling) until such time as their lack of value becomes apparent. One good example would be the National Centre for Popular (sic) Music in Sheffield (UK), which received an £11 million grant from National Lottery coffers and had to shut within 12 months because it only managed to attract about a quarter of the visitors it expected (and needed financially). Apparently the founders and designers of this museum attached more value to it than their citizenry but common sense dictated that they could not run it at a 'loss'. The harsh realities of life should apply equally to both the profit and non-profit sectors. No one deserves a free ride and those who do not provide an acceptable service should not be allowed to continue. We have reached a point where we need to ask what rules we want our society to follow and, until there is a better alternative, profit will remain the ruler while it demonstrates that it can produce the biggest surpluses. But its crown is slipping.

PROFIT IS AN INCREASINGLY UNPOPULAR KING

They say 'profit is king' and it is easy to see why. Running an organization without such a crystal-clear goal can easily lead to conflicting objectives. Trying to satisfy aims other than profit, such as ethical purposes, might seem laudable but is fraught with uncertainties (e.g. who should choose the public library's books?), shaky criteria of success (e.g. is the actual number of museum visitors a satisfactory criterion?) and very different expectations from different stakeholders (e.g. the charitable hospice is asked to provide euthanasia by a patient). The profit motive has managed to survive this long simply because it avoided as many of these other issues as possible (e.g. when did the oil industry really start taking the environment seriously?). It was never, ever a perfect monarch and there are plenty of examples of abuse of power but it has served society very well, for thousands of years, precisely because it was not sidetracked or distracted (e.g. car drivers wanted petrol to run their cars regardless of any environmental cost). Nevertheless, globalization has brought with it a huge growth in this old monarch's population and some of its subjects have become increasingly restless.

Whether it deserves some of the bad press it gets is open to debate but one thing is for certain, the number of ideas competing for the crown of economic rule is increasing. Now we have corporate social responsibility (CSR), the social enterprise, demands for greater diversity, environmentalists and the whole human rights movement all demanding to be heard in the court of this king. This particular ruler though will not give any ground without a fierce fight and any serious contenders will have to produce clear evidence that they really do represent a better alternative. Anyone wanting to rise to this challenge could start by trying to hit this particular king where it really hurts: they could question whether the profit motive is ever likely to produce maximum profits. If it isn't then this would be a straight, knock-out blow for profit and the capitalist system as we know it.

If capitalism and profit were still the best possible basis for a high value, social and economic system this book would not need to be written. It is because profit seeking has severe limitations, in its own terms, that we are questioning here whether it is up to the challenges that lie ahead. If the profit motive resulted in society exploiting, fully, all opportunities for the creation of the biggest surpluses then it would continue to reign supreme. Of course, the choices we make in the redistribution of those surpluses would still continue to be a major political issue but the profit motive itself would be unimpeachable as the main driver. However, as we will soon clearly see, the profit motive does not necessarily provide the highest levels of profitability, never mind the highest levels of societal surpluses. The profit motive only motivates a relatively narrow group of stakeholders, who may well be totally satisfied with the returns they achieve. The value motive aims to satisfy the biggest group of stakeholders possible and will never be sated as long as opportunities for greater value still exist.

Henry Ford could have been described as the archetypal capitalist and entrepreneur and was famous for exploiting the commercial advantages to be gained from the latest developments in mass production and the scientific methods of Taylorism in the early part of the 20th century. But not everyone would automatically associate him with the sort of philanthropic sentiment implied in his statement that 'A business that makes nothing but money is a poor kind of business'. The Ford Motor Company he founded in 1903 is struggling to survive today (with a market capitalization of $13 bn as at June 2006, a drop of over 50% in four years) and one wonders where and when this former powerhouse of the automotive market might have started to take a wrong turn. Was it just an inevitable consequence of increasing global competition? Hardly. The number one automotive company today, Toyota Motor Corporation (market capitalization $178 bn – an increase of 66% over the same period) was a late entrant into the industry back in 1937 but seems to have thrived in the same marketplace. So, is there anything fundamentally different between the ways these two behemoths do business?

Perhaps the different directions in which they have travelled are a direct consequence of the different motive forces that drive them. Henry Ford was as complex a mix of motivations as any of us. The famous Ford Model T was designed for what Ford called the 'great multitude' and he slashed prices between 1908 ($850) and 1915 ($360). He also fought a court battle with some of his key shareholders, the Dodge brothers, in 1916 over whether the company's first duty was to them or their customers. Ford declared in court that the purpose of business was to 'give employment and send out the car to where people can use it . . . and incidentally to make money. Business is a service, not a bonanza.' Yet he was hostile to unions and harassed union leaders until he had to sign a recognition agreement in 1941. So was Ford genuinely philanthropic, a clear-headed businessman, or both? Was the real motivation behind his lowering of prices just a means to open up a mass market for his mass production techniques, thereby increasing both profits and dividends in the longer term? Perhaps he was a true visionary who saw the obvious, virtuous circle this produced. His interest in serving society and making a profit were one and the same; mutually reinforcing.

Since his death the Ford Motor Company has certainly always tried its best to make a profit but now struggles while Toyota, in its own way, is serving society's needs and becoming the most successful automotive company in the process. Are these two company's relative fortunes just the result of different types of management or does it go much deeper than that? Are the two companies driven by entirely different motives, one profit and the other value? On the surface it may appear that their motives are identical and customers might not discern any differences or even care. After all, what they look for is a quality car at the right price so why should they delve any deeper when making their choice? Even if we look at the public pronouncements of the visions of both companies it might appear, to the untrained eye, that there is nothing significant to distinguish one from the other. Take this quote from Ford's own website:

> Today, the Ford family comprises employees, dealers, suppliers, shareholders, customers, and more – all those that help fulfil the vision Bill Ford has defined for the company: to create great products that benefit customers, shareholders, and society. (www.Ford.com – 5th June 2006)

That word 'society' certainly looks like it remains consistent with the values espoused by Henry Ford back in the early 20th century but what is it providing for society today? Does it provide great cars and great value? Obviously an increasing number of customers do not think so. Certainly Ford are finding it increasingly difficult to reconcile these aims with their current level of performance and both shareholders and stock analysts would take some convincing that Ford are achieving success on any front at the moment. A more philosophical question though is, to what extent can Ford's shareholders and customers be referred to separately from society? If these are really three discrete groups then they will have their own, discrete perspectives on what they value and there will be an immediate challenge for Ford in reconciling all of these.

Compare Ford's vision with another Japanese company, Canon, who seem to have a different take altogether on what their raison d'être is, which is encapsulated in the single word 'kyosei' (see Canon's 'Corporate philosophy of Kyosei' at http://www.canon.com/about/philosophy/index.html, 3rd July 2006). They do not mention shareholders at all when they define kyosei as 'Living and working together for the common good' and add that 'True global companies must foster good relations, not only with their customers and the communities in which they operate, but also with nations and the environment . . . Canon's goal is to contribute to the prosperity of the world and the happiness of humanity, which will lead to continuing growth and bring the world closer to achieving *kyosei*.' This is a much more holistic view of what an organization exists for and Canon, while it needs to produce a profit, does not see this as its ultimate goal. It is a means to an end and everything is seen as part of a journey. The world may never achieve a state of true kyosei but that does not mean that this is not a worthwhile goal. This is not a black and white, positive/negative view of the world but one of an ever-changing continuum.

Of course, these sorts of vision statements are de rigueur for any self-respecting organization these days regardless of whether they amount to nothing more than rhetoric or public relations hype. So how do we tell the genuine from the fake and do the genuine ones, where the philosophy is really lived, actually result in greater value? Let us take our third and final example from Toyota, whose Global Vision 2010 (from the www.manufacturer.com on 8th February 2006) identifies four areas of innovation that involves Toyota becoming 'a leader and driving force in the reduction, reuse and recycling of resources', creating 'zero negative impacts on our environment and society'; 'striving to create an automobile-based society in which people can live with ease, and in safety and comfort'; promoting 'the appeal of vehicles throughout the world and strengthen(ing) Toyota's brand image'; and ensuring 'Respect for all people . . . to be a truly global company that earns the respect and support of people all over the world.'

The language used here is very important as it starts to signal a genuine and fundamentally different philosophy. This is not just PR, even though Toyota are certainly not unaware of the PR value of these statements. Toyota's development of the Prius is a clear demonstration of all of these principles. It appears that Toyota really does take its wider responsibilities to society very seriously. We could have an interesting debate about what the word 'society' really means to each of these companies but we should never forget the simple fact that whatever Toyota and Ford's respective philosophies are, when viewed purely in terms of bottom line performance, Toyota are well on their way to putting Ford out of business and a company that doesn't exist cannot fulfil any of society's needs. This, however, is not just a battle between two old rivals. We could substitute the name General Motors for Ford above and the story would be a very similar (GM's market capitalization is $13bn in February 2006 and has a junk bond credit rating from Standard and Poor's) if not starker example of a general point.

What we are really seeing here are two competing management philosophies and methodologies. It would be too simplistic to suggest this is a West/East divide and there is certainly no intention here to hark back to the notion of 'Japanization'. For every good or bad example of an 'American' company there will probably be a good or bad 'Japanese' equivalent (in a global economy ascribing a particular company to a particular nationality is becoming increasingly inappropriate). This debate about value does not follow neat geographical lines. Nevertheless, no doubt over the years Ford and GM have hired in some of the best brains money can buy and employed the latest management theories from the 'best' American business schools, but none of this talent seems to have been converted into high market values or profits. Along the way they may have forgotten some of the principles cherished by their founders. Both companies have even tried to copy many of the practices that Toyota espouses but without similar success.

Toyota, on the other hand, applies some very simple principles to the way it does business. Principles it has trusted and adhered to virtually since its inception. Of course, the Toyota of today is vastly different to the company that existed before the Second World War but its ability to create huge amounts of value can be directly traced back to its own founding principles (for a full explanation of this point read Jeffery Liker, *The Toyota Way*, McGraw Hill, 2004). More importantly, it also seems to be winning the respect of society at large, including the 'hard-nosed' investment analysts. So, if one of the key distinguishing features between these competing management philosophies is the difference between being motivated by profit or value perhaps we should now have a much closer look at what value truly means to see if we can learn something from it.

CHAPTER 2

VALUE – A VERY SLIPPERY WORD INDEED

Summary It is the very process of articulating value, in clear, unambiguous terms, that makes it such a powerful motive force for meeting society's needs with limited resources.

DEFINING VALUE

When we looked at the definition of profit in Chapter 1 there was very little confusion: defining profit was a relatively simple, straightforward exercise. Admittedly, in practice, there seems to be a world of difference between gross, operating, pre- and post-tax profits and even in the distinctions to be made between EBIT (earnings before interest and tax) and EBITDA (earnings before interest and tax, depreciation and amortization) but, in the final analysis, if any profit really exists (other than as a figment of the imagination of the executives at Enron, WorldCom, Parmalat and others) then it should be physically bankable. Profit is always tangible. That is why we are still so comfortable with it as the key measure of both commercial and organizational performance. It is also the main reason why value has, heretofore, been unable to assume predominance. Profit is certainly not a perfect measure of anything but value is probably one of the most difficult things to measure in any, commonly accepted, way.

To set up value as an alternative, therefore, we have to offer an equally usable definition. What we are not going to do though is provide an *absolute* definition of value. This is an impossible task because value is inherently subjective and personal, there can be no objective standard. Consequently many who want to put value in its rightful place retreat from the task, as demonstrated in the following quote from a site that purports to practise value-based management:

> What is value? . . . the question appears to be almost identical to the question: Why do we exist? We are entering here into a very complex terrain, on the crossing of economics, strategy, finance, management, sociology, philosophy, ethics, and for many people also religion. I believe it is for me as editor . . . not appropriate to give you a generic answer to this fundamental question (even if I could). (www.valuebasedmanagement.net – 23rd June 2006)

This editor is right of course, there is no such thing as good or bad value per se. Smokers will think smoking is a good thing and many non-smokers will say it is bad. Nothing will resolve this debate because their definitions of good and bad differ. However, if we do not offer a workable definition of value how could we possibly hope to manage it effectively? So we cannot afford to duck this issue either. This book is an organizational management text so, while there will be no *generic* definition of value offered, we are going to adopt an organizational definition of value; one that will apply to any type of organization and the unique set of circumstances it faces. All that really matters, from a practical perspective, is that at any point in time the organization should declare what its intended value is in clear, unequivocal terms, and be held to account for it. But before we reach that point we do need to define our own terms as clearly as we can.

In fact, the first real problem you will encounter is the very word itself. The Oxford definition is:

value *n.* & *v.* – *n.* 1. the worth, desirability or utility of a thing.

But under the same word heading comes:

'value judgement – a subjective estimate of quality'

and

'value for money – something well worth the money spent'

Some people using computers will believe that whatever they pay for Microsoft's Windows XP it is very good value for money because it enables them to do wonderful things with their computer. Of course, it is very valuable to them but there is no good reason why they should have to pay as much as they do for the privilege of using it. They should be able to get the same value at a much lower price if there were genuine competition in the market. So perhaps we expect much too much from this single word value? It is trying to capture financial and subjective assessments under the one heading. It gets even more problematic when we use the word for an even broader range of statements relating to personal principles and ethics (e.g. I value plain speaking). So if we are going to make any progress towards one single, workable definition, which everyone can subscribe to, we had better find the commonality between all of these demands.

Now, just before you read any further please stop for a moment (and pick up a pencil if you have one handy) and try writing a list of 15 things you really 'value', before we apply any clearer definition to the term. Of course, you will not be a stranger to the word and probably already use it frequently. But you will have your own very personal view of what it is and this view will have been shaped over many years by many different experiences. If you find this little exercise difficult there is a long list of words in Table 2.1 that might help to prompt you. Try circling 15 at random (that's one out of every four shown) or just add your own in the spaces provided.

This is not meant to be a trick question and neither are there any right or wrong answers. It is not even a scientific experiment. The purpose of this exercise is to:

Table 2.1   Value words

What I really value is ...		
profit	money	share price
dividends	margin	a low cost base
integrity	market capitalization	good wine
office politics	sport	thinking time
productivity	sales	sales turnover
transparency	deadlines	my family
image	reputation	research and
diversity	management control	development
school sports day	innovation	cash in the bank
slow decision	efficiency	quick decision making
making	fairness	market share
freedom	sales volume	honesty
commitment	art/cinema/theatre	loyalty
planning	financial controls	brand
my wife/husband/	add value	marketing
partner	public relations	advertising
openness	fidelity	everything well
trust	customer service	organized
straight talking	'perks' (expense	tough negotiations
tight cost controls	account etc.)	quality
salary	awards	my car
equal opportunities		good relationships

- make you stop and think about how far-reaching and multi-faceted this word 'value' really is;
- highlight the fact that value has at least two meanings (i.e. monetary value and what we might term personal ethics);
- suggest these two meanings could almost be seen as inherently contradictory (e.g. do I sell something to make money or should I aim to enhance our reputation?);
- show how different values work to different timescales (e.g. immediate sales, long-term brand building);
- demonstrate that we sometimes use the word for hard measurables (e.g. costs, profit); and
- how we equally use the same word for what we might regard as 'intangibles' (e.g. reputation, commitment).

So what do you do with the list you have just produced for yourself? Well, first, consider what gets more weight in your mind, the 'measurables' (sales) or the unmeasurables, otherwise known as 'intangibles' (e.g. reputation)? Second, try to spot any inconsistencies or conflicts (e.g. quick decision making versus planning, family versus deadlines) and consider how you try to reconcile these in your own mind. Also, finally, consider whether the people who work with you or for you might have a very similar or different list and what implications this might have for them and the way you manage them; or indeed how it might affect organizational performance.

Now, you may have already skipped over this little exercise, for whatever reason, or you may equally have agonized about it in some detail. The only thing that matters here though is a very simple point. If everyone in your organization has a totally different set of 'values' and they *believe* that there are some inherent conflicts that cannot be resolved, what chance do you have of getting the best value out of them or your organization as a whole? The most obvious example would be an employee who really values their personal and family life more than their working life. They strike whatever balance they can to stay in a job.

Maybe, though, one way to get this equation better balanced is to make more effort to reconcile their values. If, for example, 'planning' were valued more in your organization there would be less conflict with 'family' values if the employee had more notice of meetings and could organize their personal life around them in a more effective manner.

They could assure their partner that because their employer really lived these values the chances of them ringing up and saying 'I'll be home late tonight' will be negligible. Even if they do have to work late, at short notice, they will have every confidence that it must be for a very good reason or a genuinely unforeseen emergency. Of course, this approach to values has huge implications for the way you and your managers manage. The workaholics, who don't seem to have a home to go to, would have to work around these agreed values as well. They should not expect everyone to be equally willing to stay late or criticize anyone who says they have to leave early. This simple but very common scenario really does start to reveal some of the connections between personal values and organizational value – they are both inseparable and indivisible. Some organizations still seem to think working late is one way to maximize profits but a more enlightened view of the need to generate value might prove otherwise. Is there ever likely to be a direct, causal connection between 'hours worked' and organizational performance?

A WORKING DEFINITION OF VALUE

It is time to be precise about what value really means. At its simplest, most elemental, level value could be described as 'the provision of a product or service at an acceptable cost' but this would be so open ended as to be meaningless, unless it is more clearly defined as a goal or an aspiration. So our working definition will be:

> Value is the provision to society of the best possible product or service at the best possible cost.

In other words, if you were judged against this definition you cannot declare you are producing real value if someone else provides the same or better at an equal or lower cost. Ford and GM therefore are not currently providing value because Toyota can make better vehicles (e.g. more reliable) at a lower cost. It follows that even if Ford and GM make a profit out of their vehicle sales they will still not be providing as much value as their competitors. Of course, a shareholder who managed to buy and sell Ford shares at a 'profit' would argue that they certainly gained some 'value' from the process, and they could even bank it, but society is not receiving the best product at the lowest cost and Toyota shareholders, in the long term, would be able to argue that the 'value' they receive from their shares has far outweighed what Ford has managed to produce. In Toyota's case it is a win–win for everyone. In Ford's case it would be a very one-sided, purely selfish argument.

Let us not move on too quickly though. We need to ask how the automotive speculator can make a profit on share dealings in a business performing so badly and producing so little, if any, value. The answer is relatively simple. Share dealings and buy/sell notices are derived from a whole range of data and information (even misinformation) including decisions to sell off parts of a business or asset strip others. Some stock market speculators are driven by profit, not value. It is not their concern whether customers are getting great cars or great value for money. They just have to gauge or anticipate market expectations and share price movements or even influence them if they can. One such instance happened when Citigroup were fined £14m by the UK's Financial Services Authority because they reconfigured their bank's computer program so that it was 'designed to stun the market with a blast of 188 simultaneous sell orders'. Apparently traders referred to this computer system as 'Dr. Evil' (as reported in *The Times*, 29th June 2005). It would be difficult for them to argue that this would, in some way, create greater value for society, even though the profit intentions were absolutely clear.

Such stories, unfortunately, are not as uncommon as we would hope. Those of us who fully realize that this type of behaviour is only to be expected from certain human beings will not be surprised or particularly disappointed. These primal, even feral, human urges to satisfy our most basic needs are the same source of motivation that drove some of society's greatest benefactors and philanthropists to give away millions. Consider this more recent example from *The Times* on 20th June 2006 (just one year later): 'Sandy Weill, the former high-flying Citigroup chairman who was renowned for his love of private jets, has pledged to give away his estimated $1.4 billion personal fortune as part of a "deal with God".' It also quotes him from one of Citigroup's own publications, *Citigroup Pursuits*, as saying 'Hopefully we'll be as smart in how we give our money away as we turned out to be smart in making it.'

As with Henry Ford, whatever complexities there must be in any individual's make-up and character one wonders how Sandy Weill reconciles these statements with the illegal practices that his bank sanctioned just a year earlier. It would be too easy though to slip into the sort of emotive language used in the press (what was the relevance of mentioning his love of private jets) and this is very unhelpful. Do we learn anything from these extreme and polarized views? Does it matter whether Sandy Weill says he has a deal with God or whether we interpret it as a pact with the devil? We will return later to the issue of reconciling apparently contradictory values but for now we are going to tread as straight and unemotional a path as we can towards the subject of real added value. But first, in our continuing endeavour to provide a clear definition of value it is very important to make a clear, objective distinction, both conceptually and practically, between two types of value – 'basic' value and 'added' value.

BASIC VALUE

If you are a manager just stop and think for a moment about what you do every day at work. Does all of your effort and commitment make much difference? Or is the main thrust of your job just to keep the wheels in motion? When you go home can you say the organization has moved forward or has it just survived another day?

Imagine you are a production manager in a manufacturing business. As with any managerial role, a key part of the job is sorting out day-to-day problems as and when they arise. So, if the conveyor belt stops it would be your responsibility to make sure it starts moving again as soon as possible. The main objective is to produce as much output as the operating plan dictates. If you were asked at the end of your shift whether you had 'added any value' you would feel entitled to say a resounding 'yes', unequivocally and with absolute confidence. Your experience and your drive to resolve problems quickly could be seen as adding value. You could even suggest that one way to measure that value would be to compare the output from the line for the day with what it would have been if you had not sorted it out.

Of course, you would have played a very important role in the running of the business but if you continued to fulfil this role for the next 10 years all you would achieve (assuming you were still in business) is a flat line level of performance. There would be no trend line showing regular improvements in outputs or costs. In other words, all you will have achieved is keeping the business operating at its most *basic* level. Basic value could almost be described as 'business as usual'. The intrinsic value of the business will be no greater than when you started; hence we can refer to basic value as intrinsic value. We could also say that the 'basic' value of an organization is reached by maintaining the minimum standard of operational performance required to remain in business. Another shorthand term for these activities is 'must-haves', those things that the organization cannot possibly operate without.

So, for example, in a restaurant the basic value, the 'must-haves', would be the number of covers needed every evening, at an acceptable average spend per head. Any reduction in covers or spend would put the restaurant at risk of going out of business. This is a statement of the obvious and the only reason we need to make such a statement is to make a clear distinction between this minimal level of value and what we will later call added value. Eventually, though, we will see the ultimate reason for making this distinction is so that we can measure the added value. If we are not absolutely crystal clear about what constitutes added value how could we possibly measure it?

Just before we get to added value we need to make one further distinction within this category of basic value, a distinction between critical and non-critical activities. Critical value comprises those activities we undertake to avoid risk. Most of them are usually very easy to spot because the law demands that we do them. The most obvious ones are those associated with compliance. So, in a financial services business we would make sure that all salespeople have the necessary qualifications or certification to sell our products legally. In a hospital, a consent form is signed before every surgical procedure, just in case anything goes wrong. Any failure to identify and deliver all critical activities will leave the organization open to serious risk (e.g. a fine from the financial authorities) or even being shut down (e.g. the food company suffers a salmonella outbreak).

Those activities which are not critical, the non-critical, basic value, activities also have to be carried out but the organization will not collapse if they are not. Take expense forms, for example. Whether you complete your expense form on time or not will not seriously undermine the integrity of the business. Even if your expenses are paid late you might not be happy about it but the business is not going to collapse overnight as a result. No legal authority will shut a business down for late submission of expenses.

There is one further set of activities that come under the heading of 'basic' that we have not yet covered – those activities driven by the standards we set for ourselves (as opposed to the standards set by the law, external bodies or regulatory authorities). All organizations work to a set of standards, some implicit and some explicit, and the standards that an organization sets for itself directly reflect its values. Hotels that do not regularly set a high standard of cleanliness are, in effect, making it clear that they do not value cleanliness. It also suggests they think their customers do not value it either. Hence we see tables not cleared in the coffee area and ashtrays remain unemptied.

At the other end of the scale, some companies set their own minimum standards at an extremely high level. One themed restaurant chain decided that the minimum service level that their customers should expect was for all waiting staff to have a complete knowledge of every ingredient, of every item, on the menu. Other restaurants might take a different view. They could appoint one menu 'expert' on each shift to deal with any detailed questions or they could just print a really detailed menu. These are all business decisions; the weighing up, perhaps more accurately described as the trading off, of levels of customer service with costs. As with all business decisions the only way to weigh up competing options is to have some measures for comparison (i.e. how much will it cost to train all waiting staff and how many more customers will we attract?). Unfortunately, though, these basic value activities do not lend themselves to simple or clear measurement.

In fact it would be virtually impossible for the management at the themed restaurant chain to *prove*, through measurement, that such a high standard as this was necessary for them to run their business successfully. But does that really matter? As long as the executive management team subscribe to a belief system, that customers are prepared to pay for this level of service, they will not be seeking any proof. Call it business intuition or just commercial nous but many successful businesses are run along similar lines or follow equally unprovable articles of faith. They just presume that their customers demand certain standards and know that they have to meet those standards if they want to stay in business. In other words the 'basic value' of the business is often founded on a whole set of implicit value judgements. Sometimes those judgements are made explicit (the waiter is told they have to remember every item on the menu) and the logic behind them is explained (customers like to know what they are eating) but often they are not.

However, basic value only requires basic management. In a hospital, basic medical services and ward management provide a standard sufficient to keep the hospital in operation. They do nothing to continually improve patient care or reduce the incidence of disease. Basic accounting means producing the accounts every month, it does not guarantee higher profitability. So basic value can be viewed as treading water; there is no sense of progress, innovation or continuous improvement. The only way to measure such activities in £ signs is to ask 'How efficiently is it delivered?', 'How much does it cost us to serve a customer or treat a patient to our minimum standards (say that comes to £200) and could we reach that same standard more cheaply (say £100)?' The only value to be gained from these activities, therefore, is to try to reduce their cost. Not surprisingly, few companies either want to or can afford to just tread water. They want to actually start swimming as far and as fast as they can. This requires making an *additional* impact on the bottom line, over and above a basic level of operation. This comes under the heading of *added value*.

MOVING ON TO ADDED VALUE

Our earlier working definition of value already has several distinct advantages over profit. First, it applies equally to all sectors, both profit and non-profit. The product or service provided could be anything from food to electronics or from education to prisons; the concept applies equally well. Second, it is primarily focused on outputs. Money can change hands in the stock market to create profits without any improvement in outputs. This is not the case with value. Third, although we described basic value as a static situation of treading water (e.g. maintaining the cost of a particular car at a particular time) what we are really interested in here is a dynamic model, a movable feast. This leads us to the next step, which is to clearly define added value as:

> An improvement in the quantity, cost or quality of the product or service produced.

This is not meant to signal some earth-shattering new theory. On the contrary. This is really just a simple statement of the blindingly obvious. Added value is all about *outputs* or, as one chief executive of a car rental company put it very succinctly, 'if it don't rent cars forget it'. The cereal makers Kelloggs have always had a similar mantra that says the ultimate criterion of any activity in the organization is 'will it sell more cornflakes?' Let us not underestimate for one second what insights this definition of added value will give us. Moreover, we should equally be aware of the enormous implications it has for the way in which organizations are managed.

In order to fully explain these implications let us apply our definition of added value to a specific example. Imagine you run a company producing, say, televisions. There are just four variables that will tell you whether you have added any value or not:

1. *Quantity* – that is the number of TVs you make per annum has increased.
2. *Costs* – the cost of producing those TVs has decreased.
3. *Revenue* – assuming you can sell every TV you produce then there should be an increase in income received (this could also happen simply through a price increase).
4. *Quality* – the TVs are produced to a higher standard or achieve a greater level of customer satisfaction.

When you think about it everything that the company does can be distilled down to these four variables. No other variables add value. So, for example, let us ask the PR department what they are doing to add value and they might say that they are getting press coverage for the latest television designs being launched. Our definition of added value here though does not include 'press coverage'. PR and any press coverage they manage to generate are both *inputs*. You cannot bank press coverage. Press coverage will, hopefully, lead to greater market awareness of your products and even higher sales eventually but there is no guarantee. So how accountable are the PR team for sales? To what extent are their thinking and their actions dictated by the mantra of added value?

Exactly the same argument can be applied to any department or function in any part of the organization of course. Try asking the HR department how their training programmes, pay and grading systems and employee welfare schemes are adding value. Or ask the IT team, despite all their rhetoric about what technology has to offer, which of these added value variables they will have a beneficial impact on (cost is not necessarily going to be on their list). More importantly, who is accountable for each of these variables? If you take your eye off these for one moment then you are losing sight of added value opportunities.

Of course, if we ask the television production team which of these variables they can influence they will immediately see output, costs and quality as something they have some direct control over. One thing they cannot directly control though is price (the revenue variable), which may be decided by the sales team. All of a sudden two separate parts of the organization have to work together to get the added value equation working well. We could do a few more simple, 'added value' calculations on the effect of an increase in price or even improving the quality of the product, which results in an increase in customer demand. However, there are a few unarguable, fundamental truths about added value that need to be pointed out:

- Added value is holistic both in concept and reality – any change in any of the variables of output, cost, price and quality cannot be viewed in isolation, they are all totally interconnected and a change in one is likely to impact on another (e.g. efforts to drive down costs may adversely affect quality and result in lower sales – a loss of value).
- Added value always has a monetary ($£€) sign attached. There is no such thing as an 'intangible' when we are discussing added value. Statements such as we are 'raising the profile of the business', 'increasing market awareness' or 'improving employee creativity and innovation' are meaningless unless it results in an overall improvement in measurable added value, either now, in the medium or long term.

Take a creative business like advertising and ask the question, which is the highest value advertising agency, the one with the most 'creative' people or the one with the highest billings and profit? Some creative directors may not like to have creativity reduced in this way, just as Savile Row did not like being compared with cheaper, foreign suit manufacturers but the reality of value catches up with everyone in the end. That is why added value is an incredibly simple but very powerful concept that we will explore in much more detail throughout the book. For now, though, we need to take a short but necessary diversion to look at what some people call value but isn't.

PRIVATE EQUITY PARTNERS – VALUE ADDERS OR ASSET STRIPPERS?

One dimension of our added value definition that we have not explored yet is that different stakeholders will define value differently. In the television company the management and the shareholders, for example, could have different views on whether the company should be investing for long-term value or taking short-term profits. Regardless of the direction in which the company wants to head, publicly quoted companies need to be vigilant against short-termist predators whose prime aim is to strip them of their assets. 'Asset stripping' though can be a very emotive term, as we have already seen with other terms used to describe how a company operates. Was Lord Hanson, who aggressively acquired many companies in the 1980s in the UK and eventually the US, really an asset stripper or just a very good businessman? Rather than get into that sort of semantic and rather pointless debate we should be asking cool, objective questions about whether he really created value or not.

Asset strippers certainly attracted plenty of bad press and some would describe the private equity partnerships of the 21st century in virtually the same terms. However, anyone taking this view is in danger of making the same mistake as those who rail against the profit principle rather than the practice. Sometimes Hanson brought effective financial controls to companies that did not already have them. Turning an inefficient company into an efficient one could easily be described as adding value. There is absolutely no benefit to society in inefficiency, wasted resources and disguised unemployment. There is no need to take the moral high ground when discussing our definition of value either because it has the needs of wider society already built in. So do company takeover specialists add value through their acquisitions?

Under the heading 'Acquisitions are sure losers for shareholders' (*The Times*, 18th October 2004) research by Alan Gregory (who sits on the UK's Competition Panel) and John Matako of the University of Exeter's new centre for Finance and Investment revealed that 'in five years after a deal, the total return on investment underperformed by an average of 26% compared with shares in companies of similar size'. Gregory was also quoted as saying 'Personally, if I were a shareholder in a company announcing an equity-financed bid, I would regard that as a sell signal. I certainly wouldn't be hanging around for the next five years.' A more recent survey by KPMG (*The Times*, 24th January 2006) found that 'while 9 out of 10 company directors judged their (company) purchases a success, only 3 out of 10 actually created value for shareholders'. Their Head of Integration Advice said, 'the perception gap is wide . . . 26% of deals worth over $100m . . . destroyed value'.

If the conclusions of these researchers are correct then this would suggest that those who promote and launch such acquisitions must have been doing it for personal gain, rather than to produce higher value companies. Of course, such merger and acquisition activity makes $ millions in profits for the banks and advisers involved but if society wants to turn such activity into societal value then perhaps the way we measure the performance of such banks should tell the whole story and not just part of it. There is nothing inherently wrong with private equity partnerships or M&A activity, per se, but we need to be able to distinguish clearly between those that add value and those that do not. Inevitably, we are led straight back to that fundamental question – what are their motives? This, of course, needs to be established right at the early, most formative stages of any private equity buy-out. Asking how, exactly, they intend to add or create value in the terms of our definition would at least produce the first set of simple questions to ask and glib answers such as 'synergies' would not count.

Private equity people come in all shapes and sizes, just like everybody else. Those working in private equity should not be classed as 'evil' and neither should their practices, which after all are only conventional, financial tools and techniques. But the huge growth in private equity deals (see Table 2.2) over recent years provides us with plenty of examples of the good, the bad and the ugly.

One illustrative example of this whole issue can be seen in the takeover of the UK retail department store chain Debenhams. It was taken private by CVC, Texas Pacific and Merril Lynch in 2003 for a sum of £1.7bn. In 2006 the partners were planning to float the business again with a price tag of £3bn. A business editor in the *Sunday Times* (22nd January 2006) reported on this whole affair under the banner 'A real Mickey Mouse price for Debenhams' saying that 'The £3 billion figure is patent nonsense' and that this was a prime example of '. . . how a company can be financially re-engineered' adding that 'There is a price to this engineering and it is called piling on £1.9 billion of debt.

Table 2.2 The world's biggest private equity firms (*The Times*, 4th July 2006)

Blackstone Fund V	$15.5bn
KKR 2006 Fund	$15.0bn
TPG Partners	$14.5bn
Permira	$14.1bn
Apollo	$10.1bn

The company itself has been split into an operating and property company. In doing so the backers have taken out £1.3bn against an original investment of £600m. The net effect is the company is now paying a big interest and rental bill against a backdrop where operational costs are rising...And why does it need to float? The main reasons are to crystallise a bumper share package for the top directors and repay a big slug of senior debt.'

This business writer is not criticizing those involved in this on moral grounds (although that is certainly implicit) but rather an obvious lack of added value. The figures seem to speak for themselves and appear to tell a clear story about the motives behind this deal. So have Debenhams served more customers in the meantime? Have they sold them higher quantities of goods? Have they reduced the costs of providing those goods? Have they managed to raise prices because of improvements in the quality of service or the goods themselves? Let us at least ask the private equity people these simple but highly focused, added value questions before we judge them and their motives. If they fail to provide convincing answers then we have an objective basis on which to condemn their short-termist tactics for their inability to provide more value to society.

THE VALUE MOTIVE ALREADY EXISTS

So is this view of value a new view? Does it amount to a new management invention? Most certainly not. All we are really looking at here is what any ordinary man or woman in the street would call 'value for money'. The notion that we should aim to get the most benefit out of every £ we spend is quite natural. It didn't have to be invented. All this book is trying to do is get some common ground for deciding what constitutes the most benefit for every £ society spends, the best return possible on all resources. However, it intends to go much further into the management aspects of value. What management practices will have the greatest chance of creating the greatest amount of value? Obviously, just re-engineering the finances is not the answer because it serves too narrow a group of interests. That is not the enlightened self-interest of Adam Smith but just naked greed and as such government would be quite within its societal-driven rights to outlaw it. The value motive should come top of the list in due diligence. So let us look again at the variables involved in added value in more detail and work through another very simple scenario to start to tease out the lessons for management.

In Figure 2.1 the four added value variables are expressed as bags of $s. The more value you add to your business the more $s it is worth. However, to be able to gauge added value we need to do two things. We must measure its current value, which we will call the *baseline valuation*, and then we need to remeasure its value at some agreed point in the future. The difference between the first and second measures will tell us whether any value has been added and the measures used, before and after, have to be the same.

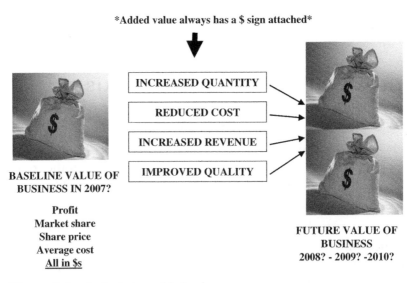

Added value always has a $ sign attached

INCREASED QUANTITY

REDUCED COST

INCREASED REVENUE

IMPROVED QUALITY

BASELINE VALUE OF BUSINESS IN 2007?

Profit
Market share
Share price
Average cost
All in $s

FUTURE VALUE OF BUSINESS 2008? - 2009? -2010?

Figure 2.1 Articulating added value

So, if someone asked you what the value of your business is now, what would your answer be? Even if you work for a not-for-profit organization you will still need to answer this first question if you are to demonstrate that you are adding value (but we will look at how added value applies to non-profit organizations in more detail later). Figure 2.1 suggests that usually the first answers for a commercial company are profit, company value (share price) or sometimes statements such as 'we are the lowest cost producer'.

Here are some similar statements of value, which we will ascribe to a book publishing business, and we will look at precisely what they mean in terms of added value:

- we made a profit of £100 million last year;
- we have 20% of the market;
- our share price is at an all time high of £10.50;
- our market capitalization is £5bn;
- we can produce our books at 10% lower cost (£2 less) than our nearest competitor.

All of these are intended to state how valuable this company is now, in 2007. They are all highly measurable and all have a monetary value attached to them. This baseline valuation of the business is the starting point for gauging *added value* because in 2008, 2009 or even 2010 you can ask the same questions and the difference will be a measure of how much value has been added in the interim. So, in 2008, if the business is to be deemed to have improved in value it needs to be able to demonstrate at least one of the following:

- we made a profit of £110m in 2007 – that's £10m in added value;
- we now have 25% of the market which is worth an extra £250m;

- our share price is at an all time high of £11.00;
- our market capitalization is £6bn;
- we can produce our books at 12% lower cost (£2.40 less) than our nearest competitor, that's an added saving of £0.40 per product.

Added value can only be measured by reference to baseline (i.e. pre-activity) and post-activity measures; the before and after pictures. In principle, the measures have to be the same, to compare like with like; regardless of any practical difficulties we might face in trying to do so. In essence, added value is that simple and there is nothing more complicated about it. More importantly, it is the language that the key stakeholders in most businesses, shareholders and financial analysts, understand.

Just before we move on though it is worth reminding ourselves that all of the four value variables are interdependent. They can all move in different directions, at the same time, and it is the net result we need to look at to answer the question whether any value has been added. Take a quick look at Table 2.3. Here are two simple scenarios of a chocolate cake making business. The first shows a cost saving of 10% (e.g. a cheaper chocolate coating is used) but this has been achieved by reducing the quality of the product (i.e. customers don't like the substandard, artificial coating). This has a knock-on effect on sales, so the net

Table 2.3 Chocolate cake value

	The chocolate cake company						
	Cost per cake £s	Sales volume	Total costs £s	Selling price £s	Total revenue £s	Profit £s	Net added value
Existing	2.00	100	200	2.50	200.00	50.00	0.00
Reduce cost (1)	1.80	70	126	2.50	175.00	49.00	−1.00
Improve quality (2)	2.00	101	202	2.50	252.50	50.50	+0.50

result could be a loss of value of £1.00. In the second scenario the company decides not to increase costs but manages to improve the quality of the finish of the cakes simply by careful handling. As a result 1% fewer get left on the shelves and sales increase. As a result, on this occasion, and only on this occasion, there is net added value, which manifests itself as a £0.50 increase in value.

While chocolate cakes help us to understand the variables of added value and their impact they can also be used to demonstrate the truly holistic nature of added value. There are many ingredients and other inputs that go into making a tasty chocolate cake. If any one of those ingredients is defective or ineffective (e.g. salmonella infected eggs, production lines that damage the finished product) then there is no cake to be sold. The whole process has to work in harmony if it is going to provide maximum value.

VALUE AS A DISTILLATION PROCESS

This is why it is useful to see added value as a distillation process. Imagine an ordinary whisky still but think of all of the inputs that go into producing the drip of the alcohol produced from the outlet of the distillation tube. Added value is that essence. It is the result of a lengthy distillation of all of the activities in which the organization and its people are engaged on a daily basis. There are the capital items (the still), fuel and the raw materials of water and malt. There is also the expertise of the distiller and their team. It is only the alcohol though that can be converted to a $ value; that is the only thing that can be sold.

Any organization can be viewed as a distillation of all of the time, effort and money that goes into it. Whether it is a commercial business producing cakes out of an oven or a social services department saving a child from abuse. Admittedly, it is quite obvious what the output from the cake making process is and not at all obvious what the desired output for the social services team or the child is. Should the child be put in a foster home or should they stay at home under close supervision? This might be a very difficult choice but somebody has to decide what the essence of what they are trying to achieve is. Both types of organization can only articulate their raison d'être in terms of the value they add. It does not matter how much time the social worker spends with the child, the only thing that matters is somebody defines what the desired output is and then gauges effectiveness, added value, against that criterion. The measures before and after still have to be the same to satisfy the golden rule of added value. This will be particularly important when we look at alternative organization types in Chapter 4.

So far so simple but obviously the crucial question now is how do you get from where you are to where you want to be? There are many ways to try to achieve value (e.g. employ better book designers, better bakers, better social workers) but value is only realized when customers pay for it. That is, they actually value 'better book design' and choose your books instead of your competitors. Book design, per se, has no intrinsic value. Yet the leaders of the publishing house, just as with the themed restaurant chain, have to make decisions on what their readers will value in terms of book design and what they will be prepared to pay for. These are precisely the sorts of decisions that split boards of directors.

Whether the business is a conventional, profit-seeking concern or not, problems often arise in trying to reconcile the different expectations and demands of all the relevant stakeholders. For example:

- The managers of the publishing company will probably *value* profit and reputation (among other things).
- Shareholders will *value* any increase in share price and dividends.

- Customers will, of course, *value* the quality and content of the books but only at a price they are prepared to pay.
- Employees will *value* what they can earn and maybe the opportunity of working for a respected business.

As we have already discussed, trying to 'value' this particular business solely in terms of its profit would be a very one-sided, limited assessment of value, even if it met the needs of the shareholders. Indeed, the usual pressures to keep shareholders happy could easily result in managers constantly trying to reduce costs in order to show ever-greater margins. A former commercial and trading director at global supermarket chain Tesco, which has earned a reputation as a very well-managed business but one that also uses its dominant market position and buying power to exert pressure on suppliers to constantly reduce prices, was quoted (*Sunday Times*, 18th September 2005) as saying at their biannual suppliers conference in 2002 'Give us better prices or watch this space.' His message was clear and unequivocal but does getting better prices from suppliers always guarantee to add value, or will it encourage them just to cut corners? The value motive will not see cost or price reductions, in isolation, as necessarily beneficial, either to the company, its shareholders or even society. Only if the quality of the goods is maintained can cost reductions produce net added value. All of the variables in this equation have to be taken into consideration at all times. The relationship between the company and its suppliers will be very different depending on whether it subscribes to profit or value as its main motive.

One of the most common conflicts in commercial management is that constant battle between those who want to build a brand and reputation, because they see their own futures resting with the business, and those shareholders who take a get-rich-quick attitude to their investment. This is bound to have an influence on employee attitudes, and we will look at their perspective in Chapter 6, but for now it is worth mentioning that if employees actually value working for an employer with integrity then the brighter, higher added value ones may leave if they sense that the purpose and focus of the business is changing (e.g. the book publisher moves down market or even chooses to publish pornography). So it is easy to see that some of these value statements may conflict (e.g. employees value integrity but shareholders just want to make money regardless of how they do that).

These are just a few examples of the normal conflicts of interest that bedevil organizations and result in them being pulled in different directions, all at the same time. Reconciling different value sets may appear to be all in a normal day's work for the management team; a constant but inevitable wrangle that managers have to manage as best they can. If that is true then anything that helps you to manage your own organization's internal value conflicts has to be worth considering. One way to do this is to produce a meaningful value statement from the start.

DECLARING VALUE IN A PUBLIC STATEMENT

The late Peter Drucker, the famous management writer, once said 'That business purpose and business mission are so rarely given adequate thought is perhaps the most important cause of business frustration and failure.' Obviously Drucker's implicit assumption is that a clear purpose or mission and business success tend to go hand-in-hand. A crystal clear mission is the necessary precursor to a crystal clear business strategy (e.g. Jack Welch dictating that GE had to hold the number one or two position in each of its markets). So why do organizations rarely get this right and what might you do to help your organization in this area?

If we look back at the value management editor's quote at the beginning of this chapter we can easily see why formulating a mission is so problematic. A mission statement goes straight to the heart of each individual's values. Corralling everyone's values towards a common purpose is the chief executive's prime task and success in this will provide a powerful platform for organizational effectiveness; but this is emotional territory and every last yard will have to be hard won. Making a clear statement about why the organization exists is always, therefore, going to be a painful exercise when it is done properly, especially the first time around.

If your own organization has already produced a mission statement that is unclear or has failed to capture the hearts and minds of your people ('we want to be the first choice for the customer') then the battle may already have been lost. You do not get many second chances. If business purpose and mission statements are to be anything more than the usual, meaningless, anodyne rhetoric that we are so used to seeing, if everyone is going to take it seriously, it is bound to push everyone into different camps. The main advantage of a clear direction statement is that it gives everyone something to agree. Some might argue that its biggest, potential disadvantage is that it equally gives them all something to disagree with. But is that really a disadvantage? Having no clear direction does not mean there are no dissenters and surely flushing out dissent is partly what organizational leadership is all about?

The dissenters in your own organization (they are present in every organization) may not openly voice their views, for obvious reasons, but their personal actions and behaviour will betray them. In effect, everyone can 'sign up' to a vague mission statement because they can interpret it how they like (e.g. a local manager gives away 'freebies' or spends too much money on trying to improve customer satisfaction in order to be the customer's first choice). The real dissenters in such circumstances, the ones who know that their own values will never be satisfied without clarity of direction, will already be looking elsewhere for an organization that knows exactly where it's heading.

The solution to this common dilemma is not just another, more meaningful mission statement but a value statement. This is not just a financial statement but one that reconciles everyone's views – explicitly. The first part of any value statement will be a declaration that the value of the organization will always, ultimately, have to be expressed in monetary terms, for the reasons given above in our definition of what added value is. This has immediate practical implications for the behaviour of everyone who works in the organization. A nurse who values care of the patient above everything else will now have to reconcile that care with their own costs. Moreover, long-term business development should maximize long-term $s and this should be reconciled with shareholders' expectations (i.e. the message is hang on to your shares – their value will continue to grow significantly over time).

So, our working definition of a value statement is:

> A clear declaration that denotes the highest level measures of what the organization intends to provide for the net benefit of society.

Just before we look at what this means in practice let us also position the value statement in a classical, strategic, planning framework. This framework is shown in Figure 2.2 and it is

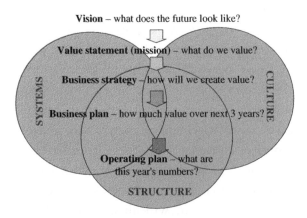

Figure 2.2 The value statement in a strategic framework

intended to demonstrate how the vision of the organization can be translated into the operating plan and any targets required to focus everybody in the organization on achieving its strategic goals. It also shows in the background, represented by the three interlinked circles, that the culture, systems and structure (we could have included other factors such as processes and organizational climate but let us keep it as simple as we can) will all play a significant part in the effective management of the organization. The only difference between Figure 2.2 and any other management textbook version of this classical model is that the value statement replaces the conventional mission statement. So, the vision sets the overall direction (see examples of Ford, Canon and Toyota in Chapter 1) and rules in, and out, what the organization will produce (e.g. the automotive company rules in providing the means for personal, motorized transport, regardless of what that transport might look like in the future, but will rule out making bicycles or non-motorized transport). Vision is at the apex of this hierarchy and will therefore drive everything that comes below it, right down to what each individual in the organization will be doing in the future. However, visions, by definition, are usually indeterminate in timescale and, more importantly from a management perspective, have very little relevance for the work currently carried out by most employees; with the exception of research and development who, presumably, will be researching future modes of transport.

The value statement suggested here is intended to be a definite departure from conventional management thinking, even though it wants to retain all of the benefits that the best mission statements have to offer. The value statement will certainly try to capture hearts and minds while declaring what the purpose of the organization is. However, it will also, immediately, start to dictate how the people who work in the organization need to behave.

Let us try this out using an airline as an example. We could choose any airline but we will look at British Airways (BA) because it provides us with an excellent example of a market that is fundamentally changing (fierce competition from low cost airlines but with air travel growing exponentially). BA is still currently a leading brand; it has an illustrious history; and has had to manage significant change while also having to respond to environmental concerns about the polluting effects of air travel. So what sort of value statement could BA formulate to address and reconcile all of these pressures with the need to provide a good net benefit to society? (It is worth noting that a visit to their website on 4th July 2006 did not unearth a vision or mission statement, although it had a full section on corporate social responsibility which we will cover in Chapter 4.)

According to BA's own figures it carries 36 million passengers and makes 360 000 flights a year. So its value statement might include a specific promise to its customers:

1. 'We will transport passengers to their destinations safely and punctually . . .'

This is really just covering basic value but we will look at compliance as a separate issue shortly. Obviously BA, as an unashamedly commercial business, has to make an acceptable profit and return on its investment so this need has to be balanced immediately with item 1. So item 2 might make a commitment to its shareholders:

2. '. . . at fares which enable the company to achieve an attractive return to investors . . .'

So far so good, but what about the impact BA has on the environment? This could be covered by a statement such as:

3. '. . . while minimizing the environmental impact wherever possible.'

If we leave it there for now it does not look dissimilar to any conventional mission statement and an impartial observer could reach the conclusion that BA is at least aiming to keep most of its stakeholders happy. Yet we have only just scratched the surface of a value statement. Value statements go much deeper than mission statements, into the very culture, systems, structure and processes that run the organization; they start to knit together the very fabric of the organization.

For example, one obvious group of stakeholders not mentioned so far are BA's own employees. What's in this for them? The value they will receive is hopefully secure employment that enables them to make a living. Perhaps that is all any employee should expect from his or her employer. If the labour market is a free and open market then any employees who are not happy working at BA, for whatever reason, are free to go elsewhere. The company does not owe them anything more. Perhaps the company could even take the view that their employees should think themselves lucky just to have a job, with such a prestigious company, so warrant no special attention or mention in the value statement. Perhaps its philosophy, like many companies, is that its first obligation is always to its shareholders.

We need to remember that our definition of value is that the organization's first obligation should be to society. Shareholders, while very important, are too narrow a group to remain as the pre-eminent stakeholder group. Value is always, first and foremost, about the best service to society at the best cost. Yet we would also argue that by doing so the shareholders will get their best returns. How else could we expect shareholders to support the value motive if they did not believe this to be the case? So what chance has an organization of achieving maximum value if employees are not a key part of the equation? Bearing in mind BA's recent industrial relations track record (with several damaging strikes at London Heathrow Airport, their main hub, between

2003 and 2005), having a workforce that is prepared to strike and keep passengers waiting for days for a flight, thereby losing the business millions, it has hardly proved to be a recipe for the highest value so far.

So, the value statement needs to include something about employees, such as:

4. 'We will always aim to employ people who share our goal of maximizing the value that the company can create.'

One aspect of value that has not been covered so far is all of the other constraints that the company faces, which we will lump together for now under the generic heading 'compliance'. These are those regulations imposed by the state or statute that we categorized earlier under the heading of 'basic value'. The most obvious element of this is health and safety, already partially covered in item 1 by the reference to transporting passengers safely. However, there will be numerous additional requirements such as following strict governance and financial guidelines and arrangements for compensating passengers who are delayed. These do not have to be spelled out in the value statement because they are already set out elsewhere and are a given, applying equally to any other airline company. There is never a competitive advantage in compliance or industry-wide minimum standards.

However, the company can still set its own standards and these should be included. For example, the airline could say it will always endeavour to ensure passengers pay the minimum fare available for their choice of seat. It could offer its own compensation scheme rather than follow the minimum imposed by law. Of course, if it did so it would immediately set up a potential conflict with item 2, which aims to give investors an attractive return. Investors could possibly be forgiven for thinking that caveat emptor (let the buyer beware) should be a key principle of running the business. Why should the airline go out of its way to make sure no passenger pays more than they have to? Of course, there is a rationale that could conceivably reconcile these two particular aims. If customers do not trust the company to help them work out the lowest fare then their relationship with the company is already starting off on the wrong foot. Whereas, customers who genuinely believe the company is doing everything it can to help them (e.g. the web booking service draws their attention to the lowest fares – try www.klm.com and try booking a flight for a real example) will inevitably refer to this when making recommendations to friends. In theory, those recommendations turn into paying passengers filling up vacant seats on other flights.

The value statement itself does not have to spell out the rationale that sits behind the business principles. All it has to do is make a clear declaration that it is satisfied that everything expressed in the statement has been reconciled. Of course, in practice, this would mean that any customer who found, after they had flown, that they had paid a higher fare than necessary, would be eligible for an immediate refund of the difference and no shareholder who subscribed to the company's value statement would see anything wrong in this (except maybe to ask the chief executive why and how someone had slipped through the 'net' of their lowest pricing system).

Yet even this example does not fully convey the power of a value statement. It is meant to be a statement of value from every dimension, in a very profound sense. Values are personal and this statement should bind together individual, corporate, customer and investor values. To fully understand this let us go back and have a look at item 3, which refers to environmental impact. Does this mean trying to minimize fuel, traffic and noise pollution? If so what do the employees of the airline do to ensure these value elements are being adhered to? Who is asking the residents living near the airport about noise; are the pilots trained to fly as fuel efficiently as possible or do they have tight schedules to meet that are burning more fuel than necessary; are the pilots being monitored for engine noise as they take off and land? But it is not just the pilots who need to be doing their best, value demands that anyone in the company that can influence value should be doing so. So, when the airline's schedules were planned did any planner ask about the trade-off between pollution and fuel savings? If anyone were to audit this company's value statement would it readily find inconsistencies and internal conflicts? Would they spot very quickly that the airline traded off fuel savings for the sake of punctuality?

Maybe now the real power of the value statement starts to appear. In essence, it serves several key purposes. It:

- covers all stakeholders and shows how it reconciles their potentially conflicting interests;
- is a clear public declaration of everything under the value label, not just profit, financial returns or even (paying) customer satisfaction;
- shows the company will be made accountable for complete value;
- will guide everyone who works for the company.

But the main reason for having a value statement is that if any organization is to maximize value in the long term it has to maximize the satisfaction of all its stakeholders. To do this means getting all stakeholders to sign up to the same agenda.

THE VALUE AGENDA

Of course we have already jumped ahead too quickly here. The previous section assumes that you can reach some agreement about organizational value between all of your stakeholders and it would be naïve to assume that all airline shareholders would be willing to forgo dividends and increasing share values in favour of reducing air pollution. They will probably need some convincing and one way to try to convince them is to start from their viewpoint – everything the organization does will have to aim to add value in terms that they find acceptable. Any activity that is not specifically designed to add value for them is history.

This may well require an education process so we are going to look at two generic agendas. One for any publicly quoted, commercial company and the other for a public sector organization. The principles behind establishing the value agenda for each will be exactly the same but the list of stakeholders will be different.

A VALUE STATEMENT FOR A COMMERCIAL COMPANY

The list of key stakeholders would include the:

- founder or founder's family (if they are still actively involved such as Walter Hewlett during the Hewlett-Packard/Compaq merger in 2002 – see below);
- board;
- executive;
- shareholders – private;
- shareholders – institutional;
- employees;
- customers;
- regulatory authorities (local or central government);
- pressure groups (environmental, business ethics).

In very broad terms, any value agenda that has a fighting chance of reconciling the interests of all the above stakeholders would have to include a clear indication of how the merged company would be more profitable, drive up the share price, while maintaining customer satisfaction, without any detrimental effect on those employees who remain with the company or on the environment. Plus, all of this would have to be achieved without increasing the risk of non-compliance with any regulatory authorities.

Having already made a specific reference to Hewlett-Packard (HP) as an example it might be illustrative to ask what value agenda was in place when the merger with Compaq was mooted. Here is an extract from the letter sent to shareowners in January 2002 (for the full version visit http://www.hp.com/hpinfo/newsroom/press/2002/020118b.html). Some words are shown in italics (by the author) to try to separate out the elements of the merger that are clearly intended to add value and those that might fall into the category of 'less well defined' or even PR related rhetoric.

Dear HP Shareowner:

Your Board of Directors and management team have completed a thorough and deliberative strategic process aimed at improving Hewlett-Packard's competitive position and delivering *greater shareowner value.*

As a result of this two-year process, we are convinced that merging with Compaq Computer Corporation is by far the single best way to reclaim a leadership role at the centre of our industry, and the best and fastest way to *increase the value of your investment in HP.*

The New HP: Stronger In Every Business

In the technology industry, market leadership drives growth. By merging with Compaq, we become the market leader in servers, storage, and management software – the essential components of business infrastructure. In one move, we dramatically improve our ability to offer the end-to-end solutions customers demand – enhancing our prospects in existing accounts and opening doors to new ones.

We immediately double the size of our services business and become a tier-one player in this important, fast-growing segment.

We double the size of our sales force, bolster our research and development budget, and extend our reach into more than 160 countries.

The merger will enable us to quickly address HP's current challenges in the personal computer business by reducing costs, *improving operating margins* and leveraging Compaq's successful direct distribution capability.

Improving the profitability of our other business segments will enable us to continue to increase our investment in innovation and R&D in our market-leading printing and imaging business. Investment is critical to maintaining our leadership in this business, particularly as we enter emerging high-growth markets such as digital imaging and digital publishing.

The merger will materially improve HP's earnings power through significant cost savings and operating efficiencies. In fact, we expect cost savings to reach more than $2.5 billion annually, adding $5 to $9 of present value to each HP share. Importantly, these benefits will enable us to achieve *higher operating margins* and *profit growth* than HP could achieve on its own . . .

Walter Hewlett: He Offers No Plan To Create Value

You may have received a letter from Walter B. Hewlett opposing HP's proposed merger with Compaq. Walter Hewlett, an heir of HP co-founder Bill Hewlett, is a musician and academic who oversees the Hewlett family trust and foundation. While he serves on HP's Board of Directors, Walter has never worked at the company or been involved in its management. His motivations and investment decisions are likely to be very different from your own.

Certainly this letter only represents one possible 'agenda' of board members as it intimates that Walter Hewlett had very different motives, different values. Also, it is a letter aimed specifically at existing shareowners so uses language and numbers that it assumes will appeal to them (profit, margins, share price). Moreover, history tells us that enough shareowners were won over for the merger to be approved. History also tells us that Carly Fiorina, the CEO who instigated the merger and fell out with Walter Hewlett, is no longer with the company. So what might we learn from this?

Well, we all know that 20:20 hindsight is a wonderful thing and we also know that if we undertook an in-depth analysis of HP's finances over the last five years there would be enough obfuscation and financial re-engineering to prevent anyone coming up with a clear and unequivocal verdict on whether this merger did genuinely create some value or not. That in itself should tell us something. Where did HP plan to follow the golden, added value rule of tracking a series of the same measures before and after the merger? In pure revenue terms total revenues increased from $78.7bn in 2001 to $86.6bn in 2005. An increase of about 10%, which probably does not cover inflation and certainly looks poor against a backdrop of market growth in most of their sectors. The real profit generator though was, and still is, the HP printer business which generates 76% of group profits and some market commentators have speculated it could be spun off and valued on its own at between $15 and $27bn. In contrast, HP only makes a margin of about 1% on its multi-billion dollar PC business compared to Dell's much higher margins which it achieves by cutting out all the sort of 'middlemen' dealers that HP relies on. This certainly does not sound like HP is a business that has made great strides in creating value.

Regardless of this conventional, financial analysis of company performance, however, what should concern us here is not what happened after the merger but what happened before it. A value agenda should give clear indications of what, exactly, a company intends to do to create value. Where are the indicators in the shareowner letter of how HP is going to work differently, more innovatively, more cooperatively after the merger and how is that going to be translated into more value? Let us not forget the lessons from the Exeter and KPMG research that showed many companies do not create value through mergers and acquisitions, despite their PR pronouncements. The reason the whole letter is reproduced here is just to illustrate that, in added value terms, very little has been italicised, denoting those statements that might actually add value. Margins and profit growth are measures of net added value but talk of efficiencies is only one variable in the added value equation.

Also, what about the societal impact? If HP relies so much on its printer business to cross-subsidize its other, lower-performing businesses, society starts to find itself in a rather perverse economic situation. In the printer business it is the printer ink that is key to high profit margins. So much so that some printer manufacturers have sold their printers for less than the cost of a replacement ink cartridge, in order to create future ink cartridge replacement sales. This desire to make profits though encourages sensible customers to buy a new printer every time they only need a new cartridge, because this becomes the cheapest option. Society should not just stand back and ask itself if this is the best use of scarce resources, it should be taking action. Either we need a different system or at least factor in the costs of the many printers that will be discarded after a single cartridge runs out. The very first action we should demand is a much clearer statement from each company of the total impact it has on societal value and how it aims to maximize that.

Free-market economists will say this is just the market working and there will always be externalities (effects on third parties not involved in the transaction). It is one thing to accept the inevitability of externalities and quite another to anticipate them, declare them and fully address them right at the outset of any business decision. Those who subscribe to the value motive, seeing it as being a superior market mechanism to profit from every stakeholder's perspective, will argue that if adopting a solely profit perspective is not producing much in the way of results at HP what have they got to lose by adopting a much more rounded, total equation, holistic approach? Certainly, if HP cannot perform significantly better as a result of a merger then even shareholders should be eagerly looking for a better alternative.

We will return to this debate in Chapter 5 when we look at how the performance of companies is measured but let us now consider what a public sector value agenda might look like.

A VALUE STATEMENT FOR A PUBLIC SECTOR ORGANIZATION

The list of key stakeholders here would include the:

- elected representatives (government ministers, local council members);
- board of trustees;
- executive;
- employees;
- customers;
- taxpayers;
- regulatory authorities (local or central government);
- pressure groups (environmental, business ethics).

This list is not too dissimilar to the commercial list except that one individual could have three different value perspectives simultaneously. For example, the employee of the council, working in the refuse collection department, is also likely to be a customer of the council's refuse collection service as well as a local taxpayer. As an employee they could be unhappy about having to achieve their own performance targets yet, as a taxpayer, happy that the other council departments have to achieve efficiency targets. Also, as a customer of the refuse collection department, they could be only too willing to complain if their bin is not being emptied promptly. Meanwhile this same person hopes that their local taxes are always being spent wisely. This brings into sharp relief the issue of always having to reconcile individual views on value, even when the individual's own views can be very inconsistent. So what value agenda could be constructed here to achieve the best reconciliation?

Taking this local government authority as our example it will be funded out of taxation (probably both local and central government) and its purpose is to deliver local services such as street lighting, libraries, refuse disposal and social services. On this level it would appear that every stakeholder should have the same view of value, providing the best services at the lowest cost. So where are the sources of any potential problems of value reconciliation? One major source will, of course, be the elected representatives themselves, the council members. They have to get elected and to do so they try to give their constituents what they want. Their own, personal political imperative is a key motivational driver for them. So, if their constituents want more street lighting they will support their case for resources against other council members fighting their own, similar, battles on behalf of their own 'competing' constituents. Of course, politicians who know what they are doing and have some integrity will tell their constituents when they believe there are other priorities elsewhere which are greater than theirs. Others will just chase the votes.

It would be helpful, therefore, if there was a value agenda that declared not only what the priorities are but how, objectively, those priorities were arrived at. This is where our understanding of basic value would come into play. So, do all streets in the area have the minimum level of lighting already? If not, then street lighting gets onto the basic priority list. Creating a clear 'must-have' list would send a very clear signal to all stakeholders. The value agenda then has to identify areas for added value. How is the local authority going to improve over the short and long term? How is it going to bring down its average running costs, how is it going to provide better housing for every £ spent?

Again, this all just sounds like nothing new except that sometimes the council has to cut costs because central government wants to reduce the amount of funding it provides from taxation. The question now becomes one of which priorities can be sacrificed (street lighting or keeping the local library open)? Yet to those whose motivation is the creation of real value this is the wrong question. Any decision to shut down the library will save money but it will not add value, per se, because no one has factored into the equation the loss of the library service to those who use it. It is this part of the equation that has to be spelled out in the value agenda. There has to be a clear statement from all stake-holders to agree on what is valued and, even more importantly, a commitment to maintain value wherever possible. Stocking 10% fewer books in the libraries for a 10% cost saving cannot be deemed to be added value, even if it has freed up money for other purposes. At best it is just robbing Peter to pay Paul, at worst it is just cutting corners. Such an agenda will immediately influence the thinking of all council employees, who will not be allowed to cut corners without explaining how they are maintaining value. If we compare how things would be different if the council were run as a profit-making concern, it would be easy for the library manager to show an improvement in the bottom line and show more profit (because of reduced costs) but customers would lose something in the process. So the profit motive does not supply a better answer.

It is worth reiterating here that this is primarily a management book, not another text on dry, cost/benefit analysis. The objective is to promote the adoption of a clear value agenda, and the principles that underpin it: to fundamentally change the management of organizations such as public sector bodies. This will be seen even more clearly when we consider the other main source of contentious value reconciliation, what we might hesitatingly call 'the politically correct agenda'. For now, suffice it to say that if a councillor wants to set up a body to look after a special interest group's 'rights' (fill in 'gay', 'women', 'ethic minorities' or any other discrete group) then the value agenda demands how such a body will either satisfy basic value needs (minimum standards) or add value. How can this be weighed up against more library books or street lighting?

There is certainly no intention here to become embroiled in the highly emotive subject of rights. The only reason this has been referred to here as the 'politically correct agenda' is to acknowledge the fact that many people do not support such causes because they can see no value in them (e.g. heterosexuals see no reason to support gay groups). Their own, individual perspective could be very different to those in the minority group and the workers who support them. Different councillors from different sections of the political spectrum will hold equally vehement but opposing views. But this is no idle debate. These sorts of decisions are already being made every day; juggling competing value propositions is already a reality. What is missing is a coherent and cohesive way of resolving them to the satisfaction of the greatest number. So what concerns us here is whether there can be any common ground on which all interested parties can firmly stand. Can the value agenda reconcile all of their views for the common good? We are not searching for that elusive absolute measure of value here. Only the possibility of giving those who have to manage resources a better chance of managing them more effectively and for greater value. A clear path to finding possible answers to these very vexing questions will be explored in more detail in Chapter 6 but let us first clear some of the undergrowth that has been getting in the way.

'INTANGIBLES' CONFUSE THE ISSUE OF ADDED VALUE

We cannot get away from some of the difficulties presented by this single word value being used in too many ways, by too many people, trying to cover too many different concepts and perspectives. It is a recipe for total confusion and one of the key causes of this confusion is a simplistic distinction made in most people's minds between what they consider to be tangibles and intangibles.

A car is something tangible you can touch and drive. The self-image it affords you is deemed an intangible. A book is something you can pick up and read but the enlightenment or joy it brings is intangible. So what about a brand or a company's reputation? What about somebody caring for the elderly who takes 5 minutes with them for a friendly chat and a cup of tea? Can you touch these in any way or do they have to be regarded as intangible? From a distinction between tangibles and intangibles it is not a very big step to a full-blown debate about how you measure them. It is easy to measure cars coming off a production line or the number of books on a library shelf. Where are the same hard measures of brand, customer loyalty and elderly care? What is that 5 minute chat over tea worth?

The main problems here though have little or nothing to do with measurement. They emanate from a false distinction being made between tangibles and intangibles. This is a complete red herring in discussions about added value and it will only take a couple of examples to expose this false dichotomy for what it is (and we will see later in Chapter 5 how this confused thinking completely undermines central government spending and the value derived from hard-earned, taxpayers' money). To do so we need to take a second look at how we defined added value in Figure 2.1.

There we looked at four ways to add value; four added value variables that it might be worth measuring, quantity of output, cost, revenue (or higher prices) and quality. It is the last of these, quality, that causes the intangibility problem. Improving quality, in itself, will not necessarily add value. It is relatively easy to find ways of improving the quality of cars, for example, but if the cost of those quality improvements is too high the increased price required might make it uncompetitive. So all of the four added value variables have to move in synch with each other, all of the time. Value will never be established if one of the variables has been excluded.

Customers will pay for what they *perceive* to be improvements in quality, relative to price. Sometimes those perceived improvements could also be described as real improvements as opposed to cosmetic enhancements (e.g. the difference between improved handling through better suspension and a 'go faster stripe' paint job). Perception is reality. That go-faster stripe really does enhance the customer's enjoyment of driving the car. It is because there is no such thing as absolute value that we can only attach worth to the things we personally value by paying for them. The only ultimate determinant and arbiter of organizational value is what the customer is prepared to pay for. That will always be true, it is a truism, but the question for the practising manager is 'so what do I need to do to make sure I am adding value?' What did the painting engineers at Ford feel like when they found that the numerous coats of paint on Ford seat frames they had recommended were seen as superfluous by Lexus engineers? The answer to that question will always be the same. They should only have recommended and delivered what the customer could see and was willing to pay for (defined as fit for purpose). Then they should have focused on the four added value variables in order to make sure any improvement in one is not negated by a corresponding diminution in another (i.e. don't stop painting the frames until you have ensured that the base metal is of a sufficient quality not to need painting). This then just leaves the separate question of *how* can you influence these variables.

There are a million and one ways to add value. Some of which are obvious, such as just working harder and many others, particularly in large organizations, which are not so obvious. Take creativity as one example. The very word seems to be inherently dealing with something intangible or will appear differently to different people's perspectives. Creativity itself, though, does not show up in Figure 2.1 because it is not, itself, an organizational output. The reason creativity is not on the diagram is because you will only know if you are being creative, and adding value, when creativity results in more output. Think of the outputs of any organization, be it a hospital or automotive manufacturer, and consider how creative approaches might add value by increasing the number of patients treated ('hey, we've worked out a different way to treat patients'); or at less cost ('he had a great idea for using fewer consumables on the ward'); increasing revenue ('customers seem to love that new colour we created for our cars and don't mind paying the extra') or better quality of service or product ('that new braking system is much safer than our competitors' and customers are happy to pay for it').

Nevertheless, although creativity and innovation are not outputs themselves they most certainly are the seed corn of huge added value so they should not be dismissed or relegated to the category of intangibles. Yet, paradoxically, when it comes to measurement, it is the outputs that we will use to measure creativity, not some qualitative survey that says 'we are creative'. All so-called 'intangibles' that are worth something, that is value adding, become tangibles eventually. Producing a new car colour that no customer wants (albeit still using your creativity to do so) will not be translated into value (more sales). So we will make no distinction between tangibles and intangibles, particularly in Chapter 7 when we start to look at how to get the best value out of people. The only distinction to be made will be between those that produce value and those that do not.

Added value can be an incredibly slippery concept though. Added value means providing more per £ spent, more for less, not less for less. Consequently, added value only really comes from getting the balance right between all of the four variables. The notion of added value is at the heart of the value agenda and something this all-encompassing in scope might sound like just an ivory tower. In fact it is also a very powerful, simple and practical tool. All it requires is for anyone to ask the question 'how will this particular activity/work/project/programme/initiative add value?' This is not a rhetorical or hypothetical question. If there is no line of sight to an increase in output, reduction in cost, increase in revenue or improvement in quality then there is no justification, business or otherwise, for continuing on that course. If, however, there is a clear line of sight then there is already a reasonable probability that the project or work in question will actually, eventually be translated into added value. Something with this much potential is bound to have a profound impact on the way we think about and manage organizations but its full potential will only be achieved when there is a simple, but radical shift in mindsets.

CHAPTER 3

THIS POWERFUL MOTIVE FORCE WE CALL VALUE

Summary We all do what we value. It is the most powerful motive force of all. All society has to do is harness that force.

HARNESSING THE POWER OF MOTIVE

Those of us who have never aspired to become a chief executive or a government minister might stand back in wonder and ask ourselves why anyone would want all of the responsibility and pressure that goes with those jobs. Presumably, while the onerous nature of these positions must also occur to those who do crave high office, the rewards, recognition and general ego trip that are part and parcel of the whole package must still be great enough for them to do anything to fulfil their ambitions. What the objective observer construes as naked ambition though is just the normal, innate behaviour pattern of the ambitious. If you ever stop, even for one second, to ask yourself the question 'am I really ambitious?' then maybe you have just failed the first test of the superambitious. To them, their ambition goes unquestioned: climbing the greasy pole and justifying their means by focusing on their ends is as natural as getting out of bed every morning.

Often such people are described as 'driven' rather than merely being motivated. They cannot change their behaviour. No one can stop them doing what they feel compelled to do. How else do you explain the behaviour of many political leaders who cling to office or business leaders like the late Kenneth Lay of Enron or Bernie Ebbers of WorldCom whose ambitions completely overwhelm their business judgement? This tremendous motive power can move mountains but it can also, equally, destroy them. The challenge for those who subscribe to the value motive is to do everything we can to harness those forces towards the ends of best societal value.

But it would be very misleading to suggest that only 'leaders' need to be motivated by value. Admittedly, business leaders who end up in court must have set their own course but why should we assume that the thousands of ordinary workers in these organizations just had to follow? It beggars belief that the only people who were at all suspicious about what was going on at Enron were just a small number at the highest level. What was motivating the Arthur Andersen employees, for example, who shredded hundreds of documents when the Enron scandal broke? Surprisingly quickly employees can be confronted with stark choices of being 'camp guards' or whistleblowers and history tells us again and again that, given this choice, whistleblowers tend to be a tiny minority. There is something about organizations that can drive law-abiding, rational people to do things that, objectively and in the cold light of day, they would never dream of doing. We should never underestimate, for one second, the power of this all-embracing, pervasive motive force.

Yet it is precisely the same force driving the 'shredder' that sends the fire fighter into a blazing building to save someone. Something, somewhere in the head of the individual drives them to behave in a spectacular or dangerous manner. The motives here, of course, are entirely different. One looks like personal survival in a highly political organizational context; the other looks like altruism. They could equally be seen by each individual as someone 'just doing their job'. We will soon return to exploring their respective motives but for now all we are interested in is the power that can be unleashed, for whatever purpose. Whether the story about James Watt (the man who refined the design of early steam engines in the 18th century) is apocryphal or not, many ordinary people must have observed on numerous occasions how the power of the steam from a boiling kettle can lift its lid. The cause and the effect were staring them in the face. However, only those with the talents of someone like Watt could make the right connections and have the capabilities to produce a working model that could harness this power. In fact, it is even worth pointing out that steam engines already existed when Watt came along but his design produced a much more powerful, and therefore more valuable, engine. An engine that was initially sought by mine owners to improve productivity but also improve safety for the mineworkers. In other words, the *outputs* of the engine were much better for everyone concerned.

So how do we link these key ideas together? The way the organization works is very much dictated by the values of those who lead it. The motive forces driving the leadership will inevitably be transmitted down through the management. This means the behaviours of individuals in the organization are determined, to a great extent, by the same motives and politics of management. Whether all of this effort is worthwhile can only be determined by the worth of the outputs of the organization.

VALUE MEANS OUTPUT, NOT INPUT

As with many aspects of this book, this just sounds like another statement of the obvious. However, defining organizational outputs is actually always highly problematic and we will soon see in Chapter 4 that, as soon as we move away from a commercial context, clarity of outputs proves to be an insurmountable hurdle for some organizations (e.g. what outputs are the criminal justice and penal systems meant to generate?). For now, though, we need at least to be clear what the difference between inputs and outputs really is and the implications this will have for the potential motive force of value. In order to do so we will obtain some of the insights we need by looking at what is recognized as the number one brand in the world, Coca-Cola. So what are Coca-Cola's outputs?

For the three months up to 31st March 2006 (see http://www2.coca-cola.com/presscenter/pdfs/ko_earnings20060419.pdf) Coca-Cola produced net operating revenues of $5 226 000 000, which is probably the main measure of its output. It certainly represents an astronomic volume of liquid refreshment and tells us, quite clearly, that millions of customers must derive an enormous amount of satisfaction from this. To produce this amount of liquid the 'costs of goods sold' were $1 726 000 000 leaving a gross profit of $3 500 000 000 (gross margin was 67.0%). In simple terms, the manufacturing costs of Coke, and most of Coca-Cola's other carbonated beverages, do not constitute the largest proportion of overall costs. However, there are considerable costs in marketing the products and administering the business as SGA (selling, general and administrative) expenses were $2 060 000 000 or 39.4% of turnover, leaving a much lower, but still remarkably attractive, operating margin of 27.6%.

If we look a little closer in order to try to establish the 'true' value to society of Coca-Cola (albeit still accepting that value is always personal), by looking at the most tangible aspect of its output, the drink itself, we could be forgiven for coming to the conclusion that all this money generates very little, actual physical, output. To illustrate this point one only has to buy a bottle of Coke and look at the nutrition table under the 'Ingredients' section of the label. There you will see the following (taken from a UK 500 ml bottle label in 2005):

Nutrition information per 100 ml

Protein	0 g
Fat	0 g
Fibre	0 g
Sodium	0 g
Carbohydrate	10.7 g (of which sugars 10.7 g)

Essentially, by Coca-Cola's own admission in its nutrition table, Coke is water, sugars and flavourings and offers very little in the way of nourishment. But then it does not set out to provide nutrition. Its customers pay for the unique taste and some even for the 'lifestyle' image it might create. So there is no point in trying to make any value judgements here about the inputs and outputs of Coke even if we might stand back on occasions and ask ourselves the question – is this worth over $20 bn worth of the world's resources every year? Coca-Cola's customers vote with their feet and their pockets and have every right to do so: one key gauge of market value here, net income of $1 162 000 000, speaks for itself. Having said that, many of them obviously need some seriously high-cost marketing initiatives to convince them to continue to do so.

Now let us move on to consider how well Coca-Cola is managed to deliver its outputs. Now we are looking at internal, organizational value. This is a hugely successful business that knows that it cannot afford to stand still because the global beverage market is an incredibly tough and competitive one. It could be said that Coca-Cola's core competence is the marketing of sugars and water, and this is genuinely intended as a compliment. Except that if this is its core competence then it seems to be slipping. Several product launches at Coca-Cola over recent years have just helped to demonstrate that the customer is always king, regardless of marketing prowess. In early 2004 Coca-Cola tried to launch its successful Dasani water brand for the first time in the UK. Unfortunately some UK national newspapers got hold of this story and revealed that the water source used for Dasani was a public mains in Sidcup, Kent (maybe if it was the public mains in Chamonix or even a Scottish glen it might have not been so bad) and the launch was eventually aborted. Another story later that year suggested that Coca-Cola was heading for a similar disaster over its C2 brand, described as 'a sort of semi-skimmed Coke'. It almost appears that Coca-Cola lives or dies by the strength of its marketing more than the intrinsic, perceived value of the product itself or the brand reputation that makes it number one. Its output really does appear to be as much about image as it is about substance.

This leads us into the whole debate about the value of brands and one business that has endeavoured to stretch its brand value to the limit is the Virgin group run by Sir Richard Branson. By 2006 this had become a conglomerate of very disparate entities and there were serious questions as to whether the brand itself had become jaded. The Virgin Cars business closed and prompted some observers to point out that this was not the first Virgin franchise that had not quite prospered under the Branson touch. Virgin Cola has been suffering and Virgin Vie, Virgin Clothes and Virgin Vodka have all proved disappointing.

So what does this tell us about the connection between value and outputs? Well, first it reminds us that customers are always the ultimate arbiters of the value of outputs. If customers do not value them they are worthless. Second, everything else in producing that output is only an input. With value we want maximum outputs with minimum inputs. This means that whether it's Coca-Cola or Virgin their marketing and brand development efforts (including the $2 bn SGA costs incurred by Coca-Cola) should always be kept to a minimum. It doesn't matter how big, or clever, or sophisticated those inputs might be, they can never guarantee a corresponding output. Now, if we change industries very briefly here and look at the pharmaceutical giant GSK we are told (GSK Corporate Responsibility Report 2005) that their already sizable R&D budget of £3.1 bn could go to as high as 25% of revenue in two to three years' time. Yet, at the same time we know that 9 out of 10 drugs that enter clinical trials never make it to market. It is amazing how much input we usually need to produce so little output. In the process, real value could be draining away and in drugs terms we really could be losing out as a society.

It does not seem to matter either what type of organizational entity society uses to deliver those outputs. In the US, where healthcare is delivered primarily through the operation of the market, healthcare costs are the highest in the world, as percentage of GDP spent per capita (see 'The US Healthcare System: Best in the world or just the most expensive?' University of Maine, Summer 2001). In the UK, by comparison, where health-care is delivered primarily through the state-run NHS, a record spend of £75 bn in 2005 produced, according to the UK Prime Minister Tony Blair, 'improvements in the NHS' while his Secretary of State for Health, Patricia Hewitt, made even bolder assertions by declaring 2005 to be the NHS's 'best year ever' at a national nurses conference in April 2006.

Of course, none of the above statistics or political posturing actually tells us how well the US or UK healthcare systems are performing in terms of 'customers' (patients in this case). Spending a certain percentage of GDP per head on healthcare looks, to the untrained eye, like an output because GDP (gross domestic product), by definition, is meant to signify an economy's output;

but here it has been turned into a measure of input. So what about the politician's views on the outputs of the NHS? Within the very narrow confines of the most limited definition of the word output Tony Blair was correct. The number of operations and patients treated increased. But did they increase at least in proportion to the extra public money poured into the NHS? Between 1998/9 and 2003/4 NHS expenditure increased by approximately 88% (from £35 bn to £66 bn) while operations carried out increased by 4% (from 6.4 m to 6.7 m) and cancelled operations (a huge draining away of value?) increased from 53 m to 66 m!

Admittedly, the NHS's output is not just measured in terms of surgical operations but it is pretty obvious that politicians who call this 'improvements in the NHS' are certainly not looking at it from a value perspective. In reality, in real value terms, the NHS organization is performing relatively worse than it used to. Patricia Hewitt's definition of 'best year' might refer to patients treated but the value equation of more patients per £ spent has certainly deteriorated dramatically. On this basis 2005 could be described as the NHS's worst year. Pouring money into an organization, especially one in crisis, is no way to increase its value. So getting the best outputs at the lowest costs must be something to do with the way the organization itself is managed, rather than the type of legal entity chosen.

With this insight let us now return to Coca-Cola and ask how well is it being run in the light of Dasani and C2? One analyst was quoted (*Sunday Times*, 14th November 2004) as saying 'You have to conclude that there are structural, managerial problems at this company that are leading to serious errors.' He even described Coca-Cola as a 'fractious empire' suggesting that 'Coke had fallen out with Coca Cola Enterprises (CCE) . . . over profit-sharing arrangements': evidence yet again that the common pursuit of profit does not necessarily produce the best or desired results. There were even strong hints that the then chief executive, Mr Daft, was having problems managing Coca-Cola's image in a rapidly changing world and was having to '. . . consciously play down Coca Cola's American image. Its Coke brand has been a particular target for Muslims fighting against perceived American imperialism.' This raises the bar considerably. Value, if it is ever to earn its rightful place as a prime, motive force, has to be seen as part of a much grander scheme of things, in a much wider context.

DEFINING VALUE AS AN ECONOMIC SYSTEM

Having looked at the competing charms of profit and value in Chapters 1 and 2 it is now time to set value in its true context. This is a much bigger context than has been suggested thus far – value as a complete economic system. Once it is put in this context profit is relegated to a very lowly, second place. The profit motive might be at the heart of the capitalist system but it requires several other systems to make up for its shortcomings. It needs a tight corporate law system (to control its excesses and irregularities), a welfare system (to ensure its benefits are distributed), a charity system (to direct resources into areas of need not provided for by the market) and a huge public sector system (to provide services such as healthcare, which some believe are not best suited to free market forces) for it to work reasonably well for the benefit of society as a whole. In effect, profit is not reconciled with the wider economic and social systems, it is more a case of the state plugging the gaping holes it leaves in its wake.

Nevertheless, anything that we attempt to organize or manage is best served by effective systems. Systems are a means for control so we had better make sure we have the best systems possible if we are to have any chance of getting the best value possible. As always, though, we need to define our terms and our definition of a system is:

> A means for making sure that what you plan to happen actually happens.

So, safety systems try to make sure no one has an accident. Payment systems make sure clients pay on time. Computer operating systems make sure the computer operates. A road system makes sure you can transport goods or people from A to B. All of these systems have checks built into them. Part of the safety system includes regular inspections; the payment system includes generating a reminder for late payers; a diagnostic tells you whether the computer operating system software has loaded properly; a series of road signs makes sure you end up where you need to be. That is why the whole concept of a system is so incredibly powerful, despite being so blindingly obvious. We get so used to systems that we stop noticing them. Moreover, the best systems are simple and make sense to ordinary human beings, which is why they become totally assimilated into our normal, everyday, behaviour patterns.

Think, for example, of what a traffic light system is meant to achieve. It has a dual purpose:

1. It is supposed to ensure that cars do not collide at intersections; and
2. It is designed to keep traffic moving as smoothly as possible.

These two purposes are totally intertwined, one cannot happen without the other. It is a very simple, easy to understand, system and every citizen should be able to see the obvious sense in it. On paper, traffic lights are probably the nearest you will ever get to an example of a perfect system. All systems need human support and commitment to make them work well though, so they are all inherently *human systems.* However, because no human is perfect there is no such thing as a perfect system. Let us look at traffic light systems again, this time in more depth, to see what the implications of this are.

When you approach a traffic light and it turns from green to amber you have to make a decision whether to carry on through or to stop. In that instant quite a few considerations flash through your mind. Will you be late? Will you be breaking the law? Will you cause an accident? Are you being irresponsible by not stopping? Systems in society inevitably become bound up with the values of society. The best systems are those that are voluntarily accepted by everyone: everyone agrees on the rules and follows them. We all believe it is morally right to obey the traffic light. Or, at least, the vast majority of us do.

A minority, however, for whatever reason, will still make up their own minds as to whether they should stick to the system or not. Some people will be irresponsible and try to jump the lights. They take a calculated risk (just like the risks many commercial companies take) and they will often get away with it. Those with even a modicum of morals will exonerate themselves by feeling that no one has suffered as a result of their actions (the same argument is applied by those who commit 'white collar' crime and suggest it is victimless). What they do not seem to realize is that their selfish, anti-social behaviour is threatening to undermine the whole system. It would not take many drivers ignoring red lights to make the lights irrelevant. If everyone ignored the lights chaos would reign. Consequently, even systems that make absolute sense to the vast majority of human beings still require laws and policing to provide a rock solid foundation and deter potential transgressors. Systems, by definition, really do mean control, whether voluntary, self-control or imposed.

Now let us immediately read straight across to a discussion of something we have all taken for granted for so many years (or at least those of us who grew up outside of the former communist bloc) – the capitalist system. We need to ask ourselves whether this really constitutes a system by the definition we have just established above. We can then revisit what was 'meant to happen' as a direct result of this system and move on to ask how well it is working.

DOES THE CAPITALIST SYSTEM DELIVER THE BEST VALUE?

The best systems, almost by definition, are those that are very well designed. They do not usually happen by chance. For example, if there were no town planning system individuals would not automatically work well together to ensure roads, housing and amenities were all positioned to mutual advantage. Yet what we loosely call the 'capitalist system' was never *designed* as such, it just evolved as a natural human system, and was never a complete economic system in its own right. The 'invisible hand' was Adam Smith's metaphor for describing his observation of how society managed itself, naturally. Smith did not invent or design this market driven economic system, he just explained it. It could be said that the capitalist system was born when the first subsistence farmer managed to acquire some capital (i.e. a surplus of crops that he didn't personally need to survive) and met another farmer in the same situation with whom he could trade (their interdependency being the defining principle of the capitalist system). Capitalism was very attractive to those who did not want to spend the rest of their lives just subsisting and the profit motive did the rest.

Since then the behaviour of capitalists has had to be controlled (e.g. anti-trust legislation and regulatory bodies such as the EU's competition commission designed to ensure fair competition reigns) in order to make sure they provide society with what it needs. In effect, there has been an ongoing development and refinement of the capitalist system. It may still look like the original but we are on the latest revision in a continuing series of iterations (Sarbanes-Oxley being one of the biggest revisions in recent years). We have spent the last 200 years modifying and adapting this system to make it work better. But should we now take a fresh look and finally accept that the fundamentals of the system are wrong and no sticking plaster legislation will correct these inherent deficiencies?

Winston Churchill said the inherent vice of capitalism was the uneven division of blessings, while the inherent virtue of socialism was the equal division of misery. What he didn't say was how to get the best out of both systems, the production of wealth and the redistribution of wealth. Communism offered an alternative to capitalism but failed to provide its society with the basic value it needed and the added value it wanted. At the height of collective farming in the former USSR the 5% of land allocated for personal cultivation produced 20% of the food. The people spoke loudly and clearly through their behaviour even if they were not allowed to do so through the ballot box.

But capitalism had to be bolstered by many other systems that inevitably grew up alongside its steady progress (e.g. welfare). From the industrial revolution onwards capitalism earned its spurs by providing huge amounts of wealth; much of which was redistributed for the good of a wide (although some would still argue a very narrow) section of society. Its predominance and the benefits it brought with it made it look like a viable system but from a 21st century perspective it could now be perceived as 'of its time', serving society very well through the huge transition from 'subsistence' economy to 'developed' economy rather than a coherent, holistic system for creating the best distribution of societal value in the widest sense. It may have been the major system and the powerhouse of economic development for an awfully long period but when viewed in the present context of the need for mutually reinforcing, high value economic, societal, political and environmental systems it is seriously wanting. In fact, we seem to be constructing a mishmash of systems rather than a unified whole (see Chapter 5 on the systems being developed for gauging organizational performance).

So, if we need to revisit the capitalist system as part of a thorough reassessment of all the systems that govern society, perhaps we have to be prepared to restate what the capitalist system has to make happen. We might struggle to find a single, common statement of what the capitalist system is or a precise definition of what it is meant to achieve, even if there is a general understanding of the term. Whatever benefits came from capitalism, it has never been clearly defined as a system for ensuring that society creates the best value possible. So why should all members of society continue to support a system that was never designed to support them as fully as possible? No wonder the environmentalists, socialists and social entrepreneurs believe they somehow occupy the high ground in this debate.

To move forward we need to build on the lessons learned in Chapter 1, where reducing capitalism to a discussion solely about 'profit' easily demonstrated the inability of the profit motive to offer the best probability of generating a profit; and Chapter 2, where we saw how the essence of value creation lies in the reconciliation of the perspectives of different stakeholders. We now, therefore, need a system that retains all the proven power of the profit motive but which also satisfies the 'what needs to happen for me' agendas of all the other key stakeholders in the system (e.g. the environmentalist's need to reduce pollution). In short, we need a well-designed, holistic, value system that produces as large surpluses as possible.

If one of global society's most basic needs is clean drinking water, for example, is the current system working and if not what system will solve the problem? Does society really need the very inefficient and expensive system that transports commercially bottled water all over the world? Should money spent on marketing water be put to better use producing ordinary drinking water, at the right quality, where it is needed? If we all agree we want this to happen we have to design a whole system to make it happen. This is just one example of a general point. Systems need to work naturally for as many people as possible, because that accords with the common sense and innate sense of fairness that most human beings seem to subscribe to. In effect, this value system will aim to tap into that incredibly powerful human force that is driven by an individual's belief in their own values (material or otherwise). So our value system will aim to ensure:

The greatest personal value for the greatest number of people.

Yes, if you think you have heard this statement somewhere before you are right. If so it was probably Jeremy Bentham's assertion that government should work to the principle that 'It is the greatest happiness of the greatest number that is the measure of right and wrong' (from Bentham's *A Fragment on Government*, 1776). So we are not treading on particularly new ground here except that Jeremy Bentham did not have to manage a car production line, a financial services office or a local authority housing department. Telling a production worker on the nightshift in a car plant that by putting wheels on a car they are fulfilling their part of a grand plan to achieve the greatest happiness of society might not cut much ice. Jeremy Bentham and other philosophers are still famous, and quite rightly so, for the fundamental truths they have taught us, their words of great wisdom and their humanity that apply equally well across the centuries. What we as managers need to do though is translate those words of wisdom into something that helps us all transport ourselves from A to B as efficiently and unpollutingly as possible. So how can we start to embed this value system into our own organizational settings? There is probably no better place to start than right at the top.

WHEN WE SAY VALUE WE SHOULD REALLY MEAN IT

It is one thing to say you 'value' something and another to actually mean it. The difference between talking the talk and walking the walk. A business leader that talks about value but does not mean it will soon be exposed. But they will already have done untold damage to the potential, latent, motive force in their workforce. Their lack of commitment to the cause will not just result in their own downfall, it will have created a level of cynicism that will deprive their successor of an opportunity to build on the natural goodwill of their employees. As we have already seen, value and personal values fit together like a hand in a glove. Individual employees will very quickly pick up any discrepancy. In Figure 2.2 our strategic framework included a value statement that was designed to make the leaders' views on value clear and explicit. Moreover, it was not meant to be plucked out of the air but born out of a clear, well-conceived, organizational vision. That is the starting point so if the vision does not set out to offer the greatest value to the greatest number of people then everything else that follows is just rhetoric. The value motive is a complete mindset. The organization has a societal purpose over and above the need to make a profit. When described in this way it hints at the vision offering the organization an almost religious or moral purpose. It suggests that those who work for the organization are doing something for a higher purpose.

This might be a new angle for some companies but we suggested in Chapter 1 that some Far Eastern companies like Canon and Toyota have always embraced this view. A further and fresher perspective is an Islamic view. Sheikh Nizam Yaquby, a leading Islamic scholar (interviewed in *The Times* on 26th April 2006) remarked on the subject of Islamic banking and Sharia law that 'What we have is not a threat to the capitalist system because we believe in freedom of ownership. Ownership is sacred in Islam and is the main block of capitalism. On the other hand there is the freedom of the market and trade. Let the market itself do the equilibrium; the invisible hand. Our scholars mentioned the invisible hand 700 years before Adam Smith.'

If Islamic scholars did observe the same invisible hand as Adam Smith it just reinforces the view that this was always an inevitable, natural state of affairs. So Islamic commercial thinking is not very different to 'western' thinking except that he continues by saying 'the Islamic banking and finance movement will not eradicate poverty but will contribute greatly to social justice . . . giving zakat (a donation of 2.5% of profits annually to charities or education) is one of our purposes'. Apparently the Islamic view of capitalism is very much bound up with 'social justice', in a similar way to the philanthropy of many entrepreneurs and industrialists. This idea of reconciling several aspects of life under one coherent system is not new at all. Let us now compare this with what is actually happening in much of the capitalist world.

If we take a company like Goldman Sachs, a very large and very successful (in conventional terms) investment bank which has made multi-millionaires out of many of its top executives we can ask whether any of them were ever motivated by anything other than personal, financial success. Scott Mead was one of their senior managers who, in 1999, 'engineered a £43 billion takeover by Vodafone of Air Touch Communications (US)' (*Sunday Times*, 6th June 2003). So what were Vodafone's motives and what about those of Goldman Sachs and Scott Mead? Was this a deal that would improve the greatest value for the greatest number of people? Was it ever intended to do so? Or was it just going to pay Goldman Sachs millions of dollars in fees that would come from the proceeds of financial re-engineering? Who was supposed to benefit, society at large or shareholders?

If we accept for a moment that society benefits from mobile phone technology, and leave aside any concerns for the environmental impact of mobile phone masts, constructing an argument for increasing the greatest value for the greatest number of people is quite straightforward. As a mobile phone company the only way Vodafone can add value (using the four value variables – see Chapter 2) is either by attracting more customers to this merged business, selling more mobile phones, providing the service at a lower cost or by improving the quality of the handsets or the service level. Ideally, it would be a beneficial combination of all four. If this were at the heart of Vodafone's vision then it would have to work hard to continuously come up with new ideas on how to run the new merged business better. So why would it have such a vision? Well, if the merger really did help Vodafone reduce costs, and these were passed on to customers in lower prices, then Vodafone would be gaining a competitive advantage. This would help customers and society simultaneously.

An alternative motive would be to unleash some extra, but purely financial, 'value' (i.e. shareholder-only value) through some sophisticated financial re-engineering. This second option would require a change in financial management but much less so a change in the way Vodafone was managed or its organizational culture, structure or systems. Whatever the motives behind this deal an article under the heading 'Vodafone's Value Destruction' (*Sunday Times*, 15th January 2006) quoted research from an analyst from Man Securities whose calculations showed a loss in Vodafone's value of £12.7bn since the deal was completed and 'not much improvement' on costs between 2003 and 2006 (operating expenses down from 22.9% to 22.2% but customer costs up from 18.1% to 23.3% – they were throwing money at attracting new customers).

So what would Scott Mead, one of the main architects of this deal, make of this? Was this a successful deal for anyone? It would appear the only ones to get any value from it were those who received the fees. Interestingly, after a long and illustrious career at Goldman Sachs he decided to leave the company and on his departure remarked 'There are many more important things in the world than M&A and equity offerings . . . I've just turned 49 and I've always said there's going to be a point in my life to pursue things I haven't had time to pursue.' Some of these 'things' included charitable works and his words could almost be construed as that classic, capitalist apology for a hard-hearted, commercial life, 'I want to put something back into society'. Is this another angle on the sort of view we heard from Sandy Weill of Citigroup and his 'deal with God' in Chapter 2?

It would be very easy to be cynical about all of this. One way to avoid such cynicism, to keep a cool head but a warm heart, is to view all of this from a value motive perspective. How could this whole situation be better served by adopting such a view? Well maybe it is about time Citigroup and Goldman Sachs and all other investment banks (but every other corporation as well) should be asked the simple question – 'do you have a vision for your company to increase the overall value of society?' Of course, we do not want to hear rhetoric, PR spin or empty mission statements. Just tell us how you are going to add value and improve shareholder value at the same time. Not only does the Vodafone deal fail on both counts, it could have been so much better if it had set out to actually add some real value.

Scott Mead and many of his ilk are obviously very bright, hard working and highly influential people and let us not detract for one moment from their many achievements. These are precisely the sorts of people who have been blessed with an extremely rare set of talents. Talents that can obviously make them very wealthy but equally talents that could make such a huge difference to the value of society. It should be a win–win, as long as their talents are devoted to that vision. After all where would society be without visionaries such as Edison or Logie-Baird? However, a common, emotional response to Wall Street and the city might be that they are cold-hearted capitalists that only see $ signs. Like most caricatures and stereotypes that would be a very false picture. We are all victims of the systems we produce and highly intelligent people like Scott Mead will know only too well that they have to work the system they are given. What a pity though that such people cannot seem to paint a better picture of themselves in people's minds as creating value for society. Also, why can they not help to influence and change the system itself?

This is not helped by the fact that such people, in their own minds, seem to make a distinction between the work they do for companies like Goldman Sachs and the 'good' works they are obviously dedicated to outside of their professional jobs. If big city deals are destroying value they are not just destroying it for shareholders, they are depriving society of many benefits. A banker cannot be truly philanthropic if they are only ever philanthropic outside of work, as the Microsoft Paradox has already shown us. Investment bankers who have a vision of value for society should be able to create a great deal for society without having to go somewhere else to 'put something back in'. The economic system on which our society is based needs investment banks. Why can't we have the best of both worlds, simultaneously? What is called for is a clear vision that shows they can reconcile their banking actions directly with society's needs. If they cannot produce such a vision then at least we all know where we stand. An investment bank that does not try to create value for anybody other than themselves and shareholders could even be described as misanthropic. If that is so then we need to get them to declare it and we will see where customers take their business. The market will always work through the invisible hand and it will work wonders when that market is judged on value and not profit alone.

A HOLISTIC VALUE SYSTEM
FOR EVERYONE

It would be very easy to argue now that there must be some moral imperative brought to bear on those unreconstructed capitalists who see nothing wrong with just making profits. If capitalists were motivated by a broader, societal definition of value then maybe the 'problem' (the need to maximize societal value) would be solved? It is this sort of thinking that leads to concepts such as the 'social enterprise' described in an analysis of this trend in the *Financial Times* (25th May 2006) as 'part of a broader push for business to behave "ethically"'. In doing so it was fully acknowledged that sometimes this 'triggers broader resentment' from some industrialists and businesspeople. As an example it quotes John Sunderland, the president of the UK's CBI (Confederation of British Industry) as saying that businesses make a contribution to society 'simply by turning a profit and paying tax'. In other words, profit, by definition, automatically already provides social benefits. That is undoubtedly true but whether they provide the most benefits is the issue. Plus, we still have to come back to the question of what are the underlying motives of such businesspeople? Especially when we realize that John Sunderland, a well-respected business manager, is chairman of Cadbury Schweppes, a company that makes chocolate, sweets and fizzy drinks. The 'social enterprise' lobby would obviously ask whether such products are marketed responsibly to youngsters and what about those whose health might be compromised by overconsumption?

The very fact that stories along these lines abound in the business pages today illustrates very clearly that the pure profit motive is under threat. It also reveals the extent to which chief executives have failed, so far, to reconcile the profit motive with the wider demands of a modern society. Ian McMahon, CEO of food conglomerate RHM, remarked (*Sunday Times*, 24th July 2005) that many years ago, when he had previously worked at the food and drinks giant GrandMet (now part of Diageo), he fell under the spell of his then boss Lord (Allen) Sheppard, saying 'Allen would tell us, "You know me, if you hit the numbers, you're fine. If you don't, I'll come to your leaving do and buy you a beer".' Businesses might appear to be a great deal easier for managers to manage when they are seen in such black and white terms, and we can easily guess what particular numbers he was referring to, but they probably did not include any numbers quantifying the potentially excessive drinking habits of their customers or the costs to the police of dealing with them on a Saturday night. Nowadays, such numbers do concern all of us; an EU commissioned report (Alcohol in Europe, by Peter Anderson and Ben Baumberg, Institute of Alcohol Studies, June 2006) estimates illness and injury linked to alcohol costs EU countries £86.5bn a year and cases of alcohol poisoning had risen 60% to 21 700 a year over the past decade. It was very damning of the drinks industry, suggesting that the company's marketing strategies were contributing to a rise in teenage drinking. We can all make our own minds up, based on these figures, of the *net* value to society of the drinks industry, even if we all still enjoy a drink.

For a really stark challenge to business ethics, of course, one would only have to look at the tobacco industry. All the available evidence shows quite clearly that smoking brings about premature death, among its many other detrimental effects to both the user and the public. If there is a simple equation, that says more cigarettes sold equals more profits equals more deaths, then a tobacco company that seeks to maximize profits will inevitably kill more people in the process. It could be seen as a strategic objective of the company. Even their own warnings on cigarette packets tell us this. Yet any attempt to condemn this business as unethical on these grounds will just be met with the view that customers are exercising their own free will and if they choose to smoke, knowing the risks, then this is not inconsistent with an ethical society that is founded on the freedom of the individual.

That is all well and good but the other main concern then becomes 'passive smoking', which results in the banning of smoking in offices and, more recently, public places and the cost of treating those who succumb to smoking related illnesses and disease. Seeing the complete value equation in the tobacco industry has been on the agenda for many years. There is nothing new in this except that if tobacco industry executives were truly to subscribe to the value motive they would have to be willing to be accountable for all of their espoused value statements.

Looking at BAT's website, they refer to YSP (youth smoking prevention) schemes of education and working with retailers to prevent underage sales but are these just inputs? If they want to deliver outputs (i.e. fewer young people smoking) then these have to be measured just as much as sales and incorporated into the total value equation. Employees of BAT have to have these numbers built into their performance objectives. But if the smokers of tomorrow are the young smokers of today then if BAT is successful in its YSP schemes its business will shrink at some point in the future. Where on the website is the clear message to shareholders that this reduction in revenue is indeed one of the strategic aims of the company? Furthermore, what sort of behaviour would it encourage in a sales manager in this tobacco firm? Their sales efforts are not easily reconciled with this strategic objective. Hitting their sales targets and not selling to young smokers could be completely conflicting objectives.

These are all good examples of what can happen when society does not have holistic systems in place. Everyone does their own thing resulting in irreconcilable differences and suboptimization of value. But this is not just an issue with commercial organizations. Admittedly, we have concentrated almost exclusively on the private sector so far but it is not just profit-making organizations that will struggle to convince us of their wider societal value. As we will see in Chapter 4, the value motive has equally serious implications for the whole of the non-profit sectors. Just because an organization says it has loftier motives than profit does not necessarily mean that it adds any more value.

VALUE HAS TO BE THE RAISON D'ÊTRE FOR EVERY TYPE OF ORGANIZATION

Summary Value is the common thread that characterizes the purpose of any organization.

ALL VALUE IS GOOD

Any book looking at better ways to manage value has to tread a very fine line between suggesting how organizations could be managed better and whether they should exist in the first place. We can all think of organizations that we would rather did not exist (and we don't necessarily just mean tax collectors) and sometimes we are all tempted to voice our opinions about the worth of a particular product or service and, on occasions, question whether there is any earthly reason for them at all. Mobile phone ring tones, for example, are an integral feature on any phone but choosing your own ring tone has become a thriving industry. The company that developed the 'crazy frog' franchise made more than £40m in 2004 and we could easily ask ourselves whether this is the best use of society's resources. Surely there are more deserving causes? Unfortunately though whether you personally love that crazy frog or feel inclined to shoot him (decide for yourself by visiting www.crazyfroghits.com) we all have to accept that trying to discriminate between one type of economic activity and another is fraught with imponderables and contradictions. One man's meat is another man's poison and it is their individual choice that we have to bow to; we cannot impose our own values on them. This is the philosophical justification for the capitalist system.

That is perfectly acceptable for individual spending habits, which are managed by price and the market mechanism. However, when it comes to allocating resources gained through taxation a different process comes into play – the political process. This has to work within the existing political system and the history of political systems thinking over the last 200 years or so, in very simplistic terms, has been the swing of the pendulum between capitalism and socialism, right wing versus left wing, individual versus state. Most of the terms we have traditionally used, however, such as left and right, are becoming completely meaningless as the pendulum currently seems to be oscillating around the centre.

For example, are we to regard an education policy, which aims to develop the brightest talent in the population to its fullest extent, as left wing or right wing? It could be either. As with all polarized schools of thought there is often a natural desire to find the best of both worlds. There is nothing wrong with developing the brightest as long as it is not at the expense of the least bright. That fits perfectly with our definition of value. As long as it is a win–win rather than one section of society benefiting at the expense of another there is nothing wrong with this. Similarly, there is nothing wrong with capitalism creating the wealth and

social democracy deciding how to allocate it. This type of thinking, rightly or wrongly, has been leading us to the possibility that
there might be something called the 'third way'; an economic,
political and social system that tries to be the best of all worlds.
Although it has to be said that it has proved to be a particularly
loose and therefore elusive paradigm. Furthermore, even though
there is currently no coherent philosophy or practice to underpin
such a system, it certainly has some apparent attractions. It just
looks and feels more egalitarian. Whether it is the best powerhouse for economic development is another matter.

Capitalism has already proved itself to be a reasonably acceptable way (abuses notwithstanding) of allocating resources the
way society wants them allocated. However, whichever system
or 'way' we choose there have always been two simple, ineluc-
table truths staring us in the face. First, we need to create the
wealth to provide the greatest happiness to the greatest number.
Although we have now decided to call that value and that, by
its own definition, must be regarded as 'good'. Second, any economic activity that contributes to that end must also therefore,
by definition, be 'good'. As long as we keep these two truths
uppermost in our minds we can now move on to consider
alternative organization forms and the economic means to fulfil
them.

VALUE IS THE RAISON D'ÊTRE OF ALL ORGANIZATIONS

The notion of value can and should be applied equally to any
organization, both conceptually and, more important, practically.
In particular, the first part of this book revisited the profit motive
and attempted to illustrate that the value motive did everything
that the profit motive could achieve and more. Now we are going
to explore the extent to which this is true for all other types of

organization. This inevitably leads us into the very muddy and potentially treacherous waters of alternative organizational entities (e.g. cooperatives, social enterprises, trusts, charities, foundations) where we will have to tread very carefully if we are not to lose our footing.

The first slippery step came when we tried (in Chapter 1) to unravel the false dichotomy usually made between profit-making and non-profit organizations. Now we have a third angle to investigate, a trichotomy of three, supposedly distinct, sectors, all of which have some part to play in delivering public services. The first two sectors are the private sector and the public sector but now we have what has been termed the third sector (see 'Exploring the role of the third sector in public service delivery and reform: a discussion document', HM Treasury, February 2005) which has been called the 'range of institutions which occupy the space between the state and the private sector' and includes community groups, charities, foundations, trusts, cooperatives and social enterprises. They are said to 'share common characteristics in the social, environmental or cultural objectives they pursue'. This thinking fits neatly (whether validly or not will be discussed in Chapter 7) into what we have just described above as the 'third way'. From a purely management perspective, all of this can lead to further confusion and possibly reduced effectiveness.

With profit-making entities the goals are usually clear and managers know where they stand. However, we would usually refer to any profit-making organization as a 'business' with a different set of principles to the other two sectors. 'Business' implies that, apart from its business objective of profit, the company will have business values (e.g. making money out of customers is morally acceptable) and business methods (e.g. the setting of performance targets). Businesses also have to regard the customer as king because the customer pays directly for the service they receive. There is always the potential for conflicts between the company's objectives (profit) and its customers (value) but the successful business manages to reconcile both.

From the 1980s onwards, during the era of Thatcherism, the public sector was encouraged to think in this business-like way; government departments and civil servants had to act like businesspeople and treat service users as customers, even though they were not customers in the true sense of paying for services directly themselves. Nevertheless this business philosophy was adopted to such an extent that organizations that had never regarded themselves as 'businesses' had to produce business plans showing income, costs and outputs. For many public sector managers this was completely anathema to their own values and the whole ethos of public service. Nowadays public sector managers do not bat an eyelid when they are asked to produce business plans. We will look at this evolution in more detail later, to see whether this business-like approach has improved the value of public services, but for now we need to ask to what extent do these same issues arise in the third sector?

Let us take a 'charity' as an example. All the connotations of the word 'charity' are altruistic, benevolent and unselfish. Words we do not normally ascribe to a business or even a second sector, public body. Who would describe their local authority as having altruistic motives, even if much of their work is obviously of great benefit to the public? When will traffic wardens, for example, really be seen as altruistic (even though surely some of them have the highest motives to keep traffic moving). Conversely, how many of us have heard a commercial manager declaring 'we're not a charity you know!' when challenged by a potential customer about the company's prices or terms of business. Such a remark implies that charities 'give things away' expecting nothing in return and as such are totally antithetical to a commercial ethos.

So, having already challenged the fundamental premise of the profit motive (see Chapter 1), it is now time to challenge the fundamental premises of both the second and third sectors. It does not matter which sector we are discussing when we adopt the perspective that they all use up valuable resources and the value motive demands that the use of those resources are justified in value terms. Those who work for the second or third sectors may wish to presume that their raison d'être is intrinsically more worthy and ethical, but is it? Do good causes and value always go together? Do commercial organizations have to do something else for society, put something else back in philanthropic terms, over and above providing customers with what they want and making a profit? Or is this all just a false trichotomy?

CORPORATE SOCIAL RESPONSIBILITY (CSR) AND THE 'TRIPLE BOTTOM LINE'

Commercial organizations have faced increasing pressures to fully address what might be called the ethical dimension. High profile cases such as Enron, WorldCom and Parmalat vividly illustrate how profit, power and corruption can so easily become a lethal cocktail. These and a whole range of other social pressures (e.g. human rights, diversity, governance, accountability, concerns over pensions, the environment) have resulted in the notion that corporations should openly acknowledge and cater for their wider responsibilities to society. So we have now entered the era of corporate social responsibility. It is an odd phrase though. It implies that corporations have to make a special effort to fulfil their responsibilities to society. The corporation is guilty until proven innocent, despite the fact that many corporations already do a great job for society, albeit making healthy profits in the process. CSR presents us with a very skewed view of the commercial world. Visit any large company's website and the chances are you will now find a specific section covering the organization's statement on CSR and the actions it is taking. Pick any one at random to see for yourself.

Anyone visiting the pharmaceutical company Merck Sharpe Dohme (www.merck.com was chosen at random and visited on 21st July 2006) will see there is a heading 'Corporate Responsibility' on the home page and when you visit that page there is a downloadable CR report (what happened to the 'Social'?). The introduction to this page states:

> At Merck, our business is discovering, developing and delivering novel medicines and vaccines that can make a difference in people's lives. But our mission also entails something more. As a Company, we seek to maintain high ethical standards and a culture that values honesty, integrity and transparency in all that we do. Company decisions are driven by what is right for patients. And we are committed to our employees, to the environment in which we live and to the communities we serve worldwide.

We will take all of this at face value without assuming that any cynical, ulterior, motives lie behind these statements. It all sounds very laudable and appears to hark back to the values of some of the earlier, philanthropic entrepreneurs. George Merck, one of the original founders, is quoted as saying: 'We try never to forget that medicine is for the people. It is not for the profits. The profits follow and if we have remembered that, they have never failed to appear.' But does it actually signify anything new, different or additional to the sort of values this business always espoused? Did companies, before the advent of CSR reporting, not 'seek to maintain high ethical standards and a culture that values honesty, integrity and transparency in all that we do'? Was that not as much the motivating force behind George Merck as his desire for profits? Let us hypothesize, for a moment, that some other capitalists do not share these principles. Would asking them to produce a CSR report actually change their own innate values?

It is a bit like the manufacturers of the breakfast cereal Shredded Wheat, CPW (Cereal Partners World-wide, a 50:50 joint venture between Nestlé SA and American food giant General

Mills) telling us that their product is simple and has nothing added. This is now a selling point in a society where we do not want to consume too much salt or sugar, but there is no new, added value here. The product has not changed, but it sounds better than it used to. It makes for good PR because it ticks all the right boxes and has all the right connotations of a healthy product and lifestyle. We will find with some alternative organizations, just as we did with Coca-Cola, that it is sometimes difficult to separate out the wheat from the chaff, the substance from the image.

Value is already a notoriously difficult concept to pin down, so perhaps false trichotomies just serve to confuse matters further. If so, you might be disappointed to learn of another concept that should pour even more confusing ingredients into this already rapidly boiling pot of the third way – the triple bottom line. So what is it? According to Katie Kross, executive director of the Centre for Sustainable Enterprise at the University of North Carolina's Kenan-Flagler Business School, the 'triple bottom line' is 'financial profitability, ecological integrity and social equity'. Again, we can all see some possible merit in this triple concept but what does it offer that is of any practical use? A company can convince us that it is satisfying the first criterion but what about the other two? Who are the arbiters of ecological integrity and social equity? How do you weigh up the potentially competing and conflicting interests of the paying customer with the ordinary citizen who feels ecology is suffering as a result?

If we distrust the exponents of our capitalist system so much that we have to impose other supposedly 'ethical' criteria on them why don't we just get everything produced by a highly regulated state? If having the healthcare system in the UK provided by the state is desirable, why not the drugs and equipment that the NHS is dependent on as well? Especially as the drugs industry accounts for a significant element of total NHS spending (drugs spending in the NHS is currently around £8bn and has risen by 45% in the previous five years).

There are many possible answers to this question but perhaps the simplest of all is that we have sufficient trust in the private sector to produce drugs on which some of us are dependent for survival. Any alternative has to achieve at least this same level of trust with its customers for it to have any chance of competing for resources. For example, do we really trust a charity that aims to help drug addicts 'kick the habit' to deliver the goods? Should part of their corporate social responsibility report tell us whether they are using scarce financial resources wisely and effectively? Or do such organizations not have to satisfy all of the same criteria as a commercial concern because it is a given that they have socially responsible goals? Visit, for example, the National Institute of Drug Abuse (http://www.nida.nih.gov), again chosen at random, and there is no mention of CSR or a CSR report. Presumably it is taken as read that they must already be socially responsible.

This is now sounding like a criticism of the 'third sector' but it is meant to be a totally impartial exploration of some very serious organizational and societal issues. There is no hint intended that capitalism equals good and public sector equals bad (or vice versa). All that matters is that the customers of all of these organizations get the best value possible. The focus should always remain on the value delivered, not the organizational format employed or the genuinely good intentions of those who work there. A clear-headed assessment of the situation is required and the main challenge here is do the distinctions drawn between different types of organization – first, second or third sector, single, double or triple bottom line – really help to add value or not? For a more well-informed but highly sceptical view of the whole debate around CSR an *Economist* survey, ironically entitled 'The good company' (22nd January 2005), provides a very thorough summary of the main arguments underpinning the conceptual foundations for CSR and challenges whether it was in any way a new idea or one of any real worth. Its main conclusion is that the whole concept of CSR does not withstand too much close scrutiny.

Regardless of our own views on this subject, this type of thinking is encroaching into, reshaping and reconfiguring the whole design of our socio-economic and political systems. In Europe, particularly, this has been encouraged and promoted by the social agenda of the EU and its EFQM management model (see Chapter 5). In the UK the government has its own website to address this and it is actively promoted by the DTI (Department for Trade and Industry). Look at http://www.societyandbusiness.gov.uk where it states that 'The Government sees CSR as good for society and good for business.' It is just a pity that it then has to acknowledge that the real business case is yet to be substantiated. In reality, CSR can cause some very intractable, practical problems.

Let us look at the implications for supply chain management. Stories about employing child labour or unethical employment practices in developing countries have caused some companies to reassess their whole philosophy on global supply chains. The associate director of design development and sourcing at sportswear retail chain JJB (*Sunday Times*, 14th March 2004) said 'Burma is a no-go country at the moment. But what are human rights like in China? Are they better than in Burma? Do we stop manufacturing in Indonesia because it is possibly a hotbed of terrorism? These are difficult decisions.' Indeed they are and it is precisely these sorts of issues that this book is designed to address.

We are on the side of the manager who already has a difficult job. Why should the choice of country be anything other than a straight commercial decision? Why not go to the lowest cost, best quality supplier? Why should a business manager have to include human rights considerations in their decision-making process? If national or supranational governments do not outlaw certain countries why should individual businesses have to make these difficult decisions? If it is not being resolved at a macro level how can it be satisfactorily resolved at a micro level? Businesses can only work within the economic systems of the world.

There is no point asking the manager at JJB to think and act ethically if there is no arbiter to tell them what 'ethically' means. In the absence of clear guidance on the matter the manager can only be expected to make commercial decisions. Will they lose customers if they outsource to certain countries? Any decision made on this basis might look like a decision that satisfies the criteria of a CSR report ('we have chosen not to source products from country X . . .') but in fact it is just like any other business decision, based on the bottom line, the single bottom line of profit.

This logic starts to suggest that CSR is all smoke and mirrors. A sort of PR game that large corporations play to keep their politically correct customers happy by salving their consciences. We get drawn into these games because no one is articulating a common understanding of value clearly. Supermarket chains, particularly, have come under great ethical scrutiny over recent years. In the US Wal-Mart and in the UK Tesco have both had to deal with challenges, on several fronts, to their business and employment practices. Yet Tesco, as far back as 1998, was a founder member of the Ethical Trading Initiative, an organization set up to agree minimum standards on fair pay and workers' rights. But what constitutes fair pay? Are the fees of a management consultant fair? The client has a choice. If they do not like the fees they can choose not to use the consultant. The market for consultancy services is such that they pay whatever they have to. The market is the only arbiter of what is fair. Equally, the consultant who believes they warrant higher fees might argue that what the client is prepared to pay is 'unfair'. But it is not a cry you will hear very often from those who chose to make consultancy their profession because the market, quite rightly, would quickly put them out of business.

Similarly, some British suppliers of organic food have complained that Tesco have forced them to cut profit margins to such a degree that they risk going out of business. Tesco have argued in return that if it prices organic produce too highly, customers simply won't buy it. Would it be unfair or unethical, therefore, if Tesco let some organic farmers go to the wall? Obviously no more unfair than it would be for them to let any of their other suppliers go out of business. Tesco is not responsible for the welfare or the business success of its suppliers and to suggest that it could be fair to some and not to others would add even greater confusion (although we will see later in Chapter 5 that perhaps Tesco could add more value by having a more enlightened attitude to its own suppliers). Trying to impose ethical standards on organizations is too indistinct. Instead, perhaps this whole situation could be expressed much more clearly and beneficially in value terms.

Nike, famously, had an issue with its reputation being tarnished by reports about its employment practices in Vietnam. Today, Nike's 'Responsibility' section of its website (what happened to the C and the S?) entitled 'Evolution: Shifting our approach to labour compliance' makes for very interesting reading when it talks about how it has been 'challenged to understand how to measure systematically the impact of our own interventions and challenged by how we play a role in enabling widespread change within the industry'. This is a great example of an individual business trying to resolve many issues outside of its own sphere of influence and it finally concludes 'No one company can solve these issues that are endemic to our industry.' Of course not. What is required is clear leadership on this issue.

If there is no global solution agreed to this global issue then one other course of action would be to let the customers decide.

If Nike offered different products, produced in different countries, at different prices (assuming for a moment that the 'cheapest' labour produces the cheapest trainers) and advised the customers accordingly, then each customer could make their own ethical choice weighed against their own, personal spending power. This would be a true indicator of how much customers are prepared to pay for their values and beliefs in human rights and it would be the most democratic solution as well.

This solution has already been introduced, of course, in offering 'fair trade' (http://www.fairtrade.org.uk/) products in markets such as coffee, tea and fruit juices. The proprietary FAIRTRADE Mark is an 'independent guarantee that disadvantaged producers in the developing world are getting a better deal'. So let us follow the logic of this. If this scheme means that more income ends up in the hands of the farmers who produce these goods, rather than large multi-national corporations, those farmers will produce bigger surpluses, which they can then choose to consume (e.g. build themselves a better house or take a holiday) or invest. Should they choose to invest in their business, perhaps buying equipment to reduce the cost of harvesting their crops, then their costs will fall and their surpluses will get even bigger. In just two short steps they behave just like any other capitalist. Then they can choose whether to keep those extra surpluses, or pass on the benefits to the customers who buy their products by reducing the price. The price mechanism will, as always, put less efficient producers, who may be other fair trade farmers, out of business. The fair trade farmer's 'ethics', in effect, would be no different to any other capitalist. This should not surprise us at all because fair trade has not changed the underlying economic system used around the world. Trotsky advocated world revolution for communism because he could see that the whole system had to change if communism was to have any chance of surviving. History taught us that capitalism won that argument and those who support fair trade would do well to learn the lessons of history.

We could look at a range of other scenarios, such as producers forming a cooperative, but regardless of the organizational format they choose it would not alter the fact that the ultimate goal would always be to maximize value, the best coffee at the lowest price, or even the coffee that gives them the biggest margin, the capitalist's golden rule. What they choose to do with any surpluses, any question of redistribution, is a secondary issue. Value is always the prime motive, regardless of the market and working conditions. So what really motivates the fair trade movement is the same thing that motivates us all – value. On that basis, what makes it 'fairer' than capitalism or any other system for that matter?

No doubt those who actively support fair trade are on the side of the poorest farmers in some of the poorest parts of the world. They probably assume that richer consumers will also support their worthy cause. This may be true but the most equitable and ethical way to test this assumption is always to let the customers decide for themselves. If fair trade coffee is better than their usual brand, and costs no more, then the decision is an easy one. But then that makes their purchasing decision no different to any other when choosing another item off their local supermarket shelf. It might look like an ethical decision but it isn't. The real test of ethics is when the quality of the fair trade product is not as good as its commercial equivalent, or it has a higher price, then the consumer would be signalling an ethical choice. They would be buying the good to help the farmers out of their existing situation, not because they get the best coffee at the best price. This is a complete value decision, based on the customer's own personal values. Either way, fair trade producers will only stay in business if they keep their particular customers satisfied.

If the declared aim of fair trade, its value statement, were to reduce prices by bringing more producers to the market, thereby increasing competition, would more customers choose fair trade?

It would certainly be the wisest decision they could make as consumers. More competition is generally a good thing. It would also support fair trade's original aim of giving these farmers a 'better deal'. This now starts to look like a coherent and sustainable approach.

Virtually every product purchase can be seen as either an ethical or a straight consumer choice. Choosing a small car over an SUV could be for either reason. Buying a soft beverage instead of an alcoholic one could be a statement of values about the dangers of alcohol. Your choice of daily paper could be a political statement or a simple choice of sports pages. Who are we to challenge any of those decisions or to enquire too closely about the motives that lie behind them? When will fair trade support fledgling newspaper publishers and ask us to pay an unnecessarily higher price? We may be stretching a point to make a point. Taking logic to its inevitable but absurd conclusion. But there is a very serious implication of this line of reasoning for those who do subscribe to some of these alternatives.

The profit motive works because it satisfies several simple, common sense and natural requirements for an economic system, albeit in its imperfect fashion, including:

- allowing individuals a choice about the allocation of their own resources;
- allocating resources to the things we value and can afford;
- a simple set of rules that are easy to understand (if you don't give customers what they want you won't exist);
- success breeds success, which seems fair and equitable.

In summary, the profit motive, the market and the price together produce a very coherent system based on a consistent set of principles. If CSR, fair trade and other initiatives are to offer something better than that they need an even greater sense of coherence and consistency. Unfortunately, many of the arguments used to support fair trade and CSR could be criticized for being neither. Otherwise, for example, we could have a situation where the principles of fair trade would support the 'plight' of UK organic farmers against Tesco.

Now, despite all of the cold logic presented above, a warm heart should still always prevail. Without a clear value proposition any organization will be left in an ethical quandary, for which there will never be any absolute answers. All that any company can do, in the final analysis, is admit what its values are and then leave its customers to decide. So, if we can articulate the real long-term vision of these initiatives, which is exactly the same standard we suggested should be adopted by any commercial organization in Figure 2.2, maybe we can make sure that when our heart tells us there is something unpalatable about an existing 'system', one that leaves poor farmers disadvantaged and corporate shareholders rich, we can suggest a better system that creates more value for everyone.

One of the necessary steps forward towards this goal is to stop disjointed thinking. Whenever we see a separate CSR statement or report on a company website, or even in their annual report, we already know that they have missed the whole point of corporate social responsibility. Devising a business strategy and trying to evolve a separate CSR strategy alongside is an open admission that the two are not integrated, coherent or holistic, either in the motivation of the directors, the direction of the organization or its culture, systems and structure. If there is no sound, strategic, business case for CSR it is difficult to see why any board of directors or shareholders would be able to fully support such a strategy. They would not be able to reconcile it with any of their clear commercial objectives. CSR, if it is to have any real meaning, has to become part of a virtuous cycle. The whole enterprise has to have a crystal clear purpose, focused on a crystal clear view of what it values and CSR has to mean more customers choose you in preference to your non-CSR competitors.

One organizational entity that some would argue fits this bill is something that has come to be called a social enterprise.

SOCIAL ENTERPRISE

Earlier in Chapter 1 we asked the tongue-in-cheek question of whether not-for-profit organizations also aimed to be not-for-value. Similarly, is the opposite of the term social enterprise a non-social (or even anti-social) enterprise? Hopefully not, but calling an enterprise 'social' seems to imply that other organizations do not have a social purpose. As we have already seen, though, any organization that does not serve a social purpose (e.g. providing chocolate lovers with nice chocolate cakes) is not likely to be around for very long. So what makes this social purpose so special? Certainly, the notion of social enterprise has captured the imagination of many people and we have to ask ourselves why. What feelings of disquiet must we already have about our present economic systems that we are impelled to produce a different organizational format? What exactly does 'social' mean? If we seek an answer to this question from the Social Enterprise Alliance (www.se-alliance.org) their definition of a social enterprise is 'An organization or venture that advances its social mission through entrepreneurial, earned income strategies.' This, it has to be said, appears to be a classic example of a circular argument – social enterprises are defined by having social missions. Yet if we substitute 'strategic objectives' for 'social mission' we would have the same definition as any commercial enterprise. So what's the difference between the two? Why isn't profit a social purpose? According to another social enterprise body, the Social Enterprise Coalition (see www.socialenterprise. org.uk), social enterprises are 'dynamic businesses with a social purpose working all around the UK and internationally to deliver lasting social and environmental change'. Again this definition of 'social' enterprises just tells us they have a 'social purpose' and deliver 'social change'. Based on the same definition a brewing company that extends the opening hours of its pubs must be an increasingly social enterprise.

In fact, many commercial organizations have delivered lasting social change; how about the commercial theatre, pharmaceuticals or publishing? All of these and more could put a very convincing argument that they have driven social change in their own way. Even oil companies are driving environmental change. So what makes a social entrepreneur unique? The Social Enterprise Coalition cites *The Big Issue* (a magazine usually sold by homeless or jobless vendors) as an example of a social enterprise so what do the proprietors of this publication believe makes them different? Their executive chairman Nigel Kershaw (*The Times*, 24th January 2006) describes the publication as 'a business solution to a social crisis'. This suggests that *The Big Issue* is a commercial business, run along the same commercial lines as any other, including attracting paying advertisers and selling each issue at a price. So apparently there is no difference in the way social enterprises operate but their aims are somehow more social, even though no one has told us yet what being social means.

The social crisis that Nigel Kershaw seems to be referring to is a combination of unemployment and homelessness and on their website (www.bigissue.com on 18th July 2006) under 'Getting results' there is a reference to 75 people getting into permanent employment and 271 being rehoused since the organization started in 1995. This actually looks like the organization is achieving something, in terms of its own strategic objectives. But is it any different to Bill Gates trying to cure malaria with the funds he secured from Microsoft? Or any different to large pharmaceutical companies that develop anti-AIDS drugs? The notion of 'social enterprise' just doesn't seem to offer any fundamentally different purpose or alternative organizational entity.

Even if it did, the common question asked throughout this book is how much value does a social enterprise generate? What has been the average cost of getting these people into jobs and homes? Could another organization have achieved more with the same funds (*The Big Issue* produced £12m revenue in 2005)? Would another organization have attracted more funds so they could do more good works? This is where we have to ask about the original value proposition. Is *The Big Issue* a charity or not? Its philosophy is that those who sell *The Big Issue* are doing a proper job, not asking for handouts. Is this true or is it just clever marketing? The same sort of marketing techniques used by any large corporation?

All of these questions might appear to be very interesting but they are all totally pointless. All we need to know is what are the expected outputs from any social enterprise; just as we would for any other type of organization. If it is a charity why not just say so? If it is a genuine publication to be read then where are the readership figures and does the editorial have a clear aim? If it is just a clever guilt trip to be laid on the public to encourage them to hand over some money then be honest about it, or would that be expecting too much from a social enterprise?

How we achieve value outputs is almost entirely irrelevant. If *The Big Issue* set out to help 75 people into employment and rehouse 271 others there is absolutely no reason why a profit-making concern, with no social pretensions, could not achieve the same or more. They could adopt a completely different approach, selling lottery tickets or artworks produced by homeless people to produce their income and taking a percentage as profit. If they managed to get twice as many people into jobs and housing with the same income level then they would, by definition, be twice as socially enterprising without being a 'social enterprise' at all.

The whole concept of social enterprise just doesn't seem to hold water even under the lightest scrutiny. Perhaps it is just another organizational red herring. Enterprises that are run as business enterprises cannot be distinguished by their aims on social grounds if there is no absolute arbiter of what constitutes 'social'. At the end of the day we are back to the customer in the street who has to decide. When they are passing *The Big Issue* seller, as they walk into their local supermarket, do they spend their money on a copy of *The Big Issue*, a lottery ticket, a theatre ticket or a tin of beans for their children. Each one of those decisions can equally be described as a social decision and we will never know what their motives are, to feed their kids, support radical theatre or win the jackpot. The most rational, social decision we could expect is that the customer will give their money to the cause they value most. For society as a whole to decide which organizations and social causes to support we need as fair competition between these organizations as possible, with a clear statement of what they are all trying to achieve. Then the best value to society is most likely to come from those organizations where customers decide that they use their resources best. As the director of the Skoll Centre for Social Entrepreneurship at Oxford's Saïd Business School said (*Financial Times*, 25th May 2006) '(Social enterprises) . . . have no greater claim to deliver value than any other form of organization . . . but plurality (of business entity) per se is good.' If by plurality we just mean more competition then amen to that.

IS THE 'PUBLIC SECTOR' AN OBSOLETE CONSTRUCT?

This now also begs the question, where does the traditional public sector fit into this? Why is *The Big Issue* doing a job that taxpayers are already paying the government to do (through employment and housing departments) on their behalf? Maybe the public sector just isn't working well enough and the rise of a third sector is proof of this. Or maybe the whole system needs to change?

In fact, as we have done with every other idea in this book, perhaps we should go back to first principles and ask whether the whole concept of a public sector is still valid? What is the public sector? It is a conglomeration of organizations (government agencies, civil service departments, local government) that get their funding directly from the taxation mechanism rather than the price mechanism. Actually that is not entirely incorrect. The public sector gets its funding from the price mechanism as well. Commercial organizations produce the goods that generate revenue of which a significant portion becomes corporation and income tax. The root of every surplus can be traced back to the same market system.

Yet again we are in danger of dumbing down what is a very serious point. If every public sector employee owes their very livelihood to the workings of the market why do they seem to think that different principles should apply to their own employment? Take this quote from Dr Jonathan Fielden, the deputy chairman of the British Medical Association's (the doctors' union) consultants' committee (*The Times*, 2nd July 2006) in reply to an initiative taken by a surgeon in Norfolk (UK) who used 'production line techniques' he learned in France to clear his ever-lengthening waiting list. This 'dual surgery' system ensured that while one patient is operated on another is being prepped, thereby significantly increasing throughput. Dr Fielden was quoted as saying 'We don't see patients as cans of beans on a production line. If people are pressing us to push patients through in a factory style manner, that would be opposed.'

The obvious question any tax-paying, production line working, patient on the waiting list would be entitled to ask of Dr Fielden is why would they oppose it? If production line management techniques have been proven to work so well in manufacturing why not in surgery? Where is the distinction to be made between manufacturing and surgery? They are both valuable activities that have to compete for valuable resources. Shouldn't doctors be subjected to the same strictures that the production line worker has to face every day on the production line? Is the NHS run for the value of patients or the benefit of surgeons? A *Guardian*/ICM poll on public services published in October 2003 showed that the overwhelming majority of people – 80% – agreed that in future private companies should be allowed to run public services if they can guarantee a better service. Based on existing attitudes from parts of the medical profession we can see why.

Common sense will always prevail though, even if it takes many, many years to do so. If the quality of surgery, or service, is right and delivered at the right cost why would anyone not vote for it, regardless of what type of organization delivers it? Yet there is still an ongoing debate about the relationship between private and public provision. Will this debate ever be decided by common sense, comparing outputs per £ spent? Only when all of the emotion is taken out of the equation. That word ethos goes a great deal deeper than just comparing costs and outputs. Otherwise, why wouldn't every doctor and nurse rush off immediately to join the private sector healthcare providers? Many dedicated doctors are totally committed to the NHS's public service ethos but unfortunately their personal values and the value they can produce do not currently match up. Nurses who still believe they have a vocation want to give the best care they can to patients. They are not interested in management theory or the bureaucracy it inevitably creates. They have an absolutely crystal clear picture in their own minds of what value means in healthcare terms. At a specific point in time it could mean anything from providing a commode to a patient urgently in need; to giving CPR (cardio pulmonary resuscitation) to save someone's life; to a kind and reassuring word just before someone enters the operating theatre. Telling them that the NHS trust they work for has a multi-million pound deficit will be a meaningless statistic. For them the level of care their patients need is an absolute, a professional standard, a minimum standard of humanity even, so the only way to put this equation right is for the government to put more money into the NHS. This is exactly the same argument as Dr Jonathan Fielden. Yet the former sounds like the genuine, value driven behaviour of someone who wants to produce the best output and the latter just sounds like someone with arrogant, selfish, vested interests.

Maybe a comment from the chief executive of Netcare UK (*Sunday Times*, 30th April 2006) suggests a way forward. He said the NHS 'is one of the things Britain has done incredibly well . . . but any business model needs to look at how it re-invents itself . . . In South Africa (where their parent company is based), we are more than just a successful commercial company, we are a values-driven organization. We do A&E, primary, secondary and tertiary care, diagnostics, hospitals and after. We also do a huge amount of pro bono work, with HIV outreach and cataract clinics in the townships.'

If the term 'public sector ethos' is ever to become meaningful again it will have to mean that the sort of ethos expressed by the nurse delivers the sort of outputs produced by the surgeon using production line techniques in Norfolk. If the British Medical Association cannot reconcile this ethos with their own interests of high quality medical procedures then society needs to question their motives. The BMA will have to feel the cold wind of competition. That is precisely what used to define the public sector – a lack of competition. Competition was anathema. Competition was seen as having totally different aims and objectives: business objectives not public service objectives. It was also about risk, with all the concomitant pressures and stresses that brings in its wake. Those who still support a 'public service ethos' seem to forget that it is precisely those pressures, even though they may seem unwelcome, that tend to generate a better performance. The surgeon in Norfolk was under greater pressure but he obviously thought the rewards were worth it; whether those rewards were financial or pure job satisfaction.

The extent to which the public sector really is not delivering was expressed clearly by the *Sunday Times* economist David Smith who, under the heading 'How to blow £50 billion without really trying' (*Sunday Times*, 13th November 2005) revealed how public spending had 'risen by 4.5 percentage points of GDP, faster than any other developed country' and 'Public sector employment has risen twice as fast (by 13.2%) as the private sector (5.7%) since 1998. Public sector productivity has, however, continued to fall. The fastest rise in public sector jobs has been among administrators and non-frontline staff, up by 66.1% in the NHS since 1998, by 47.1% in education, by 33.6% in the police and by 31.1% in the prison service.' These are huge increases in input and nowhere will you find a corresponding increase in outputs.

When state spending accounts for between 40 and 50% of GDP, as it does in most western economies, it is inevitable that questions will be asked about value until such time as convincing answers are provided. The real challenge for the public sector is can it achieve the level of outputs achieved by the private sector using a different set of values, principles and management methods. All three tend to have to work together as a coherent whole. There is no point appointing a chief executive from a FTSE 100 business to run a public sector body and hope to get the best value when everyone else in the organization works to a completely different set of values. Maybe this is why the public sector has not integrated management philosophies and methods from the private sector very well. There is the nub of the problem: the need to produce a very different paradigm for the public sector, rather than trying to bolt on one or two specific techniques (like production lines or 'lean'). The whole economic system has to change.

We looked earlier at how traffic lights are a very good example of a control system that has public values designed in. The system works because the public wants it to work and actually makes it work. The problem with all alternative forms of organization is they will only work if they become part of the overall system. They cannot work in a vacuum. Those who espouse the cause of 'social enterprise' or even 'public service' want to add, in effect, their own additional 'light' to the system. Social entrepreneurs perhaps regard themselves as 'careful drivers' and might argue that the traffic lights are not really designed for them but for the bad or inconsiderate drivers. So they suggest adding an alternative, let's say a pink light, to the existing system. Whenever this pink light is on it only applies to careful drivers like themselves. Except that they cannot move because in front of them is a driver who does not follow the pink light system. This driver only knows, understands and obeys the green light. In such a system you could add as many lights, of as many different hues, as you like but the single green light will control the whole system. So, if the whole of the economic and public service systems are predicated on the market providing the necessary surpluses for redistribution, the only way to improve the whole system is to make the market driven by value, not profit. Then those who want to distribute these surpluses need to show they can do so in competition.

The eternal debate about whether certain, particularly public, services should be provided by non-profit-making public sector organizations tends to start to appear irrelevant when both sectors are gauged on the common criterion of value. The value motive recognizes only one sector. Once the common goals are agreed there is no separate decision required about the best way to achieve those goals. The value motive does not presume that either commercial or non-commercial is best. Look at any energy or water supplier. Does it really matter what type of entity provides these as long as the right control systems are in place to help govern prices and performance in terms of output and quality? The issue then only becomes one of performance management and the methods we employ to maximize performance.

CHAPTER 5

ORGANIZATIONAL PERFORMANCE MEASUREMENT HAS TO MEASURE VALUE

Summary Setting value as the basis for all organizational performance objectives requires different conventions and methods for managing organizational performance.

TURNING HUMAN ACTIVITY INTO VALUE

Whether we come to work purely because we have to, to make a living, or because we genuinely enjoy what we do, we are all susceptible to a common disease called activity. It is part of the human condition. We generally like to be kept busy, it makes the day pass quicker, but this disease goes much, much deeper than that. If we are busy doing something we must have found a purpose in life. We don't even have to be paid for what we do, as with volunteers in charity shops, because as long as we are doing something for somebody we have a purpose. There are many other, positive reasons why we choose to work but there can be no stronger motivation than finding a personal purpose in life.

Unfortunately, this motive force is so powerful that nothing can stand in its way. As long as we are busy with activities we do not need to stop and ask about the intrinsic worth of the activities themselves. Of course very few, if any, people come to work to do a bad job or to waste their time but part of management's job is to ensure that every minute of someone's day is focused on activities that will add value. This might even mean stopping or curtailing some of their activities, such as telling people they should have fewer meetings. We might even have to suggest to some people that they go home earlier. The presenteeism, 'hours', culture that helps some people to feel valued, simply by virtue of the number of hours they spend at work, is anathema to the value motive. The only good activity is one that contributes to the organization's strategic value objectives.

Every organization has strategic objectives, or at least should have. Once those objectives are set the main task of management is to ensure they are achieved. This necessitates the construction of an MIS (management information system) from which can be drawn some performance data (e.g. costs, delivery times, revenue, complaints). Then there is normally a regular review of this data; usually at the daily or weekly team meetings and monthly by the management team. This is where the first major problem starts with conventional performance management. It's a dull routine. It's repetitive. It's a big stick with which to hit people over the head if things are not going well. Rather than inspiring you, it's decidedly uninspiring.

If you are a typical manager then you are probably already subjected to a typical performance measurement and management regime, like the one described above, and might readily identify with it. Stop and think for a moment about what you are trying to achieve this year and the chances are you will be able to put your hands on a document that spells out some KPIs (key performance indicators) and a whole series of data and measures. That is the start of the second major problem; performance becomes very personal, very quickly, but not in a positive way. So to get out of this routine ask yourself why all of this is deemed to be necessary? Why can't you just be left to get on with your job? Does your employer not trust you enough to do your best? If that is the case why did they ever bother to employ you? Whether you take this jaundiced view or not it does not alter the fact that every individual in an organization will have their own, very personal, view on what performance means to them.

Now we get into the more subtle side of performance issues. Let us assume you are highly motivated by what you do and as a manager you are already fired up about working for your organization. You are totally on board with the strategic objectives and you fervently believe that what your organization does is give great value to your customers. In that case you will not, personally, have too much of a problem with whatever targets you have to achieve. Can the same be said for everyone in your team though? Even if your team are all pulling happily in the same direction what about other teams and other departments? To what extent is your performance dependent on them? As we will see shortly, value is entirely dependent on everyone in the organization working well together. We are all part of one great big distillation process.

Then, of course, there is the other huge problem, so huge it needs a category all of its own – trying to devise really meaningful performance measures. To do this requires a clear set of working principles. After all, you cannot manage performance effectively without measuring it effectively. But beware, what gets measured gets done, so whatever performance measures you set, they will encourage the sort of behaviour you deserve. So avoid measuring things just because you can. The MIS can produce as much pointless data as it can meaningful measures. Worse still, setting stupid measures (e.g. number of training days/hours per employee per year) will encourage stupid behaviour (i.e. attendance on any course to achieve the requisite days, whether it is relevant training or not). The best measures will always be those that are simple to understand, purposeful and worthwhile in terms of size and importance.

Getting performance measurement right means, by definition, that you will end up running the organization well, that is making lots of profit. Or at least that is what the theory of performance measurement suggests. However, many academics, over many years, have produced longitudinal research data and reached the rather surprising conclusion that profit history is not necessarily a great predictor of either future performance or company value. This evidence is clear and backs up our contention in Chapter 1 that the profit motive is not necessarily the best way to achieve great profits. Once this conclusion was accepted by business academics and business management the obvious next question had to be – 'well if measuring profit isn't the best indicator of performance, what is?'

THE ADVENT OF THE SCORECARD

The short version of this very long story is that the answer the academics produced was, not surprisingly, that there would never be one single measure of performance because organizational performance is just too complex an issue. Instead there was a reasonable consensus reached that a range of measures would be needed. The analogy of a dashboard was introduced. When you drive your car you don't just look at the speedometer, you check the rev counter, the fuel gauge, the temperature gauge and other warning lights. The individual indicators are all meant to coalesce into one overall picture of a smooth running machine. As a consequence, this thinking led to the emergence of the concept of a scorecard that would be the answer to a chief executive's

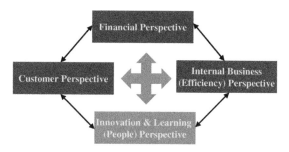

Figure 5.1 A balanced scorecard (Adapted from Kaplan, R.S. and Norton, D.P. *The Balanced Scorecard – Translating Strategy into Action*, 1996)

prayers. A sort of organizational satnav (satellite navigation device) that would show the CEO whether the organization was heading in the right strategic direction. Unfortunately turning a vision into value is never going to be a simple matter of metrics. This is not what the conventional wisdom in performance measurement would have us believe, however.

Organizations have to rely on sound management systems and probably the most well-known version of proprietary scorecards was that devised by Robert Kaplan and David Norton, the balanced business scorecard (see *The Balanced Scorecard – Translating Strategy into Action*, Harvard Business School Press, 1996) a version of which is shown in Figure 5.1. In this model there are four perspectives – four sets of measures which, when balanced together, should give the most complete picture of how well the organization is performing. The financial perspective is very much the traditional set of financial measures (costs, revenue); the internal perspective tends to look at processes and other opportunities for efficiency in operations and delivery; the customer perspective warns the organization to keep measuring how well the organization is meeting customer expectations; and the innovation perspective tends to focus on the less tangible aspects, particularly the people aspects of how well the organization is learning and how rapidly can it adapt and innovate?

If we briefly critique this latest thinking, where are its strengths and weaknesses? Certainly the shift in thinking to a broader view of measurement is welcome. Also, the scorecard is meant to serve at least two key purposes. It is meant to act as a guide for the successful implementation of strategy and it also provides a framework, the four headings, under which the performance measurement and management system can be constructed. The basic concept is simple to understand and it has a certain face validity.

Where it tends to be weak is in the innovation box. This perspective is generally interpreted as the 'people' box, requiring people measures, and organizations are very poor at measuring their people. Conventional MISs have not been able to capture and measure the latent talent, intellectual capacity, capability and creative value from people. This was fully acknowledged by Norton himself when he confessed in a foreword to *The HR Scorecard* (another book spawned by the balanced scorecard theory by HR academics Huselid, Becker and Ulrich, HBS Press, 2001) that in his experience of working with organizations 'the worst grades are reserved for their understanding of strategies for developing human capital. There is little consensus, little creativity, and no real framework for thinking about the subject. Worse yet, we have seen little improvement in this over the past eight years.' We will look ourselves in Chapter 6 at whether people or HR scorecards manage to help or hinder this situation and we will also start to address this question of whether people can be accurately described as human capital.

What is interesting though is that despite Norton's admission of this weakness he does not follow his own logic to admit that if one box in a 'balanced' scorecard is not working properly then the whole scorecard is not working properly. You cannot have a three-quarters scorecard; all perspectives are meant to be a part of an integrated whole. That is precisely what the theory of scorecards suggests. Which leads us to unearth another weakness of scorecards, particularly in practice. It is all well and good to espouse the concept of a balanced range of measures but each of the measures set might be owned by different people, who have nothing to do with each other. For example, an operational manager might be focused on costs, while a marketing manager might be measured on market share and R&D might be gauged on product development times.

The product developer rushing to get the next product out might not develop the cheapest product to manufacture, this makes the operational manager's life difficult because it imposes even more cost constraints on them. Meanwhile, the marketing manager is worrying how they are going to come to market at a low enough price to win any market share. So how does the scorecard actually reconcile these competing and possibly conflicting measures? How does the scorecard balance them? In reality, it is likely that each manager will mechanistically try to manage their own area of performance (e.g. the marketing manager says there is a maximum market price and will be ready to blame operations if they do not come in at the right cost) and they may even have these measures tied into the performance related pay scheme. In this way, pay starts to actually breed people working against each other and undermines the mutual goal of value creation. Surely it would be better to set all three of them one, common, value objective at the outset. This would involve a guide price for the product with a quality standard and an agreed margin, which also sets the upper cost limit: this is a method used very successfully by Toyota, incidentally. The most important point here is that *this value objective cannot be deconstructed into its component parts*. The organization will only create value (i.e. sell the product) if the whole comes together as planned. It can only sell the finished product from the overall distillation process.

The concept of scorecards, in effect, is working to a very outmoded way of management thinking. The sort of thinking that said everything can be managed, every problem can be solved, by being broken down into its constituent parts. It breeds old-fashioned command and control blame cultures precisely because it fragments rather than binds the organization together. Each manager can blame somebody else for not keeping to his or her part of the bargain. What this thinking fails to acknowledge is that if any part of the whole fails, the organization, and everyone who works for it, fails. Blaming each other after the event might temporarily deflect some of the personal accountability but adds no value whatsoever.

The whole point of the value motive is to produce a lean, flexible, seamless, customer-focused organization. To make sure every part of the organization is pulling together, in the same direction. So, if the principle of 'what gets measured gets done' still applies (it certainly seems to be a universal truth) it follows that if management boards want departments to work together then they had better put in place a measurement system that encourages them to do so. If not implemented carefully, scorecards can end up even more complex and complicated than the simple financial measures they are meant to improve. The cure can prove to be worse than the disease and there is even a possibility that the 'disease' was misdiagnosed in the first place. Kaplan and Norton, since their earlier writing, have come up with a new idea – strategy maps (see *Strategy Maps, Converting Intangible Assets into Tangible Outcomes*, HBS, 2004). This could be seen as the final admission that the theory of scorecards does not work because not everyone in the organization is aligned. Does bolting on another, even more complex, piece of management wizardry, however, increase the probability of them ever working? So are there any other existing alternatives?

THE EFQM BUSINESS EXCELLENCE MODEL

For probably the most sophisticated, yet generic, business excellence model of all we need look no further than the EU and its

European Quality Award scheme within the framework of the EFQM (European Foundation for Quality Management – see http://www.efqm.org) shown in Figure 5.2. It is highly sophisticated in the sense that it tries to combine a straight business management model, a continuous improvement philosophy, a focus on people and a social dimension into one whole. It is probably over-ambitious and overengineered.

When it comes down to practicalities this model has the same inherent weaknesses as the scorecard. Every box (nine in all) has to be measured and this can be done mechanistically. There is even a target number of points to be achieved if an organization wants to be given the European Quality Award. In fact, any newcomer to the scheme could be forgiven for thinking that measurement is the ultimate goal rather than a means to an end. Under several headings the phrase 'Excellent organizations comprehensively measure and achieve outstanding results' is repeated. As with the scorecard the emphasis on frameworks and discrete boxes of particular measures seems to still miss the main point. When all these measures have been religiously taken the only thing that will matter is whether the organization continues to survive in its chosen markets. Tom Peters once said that under international quality standards a company could design a concrete

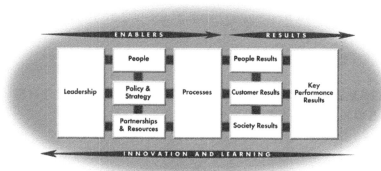

Figure 5.2 EFQM excellence model (Reproduced by permission of the EFQM. Copyright © 1999–2003 EFQM.)

lifejacket that would satisfy all of the quality conditions of the scheme, yet still kill anyone who used it. He could have been describing the EFQM.

Something often happens in organizations that makes them lose sight of their overall goals, the ultimate value that they are seeking. Even though the models described above are intended to address this very issue they seem to fall down somewhere. Edward de Bono, the lateral-thinking expert, often explains this phenomenon by recalling a story about NASA engineers. The problem they were trying to solve was how to enable their astronauts to write upside down in a weightless environment. The solution they eventually came up with, invented specifically for the purpose, was a space-age ballpoint pen. It cost millions of dollars to develop and included the ink being powered by a tiny gas canister. He then dryly remarks that, faced with the same dilemma, the Russians provided their astronauts with a pencil. There is a simple but fundamental lesson here. The ultimate goal of value has to be clear in everyone's minds at all times if they are to work together to achieve it.

Achieving that clarity means getting over all of the hurdles we have already identified. So our next task is a fresh look at what the word performance really means in a value context, building on the simple model of value we introduced in Chapter 2. Then we will consider not only *what* measures to use but also *how* to use them to provide a true gauge of performance in value terms.

AGREEING VALUE PRIORITIES USING THE 3 BOX SYSTEM

The model we established in Chapter 2 referred to two types of value, basic and added, and we made clear distinctions between them. Now we need to introduce an extra dimension to this simple model. To do so we will use something called the 3 Box System, which was designed as a simple, practical management tool with several purposes, to:

*   help everyone to articulate what value really means for the organization;
*   aid decision making;
*   assist with prioritization;
*   act as a guide on the selection of performance measures.

There is an illustrative example of this in Figure 5.3 and you will be able to try the system out for yourself very soon but first let us briefly explain the theory behind it.

Box 1 – 'must-have' activity

Organizations have become obsessed with the need to measure everything they do. They sense how important it is but do not always have the technology necessary to measure everything as

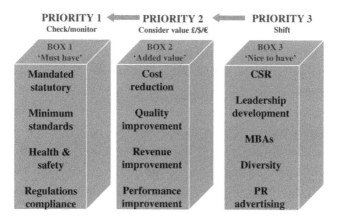

Figure 5.3   The 3 Box System

they would like. This has happened throughout history. It took 500 years for a workable thermometer to be designed to measure heat on a commonly agreed scale; even though every human being could already sense the difference between hot and cold. Sophisticated measurement systems take time to design. So, let us look at something like compliance as an activity we might want to measure. How well does your company comply with relevant legislation (e.g. having financial services people qualified with the right certificates required to do their job)? More importantly, what is the value of that compliance in £ terms? That is a difficult one isn't it? You can sense the risk involved in not being compliant – the authorities or customers might sue you – but then again they might not. Perhaps you could take a risk and hope they do not find out. How do you put a value on that?

What the 3 Box System does is take that conundrum away. It puts compliance matters in Box 1 where they are regarded as 'must-have' by the highest authority in the company. This means that they must happen; no ifs and no buts. Box 1 is a deadly serious box: you get it wrong at your peril. If you were responsible for making sure all the necessary certificates were on file, and yet failed to check or monitor this, then the Box 1 nature of this work would demand that you were severely reprimanded, if not fired. The only measurement system needed for Box 1 is a binary system – yes or no, does it comply or doesn't it? There is no need to work out the theoretical costs of being sued.

But Box 1 is not just about what the law dictates you must do. It is also about the standards your organization sets for itself. If you work in a hotel then there would be minimum standards for cleaning rooms. These would have to be expressed in some way that cleaning staff and management could check that they were being met. It does not matter in Box 1 that the measurements of cleanliness used are not set by law or by some body that can be regarded as the ultimate arbiter. It does not matter that these measures will be qualitative, rather than entirely objective, in nature. What matters is that everyone has a clear idea what the standards are and works to them. If the bedrooms do not reach the required standard then it should not come as any shock to the cleaning staff if this is pointed out to them; if they already fully understand the measures used.

At the end of each month, or each year, any organization should be able to say whether all activities in Box 1 are achieving a minimum standard. Then all they have to do is make sure that maintaining these standards is not putting the company out of business. If a private hospital suffered from an outbreak of a serious virus, dealing with it could sink the business. So Box 1 is about standards being met at an acceptable cost. This is really just another definition of what we called basic value in Chapter 2 but now it is being used as a clear management tool. But don't expect Box 1 activities to inspire anyone and they are the sorts of activities that, no matter how well you do them, you will never get a pat on the back. Box 1 provides no competitive advantage because all of your competitors are having to meet the same mandatory standards.

Nevertheless, from a priority point of view, Box 1 activities always come first. They might only keep up minimum standards but the risk of falling below those standards is very high, in reputation or litigation terms if nothing else. Whereas in Box 2 we meet an entirely different type of activity.

Box 2 – added value activities

All activities in Box 2 should clearly be designed to add value. Not just theoretically but in practice. All of the examples shown in Box 2 in Figure 5.3 will have to be designed with a very clear line of sight to a value objective. Baseline measures will already have to be in place and some estimation will have to be made of what the improvement will be worth. Box 2 activities should have a clear £ sign attached to them. The targets are the four added value variables of output, cost, revenue and quality. One way of looking at the essential difference between Box 1 and 2 is that 1 could be described as 'business as usual' and 2 could be described as the innovative, new-ways-of-working box.

So what ends up in Box 3?

Box 3 – nice-to-have activities?

Have you been on a management training programme or any form of development activity over the last six months? If so, consider now which box you would put it into. Let us take a leadership development programme as an example. It might have been a few days away at any one of the many residential management colleges that offer this type of programme. The first possibility is that someone told you that you *must* attend. That immediately makes you think that the programme should go into Box 1 but there is much more to this system than meets the eye.

If your boss said you had to attend, did you ask why? What difference would it make if you didn't go? So the boss says that everyone at your management grade has to go through the programme before they can be considered for further promotion. This definitely sounds like Box 1 now but it still has not qualified yet. We would need to know how you were to be assessed on this programme. Is attendance the only requirement or are there some tests included? What if you fail a test, is that your promotion hopes dashed?

It would be very difficult to measure what difference the programme actually made to any leadership skills or potential you might have but in Box 1, just as with the hotel cleaning, it does not matter. What matters is that you know where you stand and what you have to do to reach the standard. So you go along and do your best only to find, six months later, that somebody who did not attend gets a promotion. Their boss did not let their non-attendance stand in the way of their recommendation. Now you realize that this was not regarded as being in Box 1 across the whole organization.

A totally different approach would be to put this programme in Box 2. However, for it to qualify for Box 2 several criteria would have to be satisfied:

1. The diagnosis would have to be correct. An analysis of inferior performance of the business would have had to come to the conclusion that senior people did not exhibit sufficient leadership qualities.
2. A group requiring this particular intervention would have to be identified.
3. Each participant would have to be briefed about the line of sight between the diagnosis, their part in the process and what business measures would be used to indicate success.
4. Baseline measures would have to be agreed in advance of attending the programme.

This all sounds like too much trouble, so nobody bothers with this idea at all. That means that the leadership programme has to be relegated to Box 3. What this box signifies is that the organization *feels* that it needs better leadership (whatever that is) and is prepared to spend some money in the hope that some leadership qualities might rub off on a few executives. But there is never any real commitment to Box 3 activity, that is almost how it is defined. It would just be nice if things improved but no one has any measure to show that they have. Unfortunately, because no one takes Box 3 seriously, most executives would not turn up, even if nominated. Those who did would more likely be the ones who like going on courses rather than those who really need some development.

By now you should have a clear idea of the distinctions between the 3 Boxes. Normally activities that are vague, or deemed 'intangible', or difficult to measure end up in Box 3 simply because we don't know where else to put them. Figure 5.3 shows diversity in Box 3. This does not mean that diversity cannot be in Box 1 or 2. What it means is that the value of diversity is not articulated. Or the motives behind the diversity initiative are unclear. Is it to keep the company out of court (in which case it would be Box 1), does anyone see a line of sight between diversity and hard measures (Box 2) or is it in Box 3, that is being promoted (without any commitment) just because there is an uneasy feeling that not enough women have made it to senior management levels?

What the 3 Box System really does is force the organization to have an honest dialogue about what the organization really values and translates that into a business objective with a specific priority. It then checks that the organization actually commits to those priorities. It is, in effect, meant to be the creation of a virtuous circle of value. It is also very practical. If you were to sit down with a colleague tomorrow to discuss performance issues the 3 Box System could be used straight away to help focus that discussion on value using a simple, common language that is easy to understand and apply, even to complex performance issues.

THE GULF BETWEEN PERFORMANCE MEASUREMENT THEORY AND PRACTICE

Having established some principles of performance measurement we can now ask how far organizations are from where they need to be if their performance measurement system is to tell them something about creating value. To do so we need to quickly revisit the original purpose of performance measurement in order to suggest ways in which the original purpose itself might need to change. So what was the original purpose of performance measurement? Was it to tell the organization how well (or badly) it was doing? Was it a means for managing people more effectively? Like most management practices the whole subject evolved as much by default as by design. Some credit Peter Drucker's 1954 book *The Practice of Management* as outlining MBO (management by objectives) as a well-defined management practice. The basic idea is extremely simple and makes sense. The organization defines its objectives, these are cascaded (just as in the framework in Figure 2.2) and then fed back, through the MIS, to check achievement, while also ensuring everything is on track or remedial action is being taken where necessary. However, MBO is now seen as a very old-fashioned, rather simplistic approach, even though most current performance systems still follow a not dissimilar path. So what lessons has management learned from this about the way it sets objectives?

The quality guru W. Edwards Deming was probably the first high profile management writer to suggest that the whole philosophy of target setting was misplaced. Setting targets actually puts a cap on expectations and does not free people up or encourage them to do their best. He also criticized the use of performance measures as a means for quality inspection, pointing out that quality assurance was a much more important principle to follow. These are certainly lessons that successive governments have failed to learn when attempting to manage the public sector. The Labour government that came to power in the UK in 1997 had set 239 key targets by 1998 of which 90 were either missed or, worse still, unevaluated (*Sunday Times*, 6th July 2003). The feedback loop of MBO had not been used at all. However, it is not just the adherence to the discredited practice of target setting that is worrying. Underpinning all government attempts to 'reform' public services is a philosophy of inspection. Schools are inspected at least every three years, hospitals are inspected, so are police forces and the National Audit Office and the Audit

Commission have strict regimes in place to inspect every aspect of public sector organizations that come under their scrutiny. There is very little evidence that any of this has managed to drive up performance though.

For example, a report by MPs on the House of Commons Public Accounts Committee revealed (*The Times*, 21st June 2005) that a £1 bn fight against crime had apparently delivered 'results' even though there were no measures in place to say what the results were. The permanent secretary at the relevant department, the Home Office, tried to justify this nonsensical situation by admitting that 'In the early days . . . we did think it was right to let a thousand flowers bloom and see what the results would be.' In other words, casting the seed to the winds, in the hope that some of them would set and bear fruit, was obviously deemed to be an acceptable management practice.

Even when the public sector declared that it had achieved real efficiency gains the Chairman of the Public Accounts Committee had to admit that 'There are inconsistencies in how the savings are measured and . . . we really don't know whether efficiencies are being achieved at the expense of service quality' (*The Times*, 21st February 2006). Obviously the chairman had some intuitive understanding of the added value equation (as we all do) and was aware that increasing one variable while reducing another could actually cause a reduction in overall value. What the chairman was unable to do was to articulate his misgivings precisely using a common definition of value. Anyone with any common sense would readily accept that cost savings, which reduce quality, could prove to be a diminution in value rather than an improvement.

Nevertheless, because organizational performance is always the ultimate goal, trying to measure it will always be imperative. There is no way out of this and that is partly why hope always seems to continue to triumph over experience. John Philpott, the highly respected chief economist at the CIPD (Chartered Institute of Personnel and Development) wrote a piece for *Personnel Today* (26th April 2005) entitled 'Public sector haunted by poor productivity tag' commenting that 'Public service outputs – for example, the number of hospital treatments in a given year or the number of school pupils passing exams – may not adequately reflect improvement in public service outcomes, such as the impacts on health in society or employability, which are ultimately what matter.' He was expressing exactly the same concern that it was only the final value that mattered and, somehow, this was what had to be measured.

He was only too aware of the problems in doing this, suggesting that '. . . output measures might not always identify improvement in the quality of outputs. The apparent fall in productivity (may be) due to a lag between . . . spending and increased outputs . . . (due to the need) to build public sector capacity.' Philpott not only recognizes the inherent difficulties of outcome measurement but, as any good economist would, also fully acknowledges that finding a clear, causal connection between inputs and outputs, when significant time lags are involved, may also present an insurmountable obstacle. He ends by making some observations about the latest in a very long line of fresh attempts by economists to address these fundamental issues by reference to the Office for National Statistics (ONS), which had just launched a measurement procedure called 'triangulation'. He concluded '. . . this seems a sensible way forward (but) . . . will doubtless leave ample scope for future disputes about how productive the public sector really is'. It is a founding principle of performance measures that they are only as good as the confidence and credibility they produce. John Philpott already seems to be suggesting that new techniques, such as triangulation, will not succeed in producing measures in which we should have any greater confidence.

One of the biggest problems with economists' theories of measurement is just that, they are theories. The 'bible' of measurement produced by the UK's Treasury Department is called the Green Book (see http://greenbook.treasury.gov.uk but particularly Chapter 2 on appraisal and evaluation) and mandates that the rationale for any public project should be clearly stated at the outset (i.e. what are the objectives and are the benefits likely to outweigh the costs) and should include a proper evaluation of whether the project ultimately delivered on its promises. The whole thing is predicated on closed loop feedback system thinking. So how well does it work in practice?

This is cost/benefit analysis by any other name and any economist will tell you that the costs, particularly of public projects, are generally easier to calculate than the benefits. Take, for example, a government initiative to try to raise employment in high unemployment blackspots around the country. Imagine that it wants to make grants available in areas of industrial decline, not only for the beneficial impact it could have on the local economy but also the knock-on effect it could have elsewhere. So, if someone in the locality receives a grant to start a new business (we will take the real life example of a small boatbuilding business, by the coast, to service the growing demand for sailing) this will create extra demand elsewhere (e.g. for yacht varnish manufacturers, timber merchants etc.). Of course, while this all sounds very worthwhile, if it were left completely to the market the new boat builder would survive or fail simply by virtue of their ability, or inability, to sell boats at a viable price. Introducing the grant into the equation means it lessens their own risk but the government economists at the Treasury want to make sure these grants prove to be a sound investment. So anyone applying for the grant has to fill in a form indicating the size of business they are planning and the likelihood of it having the desired, knock-on effects. It has to be a win–win for all stakeholders.

This, very quickly, becomes a mounting hypothetical exercise. No one knows exactly what job opportunities might be created elsewhere and no one will ever know, in advance. Surveys could be carried out asking varnish manufacturers a multitude of 'what if' questions but their best answers would always, at best, be a guess. So everyone involved has to start making the numbers up if they want their grant application to be approved. Any rational varnish manufacturer, of course, will err most decidedly on the side of their most optimistic forecasts as they have nothing to lose by doing so. If the boatbuilder increases their demand they scale up to meet it. If they go bust they have not lost anything because they never had to invest anything in the first place. So what do the Treasury economists do with this information?

Economists can tell us that there are several well-known effects that happen when investments are made in an economy. One is the multiplier effect. A job created at the boatbuilder's is not just one job but possibly two or three jobs elsewhere, and not just in associated industries. The new boatbuilding employee spends money at the local pub and this creates extra bar staff jobs too. This is easy to understand, in theory, but impossible to demonstrate in practice. The National Centre for Popular Music (see Chapter 1) was just one example, of many, that was probably supported financially following this sort of rationale. But does it matter whether the theory can be put into practice or not? Surely, if the multiplier effect makes sense can it be turned into a practical management tool? Well, let us look at the implications if it were. If the Treasury's forms were changed to force the boatbuilder to consider, in detail, what impact their business would have on the wider economy, would it change their whole approach to their business? Would it alter the probability of the boatbuilder succeeding? Would it increase the chances of taxpayers' money being invested wisely?

One thing any budding entrepreneur would have to do, if they were seeking any form of finance, including this boatbuilder, would be to produce a business plan predicting costs, revenue and outputs (numbers of boats made and sold per year). Those figures could immediately be translated into estimates of yacht varnish required. An entrepreneur, using his or her own finance, might leave it at that. The entrepreneur seeking a grant would have to look at the multiplier effect though. They would have to ask at least one varnish manufacturer whether the demand they might create could be met with their existing yacht manufacturing capacity (as we showed earlier, when it comes to value, we are all part of the same distillation process). If the answer were yes then the first attempt at answering the multiplier question would result in a zero.

Let us not follow this logic in any more detail. It might already appear to any entrepreneurial types reading this book that this line of reasoning could produce a great deal of wasted effort. The true entrepreneur's argument is that business is inherently risky. There is absolutely no way to rule out all risk. There is also the belief that many business decisions are based on gut instinct, rather than cold logic. There is certainly more than a grain of truth in both these assertions but these views have to be set against the number of business failures across the globe (approximately 33 000 in US and 18 122 in the UK in 2005 – sources Euler Hermes/Experian) or VAT registrations (181 400 new registrations against 179 400 deregistrations in the UK in 2004). The pursuit of profit has produced some spectacular successes but our question is whether the pursuit of value warrants a different approach, or at least a different emphasis. Profit will always give birth to many sustainable business models but the search for maximum value will not happen by chance. The suggestion here is not so much that business risk can be avoided but that a great deal more can be done, especially when the germ of a business idea is born, to do everything possible to check that the idea has a fighting chance of creating some value. The enthusiasm that can be generated when money-making ideas are flying around the management table, and everyone sees only opportunities, can very soon be taken over by the harsh realities of commercialism when the time comes for action.

Value is a higher and tougher discipline than profit. Questions such as 'how exactly is this going to create value' and 'who has to do what' to create value have to be answered, in advance. In the real-life project, of which the boatbuilding scenario painted above was just a part, a whole project team was created to promote and expand the leisure marine industry in a particular coastal region of the UK. Somebody employed by this project team decided that it would be useful to develop a network of businesses involved in the boatbuilding industry in this particular region. The aims and objectives of this network were very vague though. Was it just a talking shop, an opportunity for businesspeople with similar interests to share ideas or a genuine business network where each company would be able to discuss possible opportunities that might be of mutual benefit? Moreover, it had already been decided that the group would need a network coordinator (at more expense). However, they would need to be clear about the group's objectives because this would dictate how they ran the network meetings. A talking shop would be a very different gathering to a proper, collaborative business group. Of course, all of this was to be funded out of the public purse. So the first question that should be asked is if the companies themselves valued this network group why did they not fund it themselves? The counter argument, from the regional development agency that was funding the project, was that one of the objectives was increased employment and so pump-priming this group was a worthwhile investment for the economy and justified the use of taxpayers' funds – in theory.

This might sound like it makes some sense but actually it is just a classic case of a lack of value clarity. If the network was being set up to offer genuine business opportunities (which should simultaneously match the business objectives of each of the companies involved) to those who attend then this should have been declared, loudly and clearly. If a by-product of these business opportunities was to increase employment in the region (a regional development agency objective) then this might justify their initial funding. This starts to make the two value statements look reconcilable but there are two further questions that need to be asked. First, if the business opportunities materialize should the regional development agency recoup their pump-priming money from those who benefited? Second, how exactly should the group be run: what performance measures or indicators will tell us it is doing its job properly? This is where the value motive starts to come into its own.

The reality was that the only measures put in place were input measures, not because anyone thought input measures acceptable but because it is always easier to measure inputs. There were no output measures of the benefits that might come from this networking group. As is so often the case, there was just an assumption that some benefit, however indeterminate, might happen. Once the two key value propositions (profit and employment) are declared, the main purpose for doing so is to gain commitment to them and the best way to gauge commitment is to agree performance indicators that all participants in the scheme will share. However, the performance indicators themselves must be value based. So how can we tell when we have added value indicators rather than mere activity measures?

ACTIVITY, PERFORMANCE AND ADDED VALUE MEASURES

Attempts at measuring organizational performance can be split into three discrete categories. Some measures only tell us that an activity is taking place. So, for example, the number of sales visits or social worker visits per day would indicate that visits are taking place. This number does not tell us anything about the quality of those visits (did the customer value the visit?) or the outcome (did the customer buy or did the school truant eventually get a decent education?). In effect, the number of visits per day, on its own, gives no indication of the performance of the salesperson or social worker.

To move up to a proper performance measure we might ask the salesperson/social worker to get a feedback sheet completed by their customer. This might be a simple checklist of points ('did the salesperson turn up on time, did they explain everything in detail'?) and if we set a standard ('90% of customers should be happy with the service') we can then start to suggest that the individual is 'performing' against a given set of criteria. From a value perspective though neither activity nor performance measures tell us anything meaningful.

To produce an added value measure the organization needs to decide what it values, the ultimate outcomes that John Philpott referred to. Is it profitable sales, lower truancy rates or what? Then a connection needs to be made between the visit from the salesperson/social worker and those outcomes. It is very easy to see, however, that whereas activity and performance measures relate to individual employees, added value measures relate to the whole organization, or even external organizations as well. So, profitable sales depend on everyone, including the production team, marketing, product development, even logistics, if poor deliveries impact on customer service and thereby future sales. Equally, truancy might be dependent not only on the social worker but the education department and the student's school as well as the attitude of the parents.

Added value measures set a much higher level of criteria. It is a much tougher standard to try to meet. It makes everyone in the value chain accountable and one person blaming another (the school blames the parents and vice versa) becomes pointless because it does nothing to add value (lower the truancy rate). The only way to ensure the organization achieves the right level of value is to ensure every part of the value chain works towards that end.

In summary:

- Activity measures tell us nothing about output quantity or quality, revenue or cost (i.e. activity measures do not relate to the four added value variables).
- Performance measures tell us the individual or organization is doing what we expect them to do (performance measures should at least indicate which direction we regard as desirable, e.g. we want the customer to buy more products).
- Added value measures tell us the outcome is right at the right cost (we make a profit, the truant child eventually gets a job as a result of completing their education).

Now let us return to the business networking group we discussed earlier. Measuring the number of people who turn up to the weekly meetings would be a pure activity measure. Setting a target of managing directors or CEOs might be regarded as a performance measure, if everyone on the project agreed that attracting these sorts of people would be regarded as a meaningful indicator of potential success. Handing out a feedback sheet asking whether the attendees found the meeting useful or interesting would still only be a performance measure, at best. The only true added value measures would be the ones originally set, profit and employment. If the lead-time for the opportunities to feed through to profit and employment were expected to be at least six months then a system for measuring a trend over that period of time would have to be instigated. Here is where the added value measures score significantly over traditional management by objectives. If, for example, employment numbers were a key issue then at each meeting employment would have to be on the agenda. The structure and content of the meeting would have to be tailored accordingly. More importantly, over time, some companies would create employment and others would not. Those attendees unable to show a contribution to the value of the group could be threatened with exclusion. All of this should significantly improve the probability of success, do you want to be in the value-generating club or not? Those who pass the test and show commitment will make it work. Those who are half-hearted will keep away. It is a wonderful, self-reinforcing, virtuous circle of value.

Value makes people work together towards common goals. Conventional performance management thinking that believes the setting of a whole range of disparate measures, for different groups and individuals in the same or collaborating organizations, will somehow produce a total that is greater than the sum of its parts is fallacious. Performance measures will not naturally coalesce into value. The only way to get value is to measure value and ensure that everyone involved is held to account against those same value measures; no one can escape. If we want to see evidence of how to get performance measurement badly wrong we only need to look again at the experience of target setting in the public sector that we have already highlighted. As with all poorly set performance targets, there is rarely any real commitment to them when the going gets tough. It is time for the whole purpose of performance measurement to be revisited.

TAKING A FRESH PERSPECTIVE ON THE PURPOSE OF PERFORMANCE MEASUREMENT

Performance measurement is one of those subjects that you tend to love or hate. There is not much in the way of a middle ground. Either you achieve something, you move forward or you don't. An athlete running the 100 metres will always want to know what their time is. That is the only thing that matters and it is entirely down to them on the day. They will obviously be disappointed if they do not win but if they can achieve a personal best that is probably the next best thing. The same cannot be said for those of us who have to work as part of a team or as just one step in a lengthy process. The engineer that designs just one part of the aeroplane hopes that the finished product will fly but how do they know that everyone else in the complete process is doing their bit just as well? So before we go any further we need to establish some clear ground rules. If people do not buy into performance measures we are wasting our time before we even start. Therefore, any good performance measure will have to satisfy two simple tests first, from each individual's perspective:

1. Will it motivate me?
2. Will it tell me what my contribution to the whole is (i.e. will my own contribution add some value)?

If the measure fails on either of these counts it fails utterly. Let us apply this principle to a measure used in healthcare, the number of patients who use a bed in a year. This is meant to be a measure of throughput and it is only a performance measure if we presume that increasing this number is desirable. So will it motivate the nurse who has to care for these patients? Probably not if their own values tell them that the only thing that matters is the 'right' level of care for each patient, not the time taken between their admission and discharge. If the nurse does not value the performance measure none of their innate motive force will be brought to bear on it. So any measure might immediately fail the first test but what about the second?

It might be possible to convince the nurse that a speedier throughput of patients will increase the capacity of the hospital, meaning more patients can be treated and waiting times reduced. If so, then the complete picture would have to be presented. The nurse might want to see the total numbers treated, the average waiting time being reduced but, perhaps much more importantly for their own values, the readmission rates also need to be included. If a patient goes home sooner, only to be readmitted later because they had not fully recovered from their operation, then the quicker turnaround times become meaningless, even detrimental to the whole. The nurses know this, they are not stupid, and the hospital's mission statement will not be motivating them if they know that the reality is so different.

To pass these two crucial tests means much greater involvement for the nurse in the whole management of the hospital. Some doctors and managers might suggest that the wider aspects of hospital management are of no concern to the nurse. However, shutting people out of the complete process is hardly likely to engage them in it and failing to engage people in the pursuit of value maximization is both foolhardy and short-sighted: not least because the other aspect of performance measurement that we now need to explore is moving from a static model to a dynamic one. Any performance improvement today is just the starting point for another improvement tomorrow. Performance measurement and management is meant to be an iterative, continuous process or it is nothing. It is hardly likely to gain a momentum of its own unless everyone sees it this way and does everything they can to support it.

The other, prime, purpose of performance measurement is that it should be right at the heart, the epicentre of the way the organization learns. If readmission rates increase in line with rises in the number of patients per bed, per year, something is going wrong somewhere. Someone therefore has to diagnose what the problem is (we could be forgiven for wondering why *diagnosing* problems seems to be so difficult in an organization run by doctors). Are the readmissions due to insufficient healing time or were the original medical procedures at fault? Even if this results in a fall in readmissions, what other actions are required to deal with the other possible causes? Approaching this performance loop with a mindset that is making an iterative search for never-ending improvements starts to become the way the organization not only works but also thinks. Once an organization starts thinking differently it has much more powerful momentum and greater sustainability. We start to see what some would call a learning organization. People work together to solve problems. Solving problems adds value.

This, as with everything in this book, is meant to be common sense except that we have not discussed yet all of the factors that can undermine and militate against such a simple idea. Many of these factors will be covered in Chapter 6 because most of them are to do with people, the way they think and behave. However, there is one more, huge hurdle to overcome first and that is the common but fallacious belief that not everything worth measuring can be measured.

MEASURING AND MANAGING 'INTANGIBLES'

In Chapter 2 we briefly alluded to the notion that there is no such thing as an intangible. Coca-Cola's well-developed, corporate image and reputation did not count for anything, in the face of adverse press coverage, when it tried to launch Dasani water in the UK. The only thing that ever matters is the value of output. Yet we all fully recognize the importance of factors such as reputation, culture, attitude, initiative, judgement and drive. We have also just briefly touched on the way organizations learn, the extent to which employees are engaged and even whether they are empowered to contribute more. These can often be the key differentiators between high and low performing organizations. Yet all of them appear as though they would not be amenable to measurement in any scientific way. You can sense them. You can even observe them happening. But you cannot touch them. So they immediately seem like candidates for the intangibles pile. Once they get tarred with this brush they are deemed to be immune to conventional management practices. This is a serious mistake and omission.

How many times have you been in a meeting where there are mainly negative vibes? Often, at new product meetings or when discussing launching into new markets or new ways of working, it is so easy for everyone to think of the negatives and likely obstacles. Everyone makes excuses, there is no can-do attitude prevalent. We all know it can happen and we all know it can make a big difference to the likely success or failure of a project. But the crucial question is how do you manage it? Especially if you cannot measure it. Should we invent a 'can-do attitude indicator' showing a score from 1 to 10? Do you tell the team they are currently showing a 3.5 on the 'lack of initiative' Richter scale?

If a company's reputation has dipped recently, based on mystery shopper scores or market surveys, what do you do to improve those measures? Spend lots of money on advertising or do you accept the truth of the figures and accept that customer service has to improve significantly? These are the difficult, often apparently intractable, decisions that organizations have to make every day. Then there is a whole raft of other typical people issues. I wish manager Bill had better judgement. Wouldn't it be great if Judy took time to listen to her people more? Why doesn't so-and-so show a bit more initiative? We can all spot the weaknesses in our colleagues and it is very tempting to think we might find a magic wand somewhere to put them right. That's why we send them to management schools.

Conventional management techniques have never really come up with a simple, effective answer to the question of measuring and managing intangibles. So is that because the question is just too difficult or is it because it's the wrong question to start with? If we believe something is intangible then we are admitting defeat, by our own definition, before we have even started. If we truly believe intangibles exist and cannot be measured effectively then the only other management method we can resort to is our own judgement. If the CEO thinks the company has earned a poor reputation or the attitude of the employees is all wrong they just have to make decisions as best they can, using their own experience and judgement, to try to put them right.

Unfortunately, it is precisely this type of thinking that usually produces the most illogical and un-common-sensical management initiatives. They usually come as a vague-sounding, single solution, programme or initiative under generic headings such as 'change management', 're-engineering', 'culture shift' or 'refocusing'. What they all have in common is no clear definition of what value they are trying to create, how they are meant to work and who is accountable for what. Here is a classic example of this management genre.

A very large, highly reputable, retail organization started to encounter a significant drop in business and customer satisfaction. It went through several, very painful and high profile changes in senior management in an attempt to get back on track. While sales plummeted senior managers were reading the regular, dire, customer satisfaction reports and obviously concluded that there must be some sort of causal connection between the two. Consequently, after one particular change at the top (the commercial director) the company mantra inevitably turned to aiming to improve customer satisfaction. However, the management's perception of the fundamental problem, regardless of how complex it might have been, started from a premise that this was, in some way, an intangible issue. Somehow, staff were not engaging with customers in a way that would make them want to open their purses. This logic led to a 'programme of change', whereby every member of shopfloor staff had to undergo a short burst of training on how to engage the customer and develop more 'intimacy' with them (whatever that means). This programme was going to cost millions and involve over 2,000 staff over a period of 18 months. At no stage in this initiative, however, did anyone, including the commercial director, ever articulate what value this programme would add or even how it would have any chance of adding value. This, by the way, is a very common problem.

How could such a long-standing, well-respected, retailer make what appears to be such a stupid decision? The only way customer engagement, intimacy or satisfaction (all deemed to be intangibles) will add any value is when customers decide they value this approach so much that they are prepared to spend more with the company or recommend it to their friends. This 'intangible' relationship issue with the customer will very quickly become tangible, measured in £s, or prove to be a waste of time and money. However, while management continues to make a false distinction between what is tangible and intangible, opportunities for value will be missed. Assuming that management is not that stupid, one possible answer for why these sorts of decisions are made is simply that the time lag between the activity of improving customer service and the increase in revenue makes it difficult to connect the two.

Whether this is a concern or not, all that is required to convert, or translate, the supposedly intangible into tangible is to apply exactly the same criteria as any sane management team would to any other business investment. If the commercial director can see a line of sight between customer intimacy and sales revenue why not at least articulate this theoretical possibility, in tangible terms, from the outset? The simplest way to do this is using a basic return on investment formula as shown in Figure 5.4. To use this for the customer intimacy drive all we have to do is *assume* what difference, in theory, this programme might make to sales revenue (or for ultimate value, increased profit on sales). A simple assumption might be that any significant management initiative might be expected to achieve at least a 1%

Net ROI $= \dfrac{\text{Gross benefit from programme (£)} - \text{Cost of programme (£)}}{\text{Cost of programme (£)}} \times 100\%$

Which we can reduce to:

Net ROI $= \dfrac{\text{Net benefit (£)}}{\text{Cost (£)}} \times 100\%$

And if we insert some numbers:

Net ROI $= \dfrac{£100\,000 - £50\,000}{£50\,000} \times 100\%$

Net ROI $= \dfrac{£50\,000}{£50\,000} \times 100\% = 100\%$

Net ROI is therefore 100% per annum.

Figure 5.4   A simple return on investment (ROI) for 'intangibles'

improvement. Using the figures in Figure 5.4 this produces a net benefit of £50000 and a net ROI of 100%. At what point though does the theory cross over into reality? Very quickly indeed, is the answer.

Once the commercial director stops thinking intangibles and clearly articulates what they are planning, using hard numbers, all other managers have something common to respond to. These responses will vary enormously depending on their own personal perspective. The store manager, who is just about to undergo a store refurbishment, might ask for a six-month delay. The manager who already gets the best mystery shopper scores might even ask to be exempt from this particular programme because it is not appropriate for their store.

Assuming that some store managers accept the basic premise of the simple ROI formula, they would be entitled to ask how any improvement in sales revenue would be measured? This is where the practicalities of performance measurement come back into play. Sales over the succeeding months could increase due to a range of factors; a new housing development in the vicinity, a large employer comes to the area and increases incomes or a new range of products is being launched at the same time. The ROI might pass the first test of motivating the store managers but it could fail the second because too many other factors will distort the figures and not reveal the individual store manager's own contribution.

We will deal with this issue very shortly but if nothing else, this simple scenario reveals how unfocused generic, single solution, change initiatives can be. It also illustrates that the potential value of anything founded on the premise of intangibles is likely to be questionable. Furthermore, it suggests that across-the-board performance targets are just too blunt a management instrument to work effectively.

Now we need to get back to this issue of convincing everyone that his or her performance is contributing to added value. We will do this by looking at the thorniest management issue of all, evaluation.

E-VALU-ATION

Maybe it does not need to be spelled out as clearly as the heading suggests. It should come as no surprise that a book on value eventually gets around to the subject of evaluation. After all, evaluation is the very process of putting a value on something. Most people agree that we must try to evaluate what we do but they also tend to feel that it can be a thankless task. Regardless of how much effort we put into evaluation there can still be so many questions left unanswered. Was there a causal connection between the action and the result (e.g. did the doctor's prescription make the patient well or would they have improved in time anyway)? Was another factor, outside of our control, the key one that made the difference (e.g. our sales improved simply because one of our competitors went bust)? How do we prove our intervention had an impact? The questions go on and on and unfortunately this makes it a subject where everyone assumes the devil will be in the detail. In fact, there is no devil in evaluation, as long as everyone agrees what value is required from the outset.

Just as an example, and as a test of your own understanding of the problems associated with evaluation, imagine that you go out for a meal with friends and you decide that you want to evaluate how the evening went. So, as you are all heading home, you stop everyone for a second and ask what they thought of the evening. Somebody replies that the meal could have been better. Someone else says their own meal was fine but the drinks were expensive. Another says it was OK, but maybe they were not really in the right mood to fully enjoy it. Immediately it looks like a very fraught exercise. So what has gone wrong with your approach to evaluation? Quite a lot.

First, before you look at how you evaluated you should reconsider why you wanted to evaluate in the first place. If you organized the evening out and you recommended the restaurant there may be some very personal reasons. You just want to check that your recommendations were well received and that everyone enjoyed themselves. But what if they did not like the restaurant or the whole evening? What would you do based on that sort of feedback? Good evaluators will always work out, in advance, what they will do with the data they get back. Paradoxically, a good evaluator will be more prepared for bad news than good news because it is the bad news that they would have to act on. Otherwise, on this occasion you may simply react by being very precious about the whole affair and truculently respond by saying 'well somebody else can organize it next time'. So the purpose of the evaluation should always be crystal clear from the outset, in everyone's mind.

The prime purpose of evaluation is always the same, to ensure that an activity has the highest probability possible that some value will eventually be added. The evaluation process itself will enhance value. This leads to the next obvious question – what do all the stakeholders mean by value? In this context you would have to ask your friends what they want from a good night out. Assuming everyone has already happily agreed to go out to a restaurant, you could check the choice of cuisine and price levels. You could even come up with a simple score (although do not try this for real if you want to keep your friends and avoid being seen as an evaluation nerd), a 1 to 10 scale for a combination of quality of food and price, as shown in Figure 5.5. Then you tell everyone that the aim is to get all scores in the top right-hand quadrant; the right combination of good food at the right price. Of course you could ask your friends for different variables (e.g. service, travelling time, ambience but now you really are in danger of entering über-nerd territory).

The reason there should be no devil in the detail is that you set your stall out in evaluation, in advance. Any problems or disagreements have to be settled at the beginning. If this method is not precise or scientific enough then all parties concerned should agree how it should be adapted. Those who do not wish to take part have to accept their views will not be considered

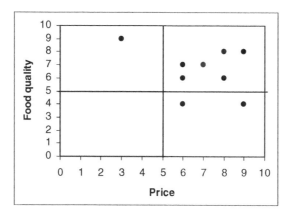

Figure 5.5 Evaluation based on two simple variables

afterwards. All you are doing is trying to match the outcome to the original value expectation as perfectly as possible. There is no point trying to do this afterwards. Without setting the ground rules first the technique shown in Figure 5.5 will just result in lots of arguments and differing opinions as to what was important and what wasn't. No one becomes engaged in the whole process after the event. They can only be totally engaged if they are invited to do so at the beginning.

The management jargon for this whole exercise is to refer to it as a closed loop feedback system. The loop is set up by the original objectives. The measures are used to feed back whether those objectives have been achieved. Whether they have or not, the loop is only completed when everyone learns something from the exercise and this sets up the next iteration. So if everyone scores the food well but the majority think the price was too high the group may decide to eat somewhere else next time. Going around this iterative loop again and again should refine the exercise until everyone agrees on the best value restaurant. Everybody's views on value will have been reconciled.

You may be wondering why we have used an evening out, rather than an operational management example, to explore the intricacies of closed loop feedback systems and the crucial part evaluation plays. The reason is this, a group of friends would not bother going to all this trouble and designing feedback questionnaires. As genuine friends they would all want each other to have as good a time as possible. There would not be too much difficulty reconciling their objectives. There would be plenty of give and take. The closed loop system works best when it works naturally with people who genuinely want to help each other. This should be the goal of any organization. It will never be possible for everyone who works together to be real friends but we can endeavour to capitalize on their need to achieve a commonly agreed goal of value. All of this eventually comes down to one thing. The extent to which those who work for, or with, the organization *want* to create maximum value becomes of paramount importance in the realm of the value motive. Value is and always will be a very human, people thing.

CHAPTER 6

VALUE IS ESSENTIALLY
A PEOPLE THING

Summary Maximum value can only be achieved by maximizing the value of people.

A FRESH APPROACH TO
PEOPLE MANAGEMENT

It is self-evident that any organization, from whatever sector, can only maximize its output and value by maximizing the contribution of everyone who works for it. Anyone who is not trained well enough; not used to the best of their potential; the uncooperative; those never asked for their ideas or suggestions; anyone unwilling to give maximum effort or just the plain unmotivated, are all sapping potential value. This is why value, ultimately, is a people thing. Profit does not demand the best from everyone, value does. So, do you get the maximum value out of your people? Or perhaps we could go back a couple of steps and ask do you *want* to get the best possible value out of your people and are you prepared to do what it takes to get that best value?

Regardless of your position or profession, assuming that you do not work in the HR function, your present understanding of the term 'people management' will probably have been shaped by two key factors:

1. Your own knowledge and personal experience of having to manage people.
2. What your HR function told you was best practice in HR.

Let us quickly take a look at number 2 first. You might like to consider whether you have ever seen any tangible value produced from the sort of activities, initiatives and programmes handled by HR. What value do job evaluation and grading systems, appraisal and personal reviews, competency frameworks, leadership development programmes, reward and recognition schemes and diversity initiatives, to name but a few, add to the organization? Do these things really have anything to do with maximizing organizational value?

Now let us look at number 1. What have you learned over the years about the best way to manage people? What is the essence of good man management? Setting clear objectives, making sure the right person is in the right job. Doing everything that can be done to aid their level of motivation. What about those who do not seem to be as passionate about the work as you are? What about the lazy, the poor timekeeper, the ones who never get their reports, or other paperwork, in on time? The ones who always have an excuse or are so eager to pass the blame onto someone else? And let us not forget those who show no initiative or poor judgement?

In theory, 1 and 2 should fit together perfectly. The HR function's job is to ensure that the people you have to manage are the best available, at the salaries you can afford. They should endeavour to ensure that all employees are already fully engaged with the organization's vision and values and are prepared to work hard for the sort of rewards package that HR deemed appropriate, after researching the market. Yet, if this is the accepted way to manage people in modern organizations, there is plenty of evidence to suggest that it is failing. Ford and GM both have huge HR functions employing the latest HR techniques but this has not helped them to keep in touch with their main competitor, Toyota. So there must be something missing in this people management equation. Perhaps an ingredient that Toyota has discovered, which most other organizations find it very difficult to replicate? An ingredient that gets everyone in the organization focused on just one thing, value.

There are many, many ways in which any ordinary manager is restricted or constrained in their freedom to manage their people as they see fit. Some of the more obvious ones that are outside of the manager's control include the fact that pay policy is decided at an organization-wide level, as is any policy on unionization. But there are many other, less obvious factors that seriously hinder any individual manager's ability to get the best out of their people. Those all-important structures and systems were designed by someone else, or worse still, happened by default. This means that who the manager has to work with, who they report to and all other working relationships are set for them. All of these factors limit the extent to which any individual manager can hope to get the best value out of their team, even if they can manage their performance (but see 'Shifting performance for value' below) in a very narrow, task-focused way.

We will soon see, however, that any fresh approach to maximizing value through people management will be subject to the same principle that underpins every other aspect of the value motive; that is, value does not happen by chance. You have to work at it strategically, continuously and systematically, over a

long period of time, for the really significant benefits to materialize. This means having a strategic, iterative, people management
system in place and this is a very tall order (just how tall an order
this might prove to be we will leave for Chapter 7). So how
would you know if you have one or not? Here are just a few
sample questions to help you to decide.

1. Does your organization tolerate underperformance from any
    employees and does it have a systematic way of dealing with
    performance issues?
2. Does it actively encourage all employees to come up with
    ideas, all the time?
3. If a new employee had an idea, which they believed would
    add a lot of value, is there a simple, well-tried system in place
    that will ensure their idea is heard, appraised for potential
    value and speedily implemented?
4. Are there any systematic, continuous efforts made to improve
    each employee's contribution?
5. Is there always a clear line of sight between any employee
    development activity (e.g. 'we want to send you on a man-
    agement course next week') and a value added objective
    ('. . . because your sales/bad debt/customer service/output
    appears to be in need of improvement . . .') with closed loop
    feedback ('. . . and we'll sit down together when you return
    to discuss what you learned and how you will apply it').
6. If you asked any employee whether they 'added value' would
    they know what you were talking about and give a simple,
    clear answer?
7. Has every employee been told they have to keep improving
    what they do and are they fully motivated to do so?

While the case for having to manage people well in a value-
motivated organization is very easily made, what is not so easy

is reaching some agreement on the best way to do this. People management or, as some would have it, human resource management is not a new subject but has yet to establish itself as a credible management discipline. This is due to many factors but the two main interlinked hurdles that it still has to overcome are a common agreement, at board level, as to its role and remit and convincing evidence of its potential value. However, rather than get bogged down here in a lengthy debate about what constitutes strategic human resource management (although if you have an appetite for this you can refer to any of the author's other titles) it is the question of value that we need to answer effectively. This will be difficult though because the most damning indictment of the latest theories in human resource management is that if you ask to see any hard, unequivocal, convincing evidence of what value they add none will be forthcoming – even though there are plenty of people suggesting they have such data.

MEASURING THE VALUE OF PEOPLE

Let us take the Saratoga Institute (acquired by Pricewaterhouse-Coopers in 2003) which describes itself in its own report 'Key Trends in Human Capital – A Global Perspective 2006' (http://www.pwc.com/uk/eng/ins-sol/publ/hrs/pwc_keytrends_mar06.pdf) as 'recognised as the world's leading authority on human capital metrics'. In this report, under the heading of 'Added-value performance', they set out to 'use a unique methodology – the human capital return on investment (ROI) – to provide a comparative measure of added value per FTE (full time equivalent – a simple measure of how many people work in an organization)'. This produces a figure, which 'compares the pre-tax profit generated to the investment in compensation (salaries) and benefit costs' and is calculated as follows:

$$\frac{\text{Revenue} - \text{Non-wage costs}}{\text{Number of FTEs} \times \text{Average remuneration}}$$

The resulting figure is described as 'the key ratio for all HR executives, as it covers all the major elements of their potential contribution'. Of course, calling it a 'key ratio' when it says nothing about value (there is no output or quality in the equation) means that this unique methodology would not qualify as an indicator of 'Added value performance' using our definitions. This is not at all unusual in the field of HR. The desire to put a value on people, supposedly the organization's greatest asset, is just too attractive a proposition to let any common sense get in the way of spurious statistics.

What we are witnessing here are the classic symptoms of simplistic correlations being substituted for causality. This is a common failing in statistics, it is what makes some statistics just 'damn lies'. Causality sets a much tougher standard than correlation. Correlations are easy to produce whereas causality is notoriously difficult to demonstrate. This crucial distinction, however, is fully acknowledged by actuarial consultancy, Watson Wyatt, whose HCI (Human Capital Index) uses 'sophisticated statistical analyses . . .' and purports to show '. . . a clear relationship between the effectiveness of a company's human capital and shareholder value creation. This relationship we found is so clear that a significant improvement in 30 key HR practices is associated with a 30% increase in market value' even though they openly admit that their methodology '*does not prove a causal link*' (HCI – European Survey Report 2000). They try to excuse their methods though by arguing 'Over time, we believe that continued (correlative) measurement will ultimately prove that superior human capital management leads to superior financial performance.' Following that sort of logic, no doubt, Watson Wyatt's methodology would prove, if it kept measuring the colour of prisoners in

American jails for long enough, that not only was there a correlation between someone's skin colour and crime but actually a direct causal link as well. How easy it is for unprofessional statistical analysis to produce such perverse conclusions – that merely the colour of someone's skin could actually *cause* him or her to commit a crime. Correlations masquerading as causation have always been a very dangerous game when applied to people and societal issues.

What is really worrying from the perspective of trying to manage value is that, despite being incredibly easy to pick huge holes in these specious statistics, it does not seem to stop very large (and profitable) organizations subscribing to them. So what does this tell us about the senior management of such organizations? Can they not see the flaws in these statistical tricks themselves? Or do they subscribe to such practices because it means they do not have to get to grips with the real issues involved in trying to manage people as effectively as possible? This latter explanation is much more plausible. Senior managers are certainly not stupid (generally) but many of them really struggle with strategic people management. Partly because they do not know how to do it properly but also because it does require a whole new mindset. A mindset that says, let us work it out for ourselves, rather than let us copy what the 'best' companies are doing. They need to offload that outmoded management obsession born out of benchmarking and a belief in something loosely called 'world class'.

The main problem with management practices based on copying others is that if you are selective about what you copy (e.g. lean production techniques) you might not be copying the most important elements or you might copy only a part of a much larger whole (e.g. supply chain management techniques without the less tangible relationship side of dealing with suppliers on a long-term commitment basis). It is this obsession with benchmarking that has led the vast majority of organizations to copy each other, all of them presuming that the others know what they are doing. Yet, as we have just seen, the data used for benchmarking does not reveal whether value has been added by these HR practices or not. So the sort of management mindset that is needed for value creation through people management is one of causation and, by definition, a relentless search for the root causes of organizational problems.

To establish causation, however, is a really tough challenge. For example, we might want to demonstrate that certain people management practices do actually lead to better performance. The raison d'être of management development, using increasingly sophisticated techniques such as assessment centres and competence frameworks, ought to result in better management and greater value. To establish such causation the companies would have to be asked, before they undertook any such developmental activity, how these managers were supposed to add value in the first place. Then they would have to ascertain how their most talented people could be put to best use. This would have to relate to baseline performance measures already gathered for each individual (but linked to the added value measures of output, cost, revenue and quality). Furthermore, not only would they have to predict which of these variables would move, but also by how much and when.

Academics and consultants desperate to prove a point may use statistical techniques, after the event, to *suggest* which way the arrow of causation points (i.e. the management development programme must have worked because the business has improved) but any attempt to actually establish the true direction of causation can only be made in advance. Management by root cause analysis demands that activity can only follow on from sound analysis. Clear logic and a line of sight have to be made explicit at the beginning; a simple, common sense test that many organizations often fail. The difference between these two, diametrically opposed, management approaches is startling. One reaches its conclusions only after the event, the other designs its management practices with a clear causal link to anticipated value. Two entirely different management philosophies. Post-rationalization versus a value-led, predictive approach that is founded on sound planning. We could almost say it is the battle between intuitive, gut-instinct management versus clear-headed, systematic management.

A more subtle, yet equally important, distinction to be made between these competing management philosophies is the whole question of trying to resolve business problems through *deconstruction*. The correlation approach suggests that every aspect of the business can be broken down into its constituent parts (e.g. what impact does advertising have, how important is R&D, will lean production make a difference, does the use of a balanced scorecard make a difference?) in order to make management decisions and resolve management problems. Whereas, the causation, value driven school of management thinking is predicated on the basis that the root causes of problems have to be identified first, and addressed effectively if value is to be added, even if those root causes cannot be deconstructed in any simplistic way.

This philosophy demands a very different type of organizational leader. Someone who can see the whole and fully understand the dynamic, inter-related, integrated nature of the whole and yet, at the same time, has the wisdom to realize that because it is a whole it has to be managed holistically. Deconstructing the whole into separate components is not the answer even though it might look like the simplest way to manage. We will revisit this concept again in more detail in Chapter 7 where we will see how deconstruction management has undermined business education for many years. But for now we will look at one key, supposedly whole, theory, which tries to totally integrate the way an organization reconciles the needs of three key stakeholders, shareholders, customers and employees.

DEBUNKING THE EMPLOYEE–CUSTOMER–PROFIT CHAIN THEORY

Probably the best known example of correlative thinking that has become embedded in what is now accepted as conventional, strategic management theory is the employee–customer profit chain. This notion is extremely simple, has high face validity and many organizations, particularly in the retail sector, even profess to adopt it as their primary business model. At its most rudimentary level this theory says that if you keep improving employee satisfaction employees will inevitably pass on their satisfaction to your customers, through being more engaged and committed to doing their best for them. This will then lead to improved sales and profit. This is the rationale behind the plethora of employee surveys that so many companies use these days to check the attitudes, engagement and satisfaction of their employees, on an annual basis.

The academic justification for this theory came from a seminal case study published in *Harvard Business Review* (see 'The Employee–Customer Profit Chain at Sears', January–February 1998). This study purported to demonstrate that a '5 unit increase in employee attitude' led to a '0.5% increase in revenue growth'. Of course, there is a high probability that satisfied employees are more likely to keep customers happier than they would be if they met disgruntled employees. We all know what it feels like to be handled by a shop assistant who complains about their employer and workplace. But to assume that employee satisfaction, customer satisfaction and profits are on an ever-increasing, causal continuum completely overplays the importance of employee satisfaction in the equation and underestimates the importance of price, market conditions, product quality and many other variables that all come into play. In Sears' case they later suffered a serious bad debt problem when they moved from their own storecard to a Mastercard. This suggests that Sears' employees were more interested in convincing customers to take a card rather than making sure they were capable of managing their finances effectively (conflicting value sets?). No doubt Sears' view on value was that the more credit cards they sold the better and this was transmitted to their employees through the performance management and measurement system.

It is not the detail of the Sears case study or its aftermath that should concern us here though. What should really concern us is the way this employee–customer theory became a mantra for many companies and the simplistic way in which a sensible notion is stretched beyond its limits to become an all-encompassing, strategic business model. This is best exemplified by award schemes such as the *Sunday Times* annual, 100 Best Companies to Work For scheme where comparisons are made between the performance of their 'top 100' and the FTSE 100 Index. Although the scheme would love to demonstrate, by correlation, that the top 100 perform better than the FTSE 100 the actual figures the *Sunday Times* produces itself do not bear this out: in 2005 the FTSE 100 achieved a return of 14.3% against only 8.3% for the 'best companies'. Because the whole concept is too simplistic it cannot cope with the vagaries of the market and the inevitable changing fortunes that come with it. There can be no simple correlation here, never mind causation.

Sometimes there is even an odd combination of theories that seem to get thrown into the management basket together, with no real conceptual linkage. In *Personnel Today* (17th May 2005) it was reported that Marks & Spencer's CSR policy 'boosts productivity and morale'. This was a community programme called 'Marks & Starts', no doubt to mirror the fact that the company is referred to by most of its customers as 'Marks and Sparks' (the ingenuity of company employee motivation schemes never fails to amaze) which provided work experience for disabled, homeless and young unemployed people. There is no actual measure of productivity included in the article but there are claims for 42%

of staff having more confidence and apparently 24% said their job was now more worthwhile (whatever that means). It does not say what impact this was supposed to have had on the business, either before, at the planning stage of this programme, or afterwards.

It sounds churlish to criticize any of these theories or the schemes and programmes they are supposed to support but until they start to demonstrate value, in any meaningful sense of the word, it is difficult to separate out the consultants' methodological rhetoric from the genuinely well-intentioned public service schemes. So how might we start to change this state of affairs so that everyone benefits? How might we get the best of all worlds? Better motivated staff, better customer service, better profits and better value.

REPLACING PERFORMANCE MANAGEMENT WITH VALUE MANAGEMENT

In Chapter 5 we reviewed organizational performance measurement conventions and found most of them lacking in some respect. Probably their biggest shortcoming is their failure to engage everyone in the organization in the search for ever-greater value. This is often due to targets being set from on high, without involving those who know, in detail, what the issues are at the workface. Also, there needs to be a system in place that personalizes performance, for every employee, in a positive way. By 'personalizing' we mean that every employee knows what he or she has to do, personally, to add some value and actually wants to. Part of this can be achieved using a very simple and very old idea, the normal distribution curve, or, as we will call it, the employee performance curve, as shown in Figure 6.1. This curve is predicated on the theory of probability. With a big enough sample size any organization will tend towards this curve in terms of the performance of its entire workforce. It is worth noting

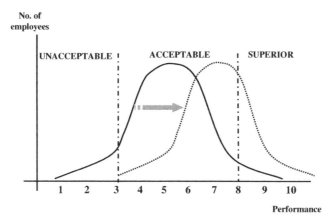

Figure 6.1 Shifting performance, adding value, through people

though that this curve will always be relative to the quality of people employed. So, even in organizations where rewards could be described as the best in the market, by external comparisons, there will always be those deemed as unacceptable in terms of their own internal standards. This truth was amply demonstrated when Jack Welch ran GE using his infamous 'vitality' curve (exactly the same as this curve) and removed the bottom 10% of managers each year. The same managers would not have had too much problem getting a job elsewhere though, where the performance standards were not so demanding.

The first thing we have to make absolutely clear is the purpose behind this curve. It has only one purpose; that is to get more value out of every employee. However, there is a basic assumption behind this particular version of this curve, which is that no employee is regarded as intrinsically bad. Of course, we have all encountered employees who, for whatever reason, just do not want to perform or are happy to get by with as little effort as possible. This curve is not designed for such people though. If they really do exist in your organization then they need to be dealt with through the usual probationary period or disciplinary procedures. We do not want this curve to have any such negative connotations. It is designed to be a positive motive force, not a punitive big stick.

This curve is a tool that should only be used on those who want to perform. It is meant to be energizing, motivating, focusing, supportive, helpful and collaborative. As Figure 6.1 already suggests, there are people on this curve whose performance is currently unacceptable (i.e. you would give them a 1) but they are prepared to listen to where and how they might be going wrong and are prepared to try to improve. Sometimes they need to learn how to do their job better or they need clearer instructions. With those provisos in mind we can now look at the curve in more detail and assess how to use it to create value.

There are three key features to this curve. It:

1. Aims to measure the performance (X axis) of individual employees (Y axis).
2. Uses a simple scoring scheme of 1 (worst) to 10 (best).
3. Forces the scorer to admit when an employee is performing at an unacceptable or superior level.

You can construct one of these curves for yourself in about 10 minutes on a plain piece of paper. Simply think of 10 people you know in your organization (they can be at any level and do not have to work directly for you) and score them from 1 to 10. Do not give anyone 3 or less unless you believe that they are not performing to an acceptable standard. Likewise, only give 8 or above to those who you might describe as high flyers, self-starters or have other abilities that mark them out as performing well above par. With the 10 individual scores you now have on your piece of paper you can roughly draw this diagram. There is one slight problem with such a small sample, however, the graph you produce is unlikely to look exactly like the one in Figure 6.1. This does not matter because our purpose is to shift the whole curve to the right. Simply giving everyone an extra score of 1 point could do this.

So far so good. That is assuming you did not get too hung up about definitions of performance, or tried to compare one individual too closely with another or were worried about the precise score (e.g. should they get a 5 or a 6?). You were not supposed to agonize about these scores. It was just meant to be an initial attempt to create a baseline. If you found that first step easy it might have been because all you were really doing was putting a score to an opinion you had already formed, and held for some time, about these people. If you gave someone a 2, for example, that person was probably one of the first people you thought of. You always regarded them as not doing their job well and this was just an opportunity to reinforce that view. That is all this exercise does. It uses a very simple scoring scheme to help you articulate what you already think, and value. So we can now move to the next step, which is, however, a little more problematic.

There is no point having a view on someone's performance unless you are prepared to share it with them. Even if they work in another department or are more senior than you it is still worth voicing your views. Either you are right about them and their underperformance is affecting yours or, alternatively, you may have your assessment wrong. This is where the problems really start. We all have different views on good and bad performance, probably because our own internal values come into play yet again. Some managers, for example, really value timekeeping and punctuality while others are more relaxed about this. Some people work better with certain managers. So, to avoid any unnecessary arguments and disagreements you had better be clear in your own mind why you scored people as you did. One way to help you articulate this is to say what would this person have to do to earn 1 extra point? It could be something as simple as timekeeping or a bit of attention to detail. Whereas those scoring 8 and above may need to be given a tougher challenge or stretched in another way.

Most employee performance measurement systems stall at the measurement stage because the actual act of measuring itself is seen as too fraught. It is so easy then to fudge it or avoid it altogether. Yet it is not the measurement that is crucial. Measurement should aid the management process, not replace it. Much more important than measuring performance is the creation of a culture of high performance. Building this culture can only start with the organization's vision setting ambitious goals that demand the best possible performance (see Figure 2.2). It requires an organization that is imbued with a philosophy of continuous improvement. Most important of all, it requires a shared mindset where discussing performance openly and honestly, and dealing with the issues this raises constructively, is seen as an absolute must. Very few organizations would currently pass this test but let us look at the opportunities such a culture opens up.

There is a widely held belief that any human scoring scheme has to be perfectly equitable and fair. This is probably a sound principle to follow but an equally important principle is honesty, producing a complete warts-and-all picture. This sets an impossibly high standard and the 'cure' (e.g. either detailed, verbal descriptors for a wide range of performance levels or forcing everyone into a few bands) can very quickly become worse than the disease. Human beings, inevitably, view measurement as a double-edged sword. We all want to be recognized for our achievements but we are much less inclined, quite naturally, to be told where we are failing. All that really matters, bearing in mind these performance scores are not to be used for disciplinary purposes, is agreement that the individual can improve in a specific way. Let us say that you marked someone down, because you saw them speaking to a customer and you felt it was barely of a sufficient standard. So you go up to them when the customer leaves and ask them whether they were happy with the interaction with the customer. They say they thought it went fine. So you say (having established the scoring scheme) that you would only give it 4 out of 10. Your '4' and their '4' might be two very different views of the same event but what matters most is that they accept they need to do better and you both agree what 'better' looks like.

The other main issue here, yet again, is not to get too confused by the distinction between performance and value. Performance is a much lesser measure than value. Performance is always an intermediate measure, never the ultimate measure of value. If the employee says 'what difference does it make how I talk to the customers' then you need to respond with a good, added value reason for asking them to modify their behaviour. What evidence is there that customers are feeling unhappy and is this having any adverse effect on sales? This is a much bigger issue than you might think. Individual performance measures can often conflict with each other (e.g. in an fmcg company the product manager might focus on profit while the marketing manager aims for market share). Both managers should be focusing, ultimately, on the combined value measure of profitable growth in market share. So although the X axis in Figure 6.1 shows 'performance' it should really show value and this makes for a much more enlightening conversation between manager and subordinate.

There are also two other dimensions to this curve that need a fuller explanation. One is the cut-off points, or goalposts, of unacceptable and superior performance. The unacceptable range fits perfectly with Box 1 in Figure 5.3. There has to be a very clear message sent to all employees that the organization cannot compromise in this area. It has to work very hard to ensure everyone comes up to a minimum standard. It will never achieve perfection but that is always the goal. Any vestige of unacceptable performance leaves the organization open to risk. Think of sterile environments in hospitals and the growth in 'superbugs'. Managing the bottom range of the performance curve is very much to do with control systems.

Whereas managing the top, superior, range is totally different. These people are potentially the future senior managers and leaders. They are the sort of people who always want a challenge, crave responsibility, and seek to innovate. Hanging onto them and ensuring they are adding as much value as possible means keeping them happy. This certainly does not mean giving them a completely free hand (we should never forget the lessons from Enron's 'talent management' programme) but within the value statement of the business they need to be empowered to achieve whatever they can.

Either way, both the lower and higher ends of this spectrum have a strong motive force behind them. The unacceptables *have* to do better and the superiors *want* to do better. This cannot be said for the very large, acceptable group in the middle. These are the steady backbone of the organization. The doctors who don't want to be consultants; the managers who have reached their natural plateau. What motive force can be applied to try to encourage such people to add as much value as possible? Especially when the performance management system tells them that they are already 'acceptable' and doing a reasonable job. They don't have to improve. Getting a higher level of performance from this bulk of your employees is the most difficult part of performance management. They need a higher purpose than just coming to work every day. This leads us onto the second dimension.

This curve is not meant to be a static model. Shifting the whole curve continuously is a critical feature. Maximizing value means never standing still. What better way to express this simple goal than to show, to every individual in the organization, that this has a direct implication for them, personally. Of course, if the leaders of the organization do not have this sort of vision then this curve will not be relevant. Yet, even without this level of leadership, the organization might have to do its best just to stand still, simply because of competitive pressures. If the latter of these two situations pertains, suddenly the whole perspective on performance changes. From something potentially energizing to something that is a laborious chore. From leading the market to surviving it. It seems common sense, therefore, that if every organization has to manage performance then why not openly admit it and set out to do it as positively as possible? Winston Churchill, as a pilot in the First World War, expressed his own attitude to always wanting to progress and move forward using the analogy of flying. Flight demands constant movement and speed. If the plane is not constantly moving it stalls and falls out of the sky. Perhaps we can stretch this analogy a little further to think of everyone in the organization as being on the same plane, rather than individual heroics. Looking at individual performance is one thing but now we need to go back to the whole.

MANAGING VALUE HOLISTICALLY

In Chapter 2 we talked about value as a distillation process. All of the ingredients (inputs) poured into the vessel, the water added and the heat, the quality and cleanliness of the vessel itself, the stirring required, combine to produce the eventual drip of alcohol from the tap. If any one of the component parts is not performing there will not be anything of value coming from the tap. So it is with any organization. Cadbury's managed to get a salmonella bacteria into its chocolate manufacturing process at one of its UK plants in 2006 and had to recall all affected products (at a reported cost of £25 million). The root cause of the problem may never be known but somebody, and we really do mean somebody, failed to ensure the cleanliness of the plant. But that somebody's behaviour was shaped by the systems and culture of the organization.

This sounds like the blame game starting again. We often search for a scapegoat so that the rest of the organization can be exculpated and shareholders and customers reassured that it won't happen again, because the cause has been removed. We could try to blame it on a piece of equipment or machinery but we all know that the human element must have had a hand in it somewhere. Who cleaned or maintained the equipment? If the equipment itself was defective who specified or procured it in the first place?

Public enquiries are often called when public service organizations are deemed to have failed. The most distressing cases often involve social services when a child has died at the hands of an abusive parent or guardian. These can be extremely complex affairs because so many different organizations could be said to have had some involvement: police, ambulance crew, social workers and teachers. The conclusions reached usually include recommending that the different organizations should work together better, in a more 'joined-up' way, and any individuals criticized for a dereliction of duty are castigated. In a recent case in the UK's Home Office, which directly led to the sacking of the Home Secretary, errors and omissions in tracking illegal immigrants and asylum seekers were described by the new Home Secretary, John Reid, as a direct consequence of 'systemic failure'. In other words, looking for a scapegoat serves no purpose when the whole system has failed. This is probably the most damning criticism anyone could ever make about any organization.

The very word 'organization' means that the entity is *organized*. There is a clear purpose, defined outcomes and objectives, with resources being marshalled and everyone working well together. Everything is meant to work together as a complete and whole system. When the system itself fails the word organization becomes meaningless. It is the opposite of organization. Disjointed activities where the people are not pulling in the same direction. In such circumstances there is little point in setting new performance measures until such time as the system starts to work properly again. Individuals can do nothing, independently, to add much value if the system has broken down. If a restaurant is purchasing substandard food and has a poorly qualified chef there is nothing the waiter can do to improve your meal.

As a consequence of these simple truths there is one simple recommendation for any organization reconsidering the best way to manage its people. That is, setting individual performance measures without linking them all to value is likely to be divisive and pull the system apart. Everyone has to understand his or her own contribution to value in the system. Their contribution then becomes synonymous with value. The waiter may think they are doing a great job by giving great service but if the meals are terrible they are adding no more value than the disastrous chef.

When the situation is not so stark, the meals are OK and the service is acceptable, focusing each employee on their own area might improve things slightly but only when they all focus on the same value will they be forced to work in harmony. Working in harmony means the waiter is empowered and encouraged to feed back any comments from customers to the chef, without any fear of retribution. They both need to trust each other. They both need to believe that the greater good, the higher purpose, is the reputation of the restaurant. You might like to refer back to the value words in Table 2.1 now and re-consider if the 'intangibles' really do contribute as much, if not more, to value as the tangibles?

VALUING PEOPLE 'INTANGIBLES'

Profit is a very clear and easy goal when compared to value. Plenty of businesses have made plenty of profits without worrying unduly about the welfare or motivation of their workforce. Some sweatshops have made big profits for their owners but sweatshops that want to turn into long-term successful businesses have to change their ways. You only get so much out of people if you are not prepared to give anything back. Treating people as very valuable assets is not only a nicer way to view the world but it also makes a great deal more business sense as well. Those employees who are well looked after should be more disposed to offering the full benefit of their efforts, skills and brainpower. In theory, creativity and innovation should be the source of great value but this presents an immediate problem for those who want to put a value on organizations. How do you value creativity, innovation, intellectual property or even more vague notions such as a 'can-do attitude'? While the importance of these factors is fully recognized they tend to be lumped together as that dreaded word intangibles simply because of the difficulties of measurement we discussed earlier.

One irrefutable fact, however, is that the valuations of publicly quoted companies are often much higher than their book values and this has intrigued many business academics and investment analysts for years. One of the top academics working in this field, Baruch Lev (John Hand and Baruch Lev, *Intangible Assets: Values, Measures, and Risk*, Oxford University Press 2003), estimates that up to 75% of the difference between market and book values can be attributed to intangibles. This is supposed to be particularly true in 'knowledge-based' businesses, even though any business could legitimately be described as such. As with much academic research any conclusion that tapping into the full knowledge reservoirs of your workers adds value can only be reached with the benefit of hindsight. Understanding the importance of the people 'intangibles' is only useful to a business leader if they know how and what they have to do to create an environment where this is possible. Perhaps the first lesson they need to learn is to release some of the shackles imposed by outdated accounting, budgeting and auditing systems.

The value motive has a very significant part to play in creating value but is of no use to those who just want to produce a slight variation on conventional accounting standards. The difference between those motivated by value and a narrow-minded accountant is one wants to set and grow the beans the other just wants to count them. Nevertheless, the debate about how to account for intangibles leads us into probably the most exciting area of people management to have surfaced in the last century – what has come to be called human capital measurement and management. The disciplines of human resource management and financial accounting have finally bumped into each other at the crossroads. This crossroads points to two future directions for organizational accounting and value. One direction follows very much the traditional accounting route; albeit newly resurfaced with Sarbanes-Oxley and other tighter regulations. The second way doesn't look like a normal road at all. The road seems wider and yet less distinct at the edges. This is not a road of financial certainties or clear-cut measures, even though the environment looks quite pleasant. Consequently anyone choosing to go down this second route will have to keep a much more open mind and learn new skills to get to the end safely. They will also have to tread cautiously because everything might not be as it seems.

If human capital management is about measuring a new, knowledge economy then should we just believe organizations when they say they are good at knowledge management? If we have to impose rigid, annual audit regulations on organizations, because we cannot trust them to do it on their own, what sort of audit will tell us that the less tangible elements of the organization are performing well, as part of a complete system? Shell have tried to be at the forefront of many progressive people management initiatives over the years and these have included setting up a global corporate university (prior to 2000) and knowledge management systems. If we looked at the tangible signs of developments in these areas there would be plenty of evidence of activity (e.g. intranet systems for sharing knowledge, corporate university courses) but the question we have to ask is not how much money has Shell spent, how many activities it is engaged in or even how 'professional' their corporate university courses are. No, the only valid question is did they add any value?

If we take a view of Shell's performance over recent years it has had a rocky ride starting with the debacle over the disposal of the Brent Spar platform, which enraged environmental protesters, the overdeclaration of proven reserves (by 20%) and as recently as July 2006 the admission that its Athabasca oil sands extraction operation in Canada was likely to face a 50% expense overrun ($6.6bn). In the process it lost its chairman Sir Philip Watts and an inestimable amount of goodwill and trust among investors. Its management style was vividly expressed in *The Observer* (18th January 2004) as an oil giant with a 'history of cumbersome bureaucracy, opaque governance, lacklustre financial performance and prickliness to outsiders'. If this description is accurate it does not paint a picture of a company that values knowledge and is eager to learn.

For a human capital analyst it is the overdeclaration of reserves that probably illustrates the true nature of the intangibles at Shell. Either the reserves were mistakenly overstated, in which case the basic competence of Shell comes into question, or Shell knew exactly what its reserves were and was afraid to declare them honestly, because it knew it would have a disastrous effect on their share price and investor confidence. Whichever is closer to the truth, their failure to face up to and deal with such a fundamental issue tells us a great deal about weaknesses in management thinking and culture at Shell.

Recent estimates (Wood Mackenzie energy analysts) calculate that before the revision of Shell's reserves it was replacing the oil it was extracting at a rate of 105%, in other words it was finding more new oil than it was depleting. This is the only way for its future stocks to rise. However, this is a very poor performance when compared to its major competitors ExxonMobil (116%) and BP (152%). After restating its reserves Shell's figure fell even further to 57%. This has a serious knock-on effect on the whole system at Shell. Before, it had 13.6 years of proven reserves; after, it had 10.9 (BP had 12.9, Exxon 13.3) and this drop meant the loss of huge economies of scale in the costs of finding and developing new fields, resulting in costs rising from \$4.27 to \$7.90 per barrel (compared with BP's \$3.73 and Exxon's \$3.93).

No one would suggest for a moment that Shell does not have plenty of talented people but there are indicators here that the whole does not come together as well as could be expected. Whatever culture Shell had in the past, perhaps where painful home truths were left unsaid and rhetoric replaced reality, the damage in terms of trust is irreparable in the short term. It is relatively easy to set up a new drilling rig compared to the many years it will take to put right a system that produced such poor figures. If we were to ask Shell what it had learned and how it was going to behave differently in future, particularly in relation to how it manages its people, it could do a great deal worse than adopt a principle of not investing in intangible propositions (e.g. corporate universities) and instead having a clear idea as to how improving knowledge management could improve its reserves. A commitment to the value motive might also win it many more friends and supporters.

Of course, there are many other, often external, factors that will have an influence on the performance of a company over time. Surely it is precisely at these times, when the mettle of leadership is most sorely tested, that makes them the defining moments. How the people who run the organization anticipate, respond or react to such events provides a good indicator of their value credentials. Non-value advocates will resort to PR and spin. It is against these criteria we might judge and we could be forgiven for taking a cynical view of BP doubling its corporate advertising budget in a '\$150m bid for a greener image . . . as it fights to enhance its environmental credentials' (*The Times*, 24th December 2005) when it had a refinery fire in Texas and more recently (August 2006) had a pipeline leak in Alaska, due to corrosion. Value observers might reasonably ask whether some of that $150 m would have added significantly more value if it had been spent on anti-corrosion measures (in July 2006 BP 'committed about $1 bn towards its American operations, about $100 m of which will go on pipe replacement', *Sunday Times*, 13th August 2006)?

Let's face it. We all know it is people who make the difference. It is a truism, but stating it and ensuring that people make as much difference as possible are not the same. In Chapter 5, when we looked at management models such as the balanced scorecard and EFQM we highlighted the fact that they had finally acknowledged the importance of people management. In both cases there is a specific 'box' for the people measures, even though this approach tends to belie the fundamentally holistic nature of any effective management philosophy. Nevertheless, we now need to look in more detail at what sort of measures will tell us whether people really are being managed for value or not.

CHAPTER 7

THE PEOPLE MEASUREMENT 'BOX'

Summary The value of the people contribution has to be assessed but don't try to consign it to a separate, single box.

ONLY MEANINGFUL MEASURES COUNT

First, we should remind ourselves why we need a people box of measures. These measures will not only help us to manage the business better, they are intended to be a source of great value. It might be instructive, therefore, to be clear about what should not go in this box. Basic numbers such as people employed, staff turnover and absence are often the first numbers any organization offers when asked about its people. Obviously a very high rate of staff turnover (or even a very low one) might be a concern, as would a high rate of absenteeism. So these might be part of the overall mix but they are not the sort of key value measures and indicators that we need. This immediately confronts us with the same problem facing all those who are interested in performance measurement; the most important factors are not the easiest to measure, but we should avoid just measuring the things we can.

If you consider for a moment what people information you would be able to extract by interrogating your own conventional MIS (management information system) the chances are it will only provide you with basic record keeping. This means that the data for the people box will have to be created from scratch. You will already have done some of this by producing performance measures based on the curve shown in Figure 6.1. You might get a tick for producing the measures but you should also get a tick for being allowed to produce this data. It signals that your organization is not afraid of grasping some very prickly nettles. This is a very rich seam of potential people value data so we should mine it for all it is worth. So the first, most obvious, number to put in the people measures box is this curve. Even though the data used to produce it would be highly subjective and often contentious. Don't forget, we are less interested in the actual measures and more interested in how we manage them. So let us consider a few scenarios here that will significantly influence the extent to which you can manage these people measures.

Scenario 1. The organization can't face up to tackling people issues

This is by far the most common scenario. If you are senior enough then try putting this issue on the agenda at the next management meeting – everyone has to create data for their own people to produce this curve, and no level of seniority can excuse anyone. The howls of disapproval and excuses why this cannot happen though may well be loud and vehement. The simple answer to this negative reaction is that the organization cannot continue to perform if it does not continue to measure, monitor and improve the performance of its people. The ancillary answer is that any organization that cannot honestly tell its people how they are performing is probably failing in the first task of management. Neither of these answers is likely to win the argument and you cannot introduce this concept into a management team that does not want to know.

Scenario 2. Let's get rid of the underperformers

In this scenario we get an equally strong reaction but not the one we want. Often senior managers will immediately try to use the performance curve to justify getting rid of the unacceptable performers. They realize that even if the data is imperfect it still sends some very powerful messages and gives them the basis for ridding the organization of all its troublemakers and underperformers. Unfortunately, you would have to explain to them again that this is not the purpose of this particular curve.

Scenario 3. The mature, intelligent approach

This third scenario is meant to be the most intelligent and mature approach. First, there has to be full recognition and acknowledgement that the organization's whole approach to performance needs to be revisited. It might be easier to do this if the organization is currently struggling to perform, there would be an immediate imperative, but it would be much better if the philosophy of building a high performance organization were the main reason. The former will change with the changing fortunes of the business. The latter is much more likely to become a constant, unchanging principle. Admittedly, introducing the idea of every manager scoring their people, honestly, would take a great deal of communication with and trust from the workforce (those intangibles become critical once again). A simple decision also has to be taken to accept that the first run of this exercise will be full of imperfections and should be regarded as such. All it is doing is opening up a more honest and open dialogue. A dialogue that will lead to more intelligent discussions about where the organization is underperforming, in terms of value, and why.

From a value motive perspective, most organizations are very immature and the games they play with performance are symptomatic of that immaturity. The most common game is to pre-determine performance bands, as shown in Figure 7.1.

Here the organization usually wants to introduce some form of bonus but decides, in advance, how much it wants to give. This leads to a simplistic division of the workforce into between three and five bands, with predetermined percentages. One should ask what the purpose of such schemes is because they are certainly

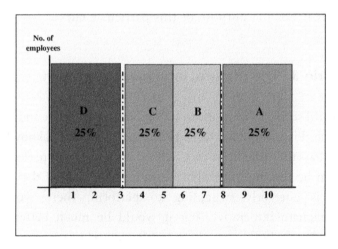

Figure 7.1 Predetermined performance bands

not designed to improve performance, never mind maximize value. Not only is this not an indicator of a value-driven organization, it can be seen as quite the contrary, bureaucratic and process-driven. Consequently these are the sorts of clues that we can regard as contra-indicators of the value motive.

Once the first hurdle of addressing performance issues is overcome the people measures box can be developed much further. As soon as possible the rather subjective 'I think he's worth a 5' needs to become much more objective. Fortunately, this is where conventional MISs do have a part to play. There should already be ample, objective data on sales, revenue, outputs and even quality and customer service to produce meaningful performance curves. It might be worth asking yourself how often you see existing business data presented as an employee performance curve. The nearest you will usually get to this will be obvious areas such as sales by each salesperson. This might already be on a spreadsheet but producing the actual curve really does paint a much more vivid picture, especially in terms of comparative performances.

As soon as real data is used there is often another obstacle to overcome. If you say to the salesperson with the lowest sales that one of their colleagues is the highest performing salesperson their natural reaction is 'ah well, they've got an easier territory than me' or 'they always get the latest releases before anyone else'. Whether this is a genuine justification for their relative performance levels or just an excuse is irrelevant because this performance curve is only intended to generate a constructive and positive dialogue. We are interested in root causes and why there might be a difference in performance levels but only because we want to improve them. All that matters is that each individual is engaged in trying to improve their own performance, their personal best. This is an extremely important aspect that is often omitted from traditional performance schemes.

This curve is devoid of blame because blame, of itself, does not add value. More importantly, it avoids the need for someone to adjudicate on who is doing best. For all we know there may well be purely fortuitous reasons why the 'best' salesperson is doing so well. They really could have the best territory with well-established customers. Conversely, the lowest selling salesperson could also be the 'best' because they are managing to sell more than anyone else could in such a tough patch. Saying to both of them that they are where they are, but they both have to improve, avoids all of these potential arguments.

A mature and intelligent attitude to employee performance will engender a mature and intelligent analysis of the real, under-lying issues. Imposing performance targets shatters any chance of genuine engagement with each individual and therefore is likely to reduce the chances of creating value. There is plenty of evi-dence that performance targets can, quite ironically, reduce value. Using examples based on sales figures readily illustrates some very sound principles because it is so easy to see a direct link, a clear line of sight, between the individual and the organization's per-formance (and hopefully value in terms of profit). But as soon as we move away from easy measurements and linkages it is more difficult to apply the same principles. Imagine, for example, trying to introduce this performance regime into the highly complex area of law and order. How easy would it be to link an individual police officer to the conviction of a specific criminal for a specific crime? The honest answer is that most of the time it would be impossible. So how do you introduce the sort of performance culture recommended here into these situations? Well, we will follow the credo we explained earlier. The purpose is value and the best way to get value is a high performance culture; the measures we use are secondary, only a means to an end. So let us explore what performance could look like in the police.

PEOPLE MEASUREMENT IS A REALLY SERIOUS MATTER

Figure 7.2 shows a performance curve based on reported rape and conviction data (including the rape of males) supplied by all 43 of the police forces in England and Wales (Fawcett Society study reported in *The Times*, 30th March 2006). This data was not published as a performance curve but as a table. Yet the power of the graphical curve is remarkable. It does not fit our model of a normal distribution at all. If one force can achieve a rape conviction rate of over 13% (whether that is good or not) why do so many forces do so poorly by comparison? This is a very skewed curve. But only the graphic highlights the skew. Yet there is nothing new in this simple, statistical analysis. What we want to do here is apply some of the principles behind the value motive to see if a significant improvement could be made. We will not be seeking to turn any chief constables into scapegoats though, as the principles we have just established tells us that the police force with the lowest rape conviction rate could, in effect, be the 'best'. No, all we are looking to achieve is an intelligent and mature debate about how to move forward.

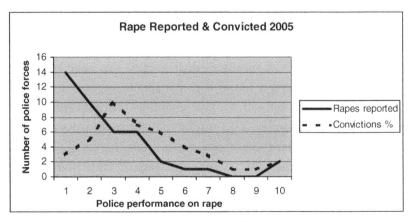

Figure 7.2 Does our society value the elimination of rape?

Rape is obviously a very emotive, contentious and highly problematic subject to use as an example but that is precisely why it was chosen. Can the objectivity of the value motive bring a fresh perspective and better results and establish some general principles at the same time? We can assume that society abhors the crime of rape and would value any reduction in the incidence of rape and ideally would want it to be zero. Or can we? Some judges have implied that women can be partly responsible for their behaviour leading to rape. Some people might not have that much sympathy for women who they deem to have 'brought it on themselves'. Nothing, when it comes to deciding on societal value, is ever clear-cut. We can never assume that everyone shares our own values. That is why the first step in the value motive is always to get a clear statement of what value is. So let us try it in this instance.

Here are a few options. The value statement could say that all rapists should be convicted. Alternatively it could say no women should be raped. It could even say we want 100% of rapes at least to be reported so that the problem can be dealt with properly. If you have fully absorbed the principle that value has to have a monetary value attached to it, then none of these statements, on their own, will suffice. The police have to allocate resources to rape allegations and they have plenty of other responsibilities competing for these resources. So a value statement could at least say that the rape conviction figures will improve based on the same amount of resources dedicated to this issue last year. That will not be perfect but at least it starts to suggest that value will be added, as opposed to, say, spending twice as much and getting twice the results. This might sound like added value but it would not be, even though rape convictions increased. 'Putting more officers on the case' would not require any more value being obtained from any of those officers. They would not have to think or behave differently or learn new and better ways of working. Whereas asking each of the existing officers to add more value would. Now we can ask what these people who work for the police can do but the value question goes right to their very soul.

Imagine the head of rape investigations being given a value objective of improving the rape conviction rate without any extra resources. In what ways could they have any chance of achieving this? They could work:

- Harder (and get their team to work harder) to get more successful cases to court per year.
- More efficiently, by cutting out any work that is a waste of time (i.e. improve the process) to get more successful cases to court per year.
- Smarter, by providing better training and improved techniques and methods (e.g. DNA evidence) to improve the chances of a successful conviction.
- Better with other agencies (e.g. rape crisis centres, the prosecution authorities and lawyers) to improve the chances of a successful conviction.
- With the victims to ensure they give themselves the best chance of a conviction.

All of these activities could improve the conviction rate but only where these are the root causes of failed convictions. If the value objective is to increase the conviction rate (%) just bringing more cases to court will not achieve this if the rate of conviction stays the same. That is, if the *way* in which rape cases are investigated and brought to court does not change then nothing will change. *Added value necessitates change* and very often the change that is required affects the whole organization and all other bodies associated with the organization. Whatever convictions are achieved it is still like the drops of whisky from the distillation process, all of the inputs in the value chain have to work in harmony towards a single goal.

So, if we quickly look at the whole chain of events here it should be illuminating. A man rapes a woman, allegedly. His defence is that he thought she had consented and let us assume that he genuinely believes she had. Now the whole case rests on two different versions of the same incident. The male investigating officer, despite being highly professional, is only human and might have his own view of what probably happened. The only problem is, once the rape has been reported police performance is being measured by successful convictions. The added problem for them is that the police do not make the final decision on whether to take the case to court; this is the decision of the public prosecutors. One figure omitted from the graph in Figure 7.2 is the fact that less than 20% of reported rapes (2689 out of 14 192) actually turn into prosecutions. Presumably because they are deemed to be weak cases, for whatever reason. This all looks a very long way away from the zero figure that the vast majority of people in society would want. Yet we are still left with the police having to improve their standing in the league table, so what can they do?

Well, what they can do is address the real issues. Get to the root causes of the problem. Or at least try to get to the root causes. Some of these root causes could be male attitudes to women. Advertising, men's magazines, TV programmes and bar room banter might have shaped these attitudes. This does not mean that this is a prescription for a lengthy academic research paper on men's attitudes to sex or a long debate about whether pornography is a contributing factor or not. If the police are tasked with dealing with rape we can immediately aim to get them to improve the value they add by first asking them which root causes they are working on. The evidence shows that whatever the police have been doing to improve the reporting of rape (up from 4900 in 1995 to 14 100 in 2004) there has been no real improvement in the conviction rate (5.6% in 2002 to 5.78%

in 2004). Maybe because the root causes are entirely outside the control or even influence of the police. This value motive is leading us into uncharted waters. We are quickly entering the realm of thinking the unthinkable and speaking the unspeakable.

The graphs in Figure 7.2 and the other statistics quoted could be seen as symptomatic of a society that does not actually value the goal of zero rapes. If it does then it is doing a very poor job of getting anywhere near to achieving this goal. Why isn't every police officer on traffic duty assigned to rape investigations? It is exactly the same as a manufacturer not taking the goal of zero defects seriously. We will never live in a perfect world but there is no reason why we should still not strive for perfection. The value motive is exactly that. Based on a vision of a perfect world that might remain unattainable yet is still a worthwhile goal. But it is much more than that, it is a complete philosophy. A view of the world and how life should be lived. It is more important for the operators on the manufacturer's production line to *believe* that they should always aim to reduce defects to zero than it is to be measured on defect rates. That belief will always carry them through when the going gets tough. They will keep trying even when the measures don't improve. But that belief will only survive while they are convinced that their organizational leaders are absolutely wedded to this philosophy as well.

So, returning to the police, is there really a shared vision among hard-bitten cops that society's goal is the elimination of all crime? Of course not. Have you ever seen a politician or chief police officer declare this as a goal? Yet we all know of the policing policy of zero tolerance, exactly the same management concept as zero defects. If you believe it is a worthwhile goal, and you do everything you can to aim to achieve it, then it does not matter that you never reach your destination because you will have added a great deal of value along the way. So, if we stick to the principles learned from the performance curve, we will not be criticizing or blaming the police for doing a bad job. We will just ask them to add as much value as they can, when they can.

The number of rape convictions by police force ranges from seven (Warwickshire) to 516 (Metropolitan London). Where police could work smarter is to capitalize, nationally, on the expertise they already have rather than be spread geographically. Plans by the UK's Home Office in 2005 to merge several smaller forces into combined forces were scrapped in 2006 because of the likely cost and resistance from some forces. Yet there is a simple question that needs to be asked, what is the best way to get the best value? What can the forces at the top of the performance curve teach the bottom? Is this best done through national initiatives or should police rape investigation teams be organized on a national rather than an individual force basis. As with all value discussions, no one will know in advance but is this option being considered or tested?

What about the wider implications though? Who is focusing on the attitudinal side of the rape equation? If rapists are not all born that way then something in their development has made them into what they are. If magazines and TV have influenced them then why doesn't society use other areas of expertise to deal with the problem? If Coca-Cola can spend millions of dollars to convince people that Dasani is better than tap water and BP can spend $150m trying to convince us of its green credentials why isn't the Home Office employing a corporate advertising agency to convince people that rape doesn't have to happen? Of course, the agency should only be paid on results. The same principle that Coca-Cola should have followed when Dasani failed in the UK market. We have plenty of evidence that throwing more resources at the police does not seem to be having much impact, so what does society have to lose? Thinking the unthinkable is bound to raise some unusual prescriptions, more of which will be covered in Chapter 8.

For now though let us retrace our steps. This has been a very lengthy digression from our search for the measures that go into the people box but a very informative one. The performance measures lead us to question how individuals (police officers in this case) are meant to add value and the extent to which their inner belief systems motivate them to do so. This inevitably leads to another consideration, what sort of people do we employ? Are they the best ones for the job and have we managed to attract the best available from the total talent pool?

DOES DIVERSITY ADD VALUE?

One measure often suggested for the people measures box is the diversity of the workforce. So does your organization truly value diversity? By diversity, do we mean equal opportunities for all and an organization whose people really reflect the society that they serve? Is this a philosophical question or one of substance? Is it an ethical question or is it business critical? A head of diversity may follow an agenda that says there is a need to encourage more women to achieve senior management positions but would this be consistent with trying to achieve maximum shareholder value? There is no reason why these two objectives should be mutually exclusive but, then again, there is no guarantee that they are mutually inclusive either.

One possible argument that should pull both objectives of diversity together is that, if talent is rare, then the net to trawl the available talent should be cast as widely as possible. Assuming no difference between men and women, or one ethnic or minority group and another, then it makes absolute sense to reduce any barriers to entry for potential talent. The '*moral*' value of equal rights and opportunities and the £ value to the business could possibly be the same value at the end of the day. The business performs better and we achieve a more egalitarian society, at a stroke. If this were possible it would be hard to see how anyone could not buy into and share the values of such an organization. But the problems really start when employees do not share their organization's values.

In the US, companies with more than 50 employees working on federal government contracts worth more than $50 000 must develop an affirmative action plan (US Department of Labor's Office of Federal Contract Compliance Programme). This lead is currently being taken up in the UK by the Ethnic Minority Employment Task Force, which is running pilot projects to ascertain whether companies tendering for work should declare their ethnic mix credentials. Having just delved into the contentious issue of rape we should not be afraid to step into an equally heated debate in the search for greater value.

Is the main argument promoting diversity one of ethics or value? If a company tenders for a government contract and only employs whites or blacks or any other colour, but is a very efficient company that is well managed, should it be barred from winning the contract just because it does not have a mixed workforce? Does this mean that a less well-managed business, albeit with a better ethnic mix, should be given the contract in preference? Even if we get a clear answer to that one, what weight should be given to the relative business acumen versus ethnic mix ratio? This sounds like a bureaucratic nightmare before we start.

Nevertheless, if we are thinking the unthinkable we should at least keep a completely open mind when doing so. Is there anything ethically wrong with just employing people of one colour? Only if that is a definite policy to discriminate. Yet in some local authorities, where there is already a significant ethnic mix, many procedures have to be put in place to demonstrate that the authority is not using discriminatory employment practices (e.g. selection and interview record-keeping notes to rule out any possibility of discrimination). This is where political correctness replaces common sense. An organization could be deemed to be discriminating if it had overt, discriminatory policies, practices or only seemed to favour one race or colour. But where this is already obviously, demonstrably, not the case then what value do these bureaucratic procedures add?

If the government promotes these policies because they are ethical and equitable is it also saying they are the best value? If not then they are stepping into very dangerous management territory. They would have to support contractors who employ a greater ethnic mix while accepting that the taxpayer may not be getting the best value for money on a particular contract. So how does the government, or any of the bodies promoting diversity, reconcile these different objectives? Is a more ethnically diverse society the goal that society should value most? Even at the expense of more expensive contracts? Is this the higher purpose that is worth the price? Even assuming that it is, we still have to get around to the practicalities.

There seems to be no point appealing to an ardent capitalist's better nature or higher motives if they don't have any. If they believe, like John Sunderland of Cadbury, that making a profit is a very valuable contribution to society, then the best way to sell them the idea of diversity is to appeal to their own motivation – profit. If they can achieve that and do it through greater diversity we have finally reconciled the apparently irreconcilable. However, if we do not choose that course then, as we all know from history, all we will do is breed tokenism. The canny contractor will build the cost of employing ethnic minorities into their bid but they will not, in their heart of hearts, be any more a devotee of diversity than they were before. This is a very strong argument against setting any quotas for diversity. The best they will achieve is numbers on a piece of paper. What they will not achieve is a change in attitudes or values. They will not win the hearts and minds of the recalcitrants. It is a pity that we have to return to the police for the best evidence of this unfortunate fact of life.

In the UK, as with many other countries, there have been accusations made about racism in the police. The Macpherson Report, which followed a public enquiry into the murder of black teenager Stephen Lawrence, was utterly damning in its description of the Metropolitan Police as 'institutionally racist' – a term as catastrophic as systemic failure: the organization had somehow become a system for ill rather than good. This, inevitably but perhaps unwisely, led to pressure for police forces to make strenuous efforts to ensure their workforces truly reflect the societies it is their duty to police. Certainly the investigation into this murder was seriously flawed but will diversity *targets* (as opposed to a philosophy of diversity and a vision of a police force where diversity is no longer an issue) stop that happening in future? Let us see if this logic makes sense if we put it another way. If diversity targets are part of the solution to this problem then the next similar murder case should be investigated more thoroughly and effectively by virtue of the fact that we have more black police officers. But will that prevent the next racist murder, which is the ultimate value required, and did everyone involved agree that this should have been the real objective? The root cause of the murder was the racist attitudes of those who committed it, not the police officers who investigated it.

We do not need to philosophize too much about this though. We should never forget that the only ultimate arbiters of the value of the police will always be crime detection and prevention figures. In the meantime a simpler question is have diversity targets actually achieved their own objectives, that is a greater ethnic mix and more women in charge? The answer to that appears to be quite straightforward if we believe Dr Mike Rowe from the Department of Criminology at Leicester University, who remarked 'The police have for several decades been investing a lot of effort in trying to increase the number of ethnic minorities they recruit and they've never been very successful at it' (http://news.bbc.co.uk/2/hi/uk_news/4329415.stm).

How many times do we have to learn that setting simplistic performance targets rarely adds value? They certainly do not change the way people think or behave. Surely the only way to make the police less racist is first to make sure that all officers joined up to reduce crime and are doing everything they can to achieve that goal. Then it would mean ridding the force of any racists. That would require an honest measure of who is and isn't (on a 1 to 10 curve?) and removing the unacceptables if they were not prepared to change. Those who were willing to consider new ways of working would have to be convinced that their crime figures would be better without racism. This might sound like the practical suggestion of a very naïve manager. Fortunately though, all of the evidence available indicates quite clearly that politicians who set meaningless targets are the ones that appear naïve. At least this proposal has the very sound basis that it is focusing on obvious root causes. When organizational leaders see where diversity fits into the value equation it will satisfy both the goals of value and ethics simultaneously.

A similar development is the recent EU legislation on age discrimination, which attempts to ensure that companies do not discriminate on the grounds of age. What is their motive? Political correctness, equity or value for the EU? At automotive company Nissan, Carlos Ghosn (*Sunday Times*, 3rd April 2005), who is credited with having transformed the company's fortunes, gave his view of age: 'I said that I embraced the Japanese concept of fairness, but that actually some Japanese practices were unfair. The seniority rule was, and is, segregation against young people. The company does not live from the age of its employees but from the contribution of its employees . . . There is a lesson to be drawn from it, and personally I think it is that the 21st century is going to be fundamentally about diversity, and about how to make people with diverse backgrounds work well together. If managers do not take into account identities and the specifics of the cultures involved, they will fail.' This is a clear value argument that sounds like it is also ethical. Not the other way around. Maybe our capitalist leaders could teach our political leaders a thing or two about the link between intangibles and real value.

In summary, there is very little point putting diversity figures in the people box. Unless, of course, you can show a clear link between these figures and the value created by the organization. But, as we pointed out earlier, simple connections and linkages are very difficult to isolate in complex organizations. Instead what we should really be aiming to do in this people box is raise confidence, to the highest possible level, so that everything we do with our people at least starts out with a focus on value. Then we have to show that all the other necessary elements of the whole are in place and functioning effectively. If we are to really get the best value from people perhaps we should treat them in the same way as any other capital investment.

HUMAN CAPITAL MANAGEMENT, A REVOLUTION IN MANAGEMENT THINKING

Let us forget having a specific box for people. The idea came from the notion of scorecards and scorecards were always just an extension of financial accounting conventions. Even the concept of 'balance' was never really the big shift in thinking it was meant to herald. Creating lots of numbers and then balancing them in some way was still suggesting the best way to manage is from the top. It did not force organizations to move away from command and control structures and cultures. There is no hint in either the scorecard or the EFQM of the full import of unleashing every last bit of human potential. What we are calling human capital management (HCM) (and there are many pretenders using the same name) really is meant to signal a seismic shift in management thinking.

The pharmaceutical CEO who thinks that the costs of clinical trials are relatively unimportant, when compared to revenue streams, is right in one sense. But if he or she wants to maximize value they have to fundamentally change their own thinking first. It is hard to overestimate the potential shift in management thinking that HCM requires, not just in people management but in general management as well. Organizations that want to adopt the tenets of HCM will have to completely rethink the way they operate. After all, Ford and GM are probably doing as much as, if not more than, any other company to try to manage their people as well as they can, with their current management methods. They do their best to recruit and select the best, they want to develop their people and encourage them to bring new ideas to the workplace and they have probably tried every 'best HR practice' in the book including performance management, sophisticated reward systems and diversity initiatives. Yet all of this effort still leaves them trailing far behind their main competitor both in terms of profit and the value they provide for society. So they will have to try something else if they want to close the gap. But what could that 'something else' be?

Perhaps we need a method for identifying the best way in which organizations can be seen to be getting the best value out of their people. One body that set out to do exactly that was the Accounting for People Taskforce set up by the UK's Department for Trade and Industry (www.accountingforpeople.gov.uk). The message and intent was quite simple. Its task was to look at the

> performance measures currently used to assess investment in human capital.

Obviously there is an underlying belief that how organizations manage their people can make a significant difference. Just how much difference though can only be measured by way of reference to how the organization is performing. After openly inviting papers and evidence from all sources, and reviewing what was being done in the name of HCM, the Taskforce produced a report in October 2003 (Report of the Taskforce on Human Capital Management) that eventually defined HCM as

> an approach to people management that treats it as a high level strategic issue and seeks systematically to analyse, measure and evaluate how people, policies and practices create value.

Even though the brief of this taskforce was wide ranging it has to be said that there was still an aim to produce a box of people measures, or at least encourage companies to produce an annual, human capital report. Not surprisingly, the case studies presented duly obliged with typical input measures of employee surveys, average training days per employee and the usual people measures of staff turnover and absence along with a liberal sprinkling of diversity statements. Whether any of this was really done 'strategically' is a moot point but the question of how these people practices create value is never shown. That is because they are still thinking that there is something called best practice HR. One organization, the RAC, even used Asda retail (now part of Wal-Mart) as a benchmark because Asda had come top in the *Sunday Times* 100 Best Companies to Work For. It is amazing how if you say someone is the best it is very easy to suggest your own organization must also be good, without either of you mentioning the word value or showing any financial figures to support this. Benchmarking has a lot to answer for.

This is a very tricky area. There are many organizations that seem to look after their employees very well but that is not the issue either. There has to be a clear philosophical, as well as an operational, link between looking after employees and getting the best out of them. One organization that purports to put its employees, welfare at the pinnacle of its goals is the John Lewis Partnership, a UK-based department store business that is owned in trust for its members and 'its ultimate purpose is the happiness of all its members, through their worthwhile and satisfying employment in a successful business'. This is a very uncommon entity. It was the son of the founder, the late Spedan Lewis, who formed what could best be described as an employee cooperative. Unfortunately, according to a present day director, no one knows exactly why he chose to do so. Did he think the business would be more successful by allowing employees some control? Was it some sort of philanthropic gesture or what? Certainly the employee 'partners', as they are now called, have some say in how the business is run through their own council. Those of us who are interested in how employees interact with their employers have learned an important lesson from the John Lewis experiment – there is no simple rule that says involving employees in the running of the business will automatically make the business more successful.

John Lewis (the company) was very late in joining the move to Sunday opening in the UK some years ago and this put them at a competitive disadvantage. Even fans of the level of service that John Lewis customers have come to expect can see that by the normal criteria of profit-making businesses, they are not performing very well. As the business editor of the *Sunday Times* wrote (10th October 2004): 'Under a different ownership structure I am sure the group could make a lot more money. But I am one of many who view John Lewis as a national treasure whose continuing existence we should seek to protect.' It is interesting what a huge discrepancy there can be between a value-laden phrase such as 'national treasure' and the reality of relatively poor operating figures, that is monetary value. It could almost be said to be a measure of the cost of letting your heart rule your head. Moreover, why should this organization warrant any protection? If it were keeping more customers satisfied, more often, the market would guarantee its protection. This confusion between values and value can colour and distort the thinking of even the most professional of business commentators. It is this emotional response that HCM has to overcome if it is to offer that breakthrough in management thinking to release so much more value. People are capital and there is nothing wrong in capitalizing on them.

PEOPLE – ARE THEY PERSONNEL, HUMAN RESOURCES, ASSETS OR CAPITAL?

That mother of all motherhood and apple pie statements – 'our people are our greatest asset' – has a great deal to answer for. It has caused more confusion than probably any other supposedly simple tenet of management thinking. First, it is entirely false. People are not an asset. They can never be, in any sense, owned (slave traders notwithstanding). They have no residual value if they fall under a bus or expire in any other way. They are not homogeneous or constant (just look at the top football stars who command huge salaries). More pertinently though, from a business management and accounting perspective, they must be the only 'asset' that does not show up on the balance sheet and anything that does not appear there is not taken seriously by the business and investment communities. It is not valued, either in the sense of having a £ sign assigned to it or in the broader sense of 'we think it's really important'. For a substantiation of this point just ask any CEO what they get for all the money they spend on training and developing staff and you will get blank looks. People and their development are definitely in the CEO's 'intangible' box.

The reason CEOs and CFOs still hold this view is that every attempt at putting a balance sheet value on people has failed. As far back as the late 1960s and early 1970s many academics and finance professionals tried to develop methods to put a measurable value on human assets. The general approach was to apply conventional accounting principles to a subject for which they were never designed. Therefore the early attempts at HAV (human asset valuation) and HAA (human asset accounting) had a very short shelf life. They were, in effect, treating people as just another type of bean that had to be counted.

Yet it is now widely accepted that the biggest potential contribution to firm performance is both the quality of the people and how well their full potential is managed. Even the performance of the hardest-nosed private equity firms has to be attributed to their partners. It is a truism that you can only manage what you measure; therefore, if you cannot measure the 'people' contribution then you cannot manage for maximum value. It is equally true, from the employee's perspective, that if they cannot measure their own contribution they will never know when they are adding value or not (did John Lewis partners think of lost sales when they voted against Sunday opening?). It is the very fact that financial and investment analysts cannot escape from these very simple truths that keeps this subject alive, despite all of the earlier disappointments. The use of the term capital to describe human beings is starting to stick and gain currency. People are now being regarded as capital, even though the measures do not exist to gauge just how much value can be gained from this type of capital.

Another reason it should stick is that it is the most accurate description of the relationship between employees and employer (profit making or otherwise). It also attaches the right level of importance to the value of people. While you have people capital in your account and at your disposal you should be making as much value of it as you can. You don't have to own capital to make good use of it but while you have it you should act as an investment manager and attempt to get the best possible return. The title capital also suits many individuals who can now talk about the development of their own capital worth, through their own personal development and acquisition of new skills, knowledge and expertise. Personal capital is a much more marketable commodity. The title 'human resources' always made people sound like victims: referring to people as capital makes them sound like masters of their own destiny. Fortunately, the word exploitation now seems totally inappropriate in a modern organizational context.

As with every other aspect of the value motive we reach a point, yet again, where we have to emphasize that while it might be a worthwhile goal to measure the value of human capital it is much more important for the organization to regard their people as real capital and to do everything they can to capitalize on it. Their beliefs and motives are the issue, not the measures chosen. A belief that 'intellectual capital' will make a huge difference will promote efforts to distil and exploit (we are now happy to regain that word in this context) every last drop of intellectual capital held by employees. But, and here is the rub, there is no point in trying to measure 'intellectual capital' per se. The value created by the business is all that will ever be measured. What we will want to see though are indicators that give investors confidence that this intellectual capital is being converted to outputs. Certainly a contra-indicator would be a simplistic view on people development such as creating a corporate university with no line of sight to any organizational value. So what might a positive indicator look like? The best way to answer that is to go back to the original question.

HUMAN CAPITAL MEASURES AND INDICATORS OF VALUE

We have to start thinking differently about the whole subject of performance measures and indicators. While the wrong questions are being asked about human capital (i.e. how do we show it on the balance sheet) it will lead to the wrong prescriptions. It is widely acknowledged that profit and loss accounting and double entry bookkeeping have severe limitations when it comes to measuring the real value of organizations. This thinking has driven organizations for hundreds of years so it will not change overnight. Meanwhile, some analysts have managed to earn a great deal of credibility for the way in which they assess the financial viability of a business. Standard & Poor's is probably one of the best known and most highly respected rating agencies so, when they say that they give Ford and GM a junk bond credit rating, most observers accept their assessment and realize there is something seriously wrong in these companies. Yet the methods they use for assessment remain secret (for obvious reasons). An S&P analyst remarked (*The Times*, 7th May 2005) that 'S&P does not allow its analysts to sit on the secretive committee that eventually decides whether the creditworthiness of a company needs to change'. Quite right, this rating is such a powerful indicator that it can add, or wipe off, millions of dollars from a company's market value. But does this sort of rating do anything to add any intrinsic value to the businesses rated? As soon as S&P announces that it is awarding a higher rating for a company the share price is likely to rise but it would be ridiculous to suggest that, from that moment on, the rating itself has added value in terms of the company's outputs.

Such ratings still adopt a primarily historical analysis rather than a predictive analysis, even though a poor rating will suggest poor performance or even collapse in the future. Did S&P, for example, predict 10 years ago that GM was heading for a fall because it could not possibly compete with Toyota? Did it identify ineffective and outmoded people management policies as part of the root cause of that fall? Are they predicting today that unless GM formulates a better human capital strategy it will never have a chance of long-term survival? This is especially important when Honda and other automotive producers are adopting similarly advantageous human capital strategies. Of course, S&P and many other analysts and researchers will offer clues as to the relative strengths and weaknesses of a management team, or the business strategy being pursued, but until there are clear indicators about the underlying value generators they will only ever tell part of the story. There is also the additional issue of how would organizations that rate businesses rate non-commercial organizations?

Maybe one way forward is to rephrase the original question. Our question is not how do we measure human capital but does the organization treat its people as capital and how do they propose to get the best value out of that capital? It is inherently forward looking. There is absolutely no point looking backwards and asking how well did an organization manage its people. If current profits are meant to be an indicator of how well an organization has been managing its people so far then it is a very poor indicator. On this basis, GM's profits 10 years ago may well have suggested that it was managing its people well. Compared, then, to its up and coming rival Toyota it was managing its people very poorly and has continued to do so ever since. Worse still, at precisely the time when it is in serious trouble and needs better people management all it seems capable of doing is reducing output, shedding labour and selling off viable parts of the business to pay off its debt. It may never have a chance to take the really big decisions to survive. One of which is to fundamentally change its relationship and attitude to its human capital (especially the human capital that also wants to be union members).

This provides a flavour of the sort of new indicators that will be required for a proper, predictive assessment of future organizational success and value. These will complement existing ratings and assessments, not replace them. This book is not going to provide great detail on what other indicators will be needed as these are covered elsewhere (these have already been covered in the author's other books and guides – see 'About the author' especially www.TheNewburyIndex.com). However, here are a few of the key aspects of organizations that need to be rated if a true impression of value potential is to be garnered. Furthermore, we should not be afraid of applying a subjective measure to our judgements on these factors, following the same principles established regarding measures for the performance curve.

People management style

If communism taught organizations anything it was that command and control from the centre was a very inefficient and, ultimately, very ineffective approach to management. Centralism is never going to be as responsive to changing customer needs as decentralism. Employees also need to be empowered to respond as they see fit, albeit within well-ordered parameters, to achieve organizational goals.

A solid, credible management philosophy

Visions and mission statements, posters in the canteen promoting teamwork and regular team meetings may all look like the outward signs of an organization with a clear and strong management philosophy. To the trained eye of the value seeker they are meaningless unless backed up by action. What is each director doing to promote continuous improvements in their own area? How do managers react when someone challenges their authority? How are decisions made and problems solved? Are there well-tried and tested management tools being used? All of these will be indicators of an organization where the senior managers actually walk the talk.

Flexible but well-organized structures

Command and control organizations tend to have rigid, silo hierarchies with fixed reporting lines. The weaknesses of such organization structures have been fully recognized for many years. Turf wars proliferate and cross-functional cooperation can suffer. One answer to this has been the growth in matrix-type organizations but these have their own problems of unclear reporting lines and shared (some would say weakened) accountability. There is no one-size-fits-all solution, which is why an insightful judgement on the effectiveness of the structure is required.

Open, not-seeking-to-blame culture

Politics, back-stabbing and covering your backside are the not so subtle tell-tale signs of an organization where everyone is more interested in protecting their own narrow interests than creating value by taking a few risks and innovating. There will never be an absolute measure of something that is inherently dynamic and inconsistent but this does not stop us spotting how such cultures get in the way of improving value (e.g. too many signatures required for new products, overlengthy development cycle times). HCM can only thrive in a culture that allows mistakes to be made but it can also only thrive where people learn from their mistakes and do not continue to make the same ones. Somebody may ultimately be blamed for making too many mistakes but it is that eagerness to blame, blame as a first resort rather than as a last resort, that is an indicator of the true culture of the organization.

'Act of faith' management practices

We looked earlier at how seminal theories (e.g. scorecards, employee–customer profit chain) become accepted as the conventional wisdom. Any management practice should be thought through thoroughly, in terms of how it will work for a particular organization and, much more importantly, not only how it will add value but how much value. This is particularly true in people management practices. 'Act of faith management' is an oxymoron, and no more effective than keeping your fingers crossed and hoping for the best.

Systems and processes

One key element in HCM, which helps to create the type of environment where human capital can flourish, is that value can only be created if the whole organization is working well together. Every organization is run using systems and processes. They, along with the prevailing culture, are the fabric of the organization. HCM works best in flexible, adaptable, mutually supportive organizations; regardless of how the organization chart is actually drawn. Intelligent, human systems and processes will aid the building of a very high value, adaptive organization. Traffic lights will only be used where absolutely necessary. The value systems (i.e. trust, honesty, cooperation) will make all the difference. Processes will always be open to review and change (anyone at Toyota can stop the production line if they have good reason to). The process is what turns inputs into outputs and ultimately produces value. Systems and processes that work well together, and are adaptable, are a good indicator of future organizational performance.

These are just a few of the elements that make up high value organizations and you will notice that all of these can be applied equally to the non-profit and public sectors. There is no need here to use any different or new financial indicators. Walk into any government department or civil service agency and very quickly we get a feel for the politics and culture. Asking simple questions about what is valued will immediately indicate where political agendas are taking priority over an added value agenda. The factors that led to Shell's inability to face up to its shortfall in reserves are actually quite easy to spot.

Against a backdrop where the public sector takes a significant, and increasing, share of GDP the need to assess government bodies and get the best value out of them is becoming of paramount importance. If a nation is not getting maximum value out of its entire working population then it is missing a huge opportunity and will be left behind by other nations whose management and political thinking has reached the level of maturity that HCM demands. Certainly, the advent of the sort of HCM that demonstrably adds value will raise the game for all companies in the same market. Once one organization shows how to get the best value out of its people, just as Toyota has done so clearly and effectively in the global automotive market, every other organization that wants to compete will have to do the same. Public sector organizations too will be seen as very low value if they do not follow suit. They cannot follow a different set of rules, they are inevitably drawn into the same, common goal of value. Taxpayers in society will always gravitate towards the best value supplier of services, even if some sacred cows have to be slaughtered along the way (as with the NHS in the UK). Moreover, higher value from the commercial sector means higher taxes available for a better social agenda. The value motive, when working in conjunction with HCM, produces a holistic, societal system based on a total win–win philosophy.

So, if the potential goal is this attractive let us move on to consider what needs to happen to start to turn this into a reality.

CHAPTER 8

HOW THE VALUE MOTIVE COULD UPSTAGE THE PROFIT KING

Summary A manifesto to encourage a different type of leadership to promote value.

THE VALUE MOTIVE *IS* LEADERSHIP

We started out in Chapter 1 with a review of the undoubted strengths, but also the inherent weaknesses, of the profit motive as a means for ensuring that society gets the best value out of the resources at its disposal. Value, as a motive, has been around for as long as profit but the key factor that has been holding it back, from becoming the predominant force in our economic system, is the simple fact that it has never been regarded as a coherent singularity. No debate about value, outside of an organizational context, could ever be resolved in absolute terms or to everyone's entire satisfaction. By keeping this book as close as possible to its chosen remit, of a management text, it should allow value to earn its rightful place. Any organization that declares itself to be driven by the value motive, which is resolute in expressing its very raison d'ére in added value terms, has to be prepared to be judged against its own public statement of value. At least then meaningful comparisons can be made between those who subscribe to the pure profit motive and those who aspire to a higher purpose, without getting lost in a philosophical debate about what is value.

It is this higher purpose, synonymous with the value motive, which inevitably demands leadership driven by a higher purpose. We may talk glibly these days about leadership but the essence of leadership is surely in its ability to pull people together in the pursuit of a common goal. One leadership organization, the Leadership Trust (www.leadership.co.uk), defines leaders as those who 'can truly inspire their people to release their personal and collective potential'. We could take this one step further and define the purpose of leadership as realizing the maximum value of human potential (or capital if you prefer). This is an extremely tough standard but why would we want anything less from our leaders or from the populace? It is, therefore, inherently a 'societal' rather than an investor or shareholder view of leadership. 'Leadership' that can only produce gains for some at the expense of others is of less interest to society as a whole and fails to satisfy Bentham's principle of the greatest happiness of the greatest number.

Leadership is also about making choices and it is often in the public domain that the starkest choices are writ large. Healthcare seems to be placing an inexorably increasing burden on the state and the boundaries of survival, health, patient preferences and cosmetic surgery are becoming more blurred by the day as new drugs and technology come into the equation. The first choice for the National *Health* Service, for example, is to define 'health' although nowhere in its Core Principles (see www.nhs.uk) is a definition offered. So let us look at the choice between allocating resources to treat cancer and IVF (in vitro fertilization) for child-less couples. One is a matter of life and death and the other is becoming a societal expectation. There seems to be an emerging view that all of life's disappointments should be resolved if we have the technology to do so. Yet every penny spent on either means a penny less spent somewhere else, where society's con-sensus may put a higher value.

Our inability to resolve these difficult choices satisfactorily, in any objective way, means they become political choices and once in the political arena the laws of political expediency take over. Politicians have to win votes and the role of leadership in making decisions to maximize societal value from limited resources can take second place. Fortunately, the choices on offer do not always have to be mutually exclusive but short-termist politicians will always choose the votes option. Political *leaders* of substance will aim to make both causes mutually inclusive and reinforcing. The only long-term, coherent answer in a democracy is to aim to create as much value and wealth as pos-sible, through competition, to allow as many desirable decisions to be made as possible. Value will never be sated though and there will always be battles to be fought with those who have a different agenda.

Irwin Stelzer (*Sunday Times*, 28th May 2006) accused the political leadership of the EU of resisting competition, saying that it reflected a fundamental difference between the American philosophy, from the 19th century, of keeping its economy open and competitive and refusing to tolerate monopolistic bullying 'by the likes of John Rockefeller's Standard Oil, "malefactors of great wealth" as Teddy Roosevelt called them'. He continues his critique by referring to an adviser at the Center for Strategic & International Studies who criticized the old Soviet Union because it encouraged a system where 'In the absence of market competi-tion old and inefficient firms continued merrily along instead of releasing resources for those newer and more efficient . . . Creative destruction (was) the true secret of capitalism that the KGB never discovered.' Real wealth and value, the argument goes, can only come from the creative destruction of systems that just do not work in the interests of the majority.

At a time when the CAP (Common Agricultural Policy) still rewards inefficient farmers, through subsidies out of EU taxpayer funds, and pays winegrowers to tear up their vineyards rather than leave them to the vagaries of the global wine market, there are obviously still some serious lessons to be learned on all sides. However, Stelzer should also be reminding America to continue to follow its own philosophy in the 21st century in the face of the monopolistic bullying of Microsoft or Intel and the restrictive practices that some of its own industries fall back on (including tariffs on steel and foreign agricultural products) with full political endorsement. The leadership challenge here is immense and we should not be surprised by the extent to which leadership is so conspicuous by its absence. Leadership, by definition, will always remain the domain of those rare individuals who are able to resist the clamour of the vested interests and the short-sighted and yet reconcile any legitimate demands where necessary.

Lord (John) Browne, chairman of BP, has been voted as number one business leader in several polls over as many years. There is no doubting that people of his calibre do not come along very often (one only has to compare him with his own predecessors for clear evidence of this) but what is the full list of criteria that should be applied to give us confidence that such leadership really does equate to societal value? The two sides of the profitability/ecology equation are difficult to balance but when more money is spent on a company's image than its pipeline renewal it is difficult to regard this as the right balance.

Let no one reading this be in any doubt, the value motive really does present leadership with the ultimate challenge. That is why one of the main recommendations here is that we start to recognize and reward the sort of all-round, value leadership that we all know we need but so rarely witness. We can still admire and respect the entrepreneurs for the great work they already do in setting commercial seeds and cultivating huge amounts of wealth. We can also continue to appreciate the difficult decisions that all organizational managers have to make every day, and be thankful when they make the best decisions. Nevertheless, we need to reserve a totally different category of recognition for those leaders whose force of character, integrity and brainpower is devoted solely to the pursuit of societal value.

Any prospective leader wanting to set a course of value will have a tough task in framing their value statement, articulating it clearly and gaining buy-in from everyone concerned. One example of the type of leadership we need might be the sort espoused by Stephen Green, chief executive of HSBC, who wrote about the connections between his religious and commercial beliefs and personal values in his book *Serving God? Serving Mammon? Christians and the Financial Market* in 1996. In his book and his sermons (as a lay preacher) he stressed that businesses like HSBC could demonstrate their moral standing by always acting responsibly toward employees, customers and local communities. Referring to how his Christian beliefs affected his management style, he told *Institutional Investor* (April 2003), 'There's a very clear focus on doing the right kind of business, on long-term relationships with clients, on honesty and transparency' (you may wish to compare this philosophy to Citigroup's 'Dr Evil' computer programme discussed in Chapter 2).

Green said that his number one priority in management was meeting what he called the 'people challenge', that is, preserving a strong sense of teamwork through a management and working group that was spread across the globe. Analysts noted that he emphasized instilling integrity and professionalism in all HSBC staff. He stressed a moral business code of always giving the customer a fair deal. 'I can't think of another management challenge more important than that', he said. 'If you get that right everything else will fall into place. If you don't, you will lose something very precious' (*Business Times*, 13th November 2003). Green also looks for certain characteristics in employees and the most important characteristic, regardless of the employee's faith, was a view of the importance of morality and integrity in business life. 'I happen to believe it is the only basis of sustainable success over the long term', he said (*The Guardian*, 18th October 2003, or see http://www.referenceforbusiness.com/biography/F-L/Green-Stephen-K-1948.html).

HSBC, by any conventional criterion of business success, are currently very successful and much of this success has been attributed to its recent chairman Sir John Bond. It is also worth adding that there is no intention here to diminish any of their achievements in any way but any objective judge of value still has the right to ask some searching questions. In the UK, HSBC has been closing down branches, like most retail banks, presumably in response to the increasing use of Internet banking by its customers and to keep its cost/income ratio down. So we should challenge them, and all other banks, on whether these closures could be deemed to be adding value and, if so, to whom? This may be just one detail, and a relatively minor one at that, in a much grander scheme of things that might reside in Stephen Green's head but it should, nevertheless, be part of a coherent, holistic approach to managing value.

Some business managers, who still cling to the notion that profit is king, will have a very simple answer to this question. Any business decision is likely to have some winners and losers (you can see how this sort of mentality has not fully understood the win–win mentality of value). Some customers will lose their local branch and will have to travel further for their banking services. A proportion of these may choose to change banks so that they still have a local branch, albeit with a different bank.

All that matters to the bank though is to retain enough customers, who like the service and pay accordingly for it. If the bank can reduce its costs then its profits could improve. However, if too many customers go elsewhere this could equally be reflected in the profit and, probably, the share price. The profit motive should provide a perfect mechanism for regulating the market and keeping it in equilibrium. This is a classic economist's and capitalist's view and, in value motive terms, it is very short-sighted. It is also likely to breed a 'cutting corners' rather than a value added mentality in the minds of bank employees.

Regardless of the purpose of a bank's network of branches, customers use them because they must value the service they offer. That offering is part of the whole banking system, not just the local high street. Depositing cheques and cash is one of the services local branches provide because our financial system has not yet managed to eliminate them. So, if you have to visit a branch to pay in cheques the extra journey it takes will be an extra cost to you (mileage) and the environment (pollution, congestion, queuing times). The bank measures what it can (number of customers, transactions, ratios) and reports on profit but who measures the other costs? The key point here is that the bank can make it appear that it has added value (its cost/income ratio improves) by reporting bigger profits but all they have done is displaced the costs they saved with extra costs, elsewhere in the community and the economy. In fact, the total, societal, value equation could be negative (extra mileage costs for all customers exceed the banks cost savings).

We are unlikely to get a change in company reporting on this scale, at least in the short term, but it would be interesting to hear the bank's views on this. It would be even more revelatory if the bank did its own survey, before it shut any branches, to try to weigh up the full costs in the equation. It is their willingness to do so, the efforts they are prepared to make towards that goal, their public support for a wider definition of value, that we should applaud. If the resulting equation showed that shutting branches was the best option available (and the bank was prepared to share the savings with customers through reducing its charges or improving its savings rate) then perhaps we can ask the bank to do no more. Unfortunately, those truly driven by the value motive will go into it knowing that value is never sated.

Not only should we, as customers, ask for everything we can get out of the banks, and every other service provider for that matter (and why not?), the bank itself should be doing absolutely everything within its power to give us the best, lowest cost, service it can. This is not likely to happen when attitudes in banking lead some staff to refer to customers who change mortgages or credit cards regularly, derisorily, as 'rate tarts'. As though there was anything wrong with a customer exhibiting natural, common sense behaviour to achieve the best deal. It is not just doctors who seem to think they are more important than their customers. A story from www.thisismoney.co.uk dated 14th January 2006 under the heading 'The demise of the rate tart?' revealed that 'TESCO Personal Finance is considering plans to actively reject credit card applicants that have a history of switching their balance to take advantage of 0% interest offers, signalling the demise of the rate tart.' When all banks start to move our money around for us, every day, to ensure we are getting the best returns possible on our savings we will be able to truly say that the banks have been following the value motive. But that will never happen until and unless they declare that to be one element in their value statement. Whether this sounds a naïve hope or not, we can use it as a real yardstick or benchmark to judge our existing banking system – an objective set of value criteria, which no bank would currently satisfy, including those who profess to have ethical banking policies.

When we look at value in this way it is a very short step to argue that it is every citizen's *moral* duty to demand the earth and complain like mad when they don't get the service they are entitled to expect. We are all each other's customers, 'employees' and pension fund providers. Shareholders might have purely selfish interests but even their best interests are served by ensuring the people who run organizations do so to maximize true value. We're all in this symbiotic relationship together and, if we are to aim for the goal of best societal value for all, it behoves us to make these demands. Just look at what happens when we don't.

'Five years after Enron, a culture of greed is back.' Gerard Baker averred in his 'American View' (*The Times*, 20th June 2006), highlighting the dubious practice of executives backdating their own share options. There were investigations under way by the US Securities and Exchange Commission and Justice Department but he saw this as a serious flaw in America's system of corporate supervision. More pertinently though he suggests that 'Sarbox' (Sarbanes-Oxley), while being seen by some business observers as a sledgehammer to crack a corporate governance nut, was looking as though '. . . it might not even have cracked the nut . . . some of it is the result of a deep and continuing systemic problem in many companies, where incentives for executives and for shareholders are badly out of sync'. It is really not good for society when organizations have systemic failures and the interests of executives and the society they are meant to serve are so completely out of sync. Clear leadership is needed on this, so where is it ever going to come from?

THE POLITICIAN'S DEFINITION OF VALUE

It is probably too cynical to suggest that the politician's view of value is that which is likely to give them the most votes. Nevertheless, following our principle that if you want to influence somebody's behaviour you had better tap into their own individual motivation pattern, then if we want our politicians to help us maximize value we had better make sure they see it as a vote winner. Politicians may be masters of expediency but they are not, generally speaking, stupid. They allocate huge resources provided by taxpayers so they had better make sure that, if any party is going to get the best value out of those resources, it is seen to be theirs.

What we don't want to see are the sort of public declarations that politicians are so fond of, the grand or magnanimous gesture. When a minister is reacting to increasing crime figures, or lengthening hospital waiting lists, their simplistic statements that they will 'double the number of police officers or doctors' (or just insert whatever sector is currently in trouble), as if throwing money at such complex problems has any chance of success, should worry the electorate rather than reassure it. The voters (and more value focused opposition parties) should howl with derision at any attempt to improve outputs (reduce crime) simply by increasing inputs. We all know this to be true, so we need to demand value-driven solutions, based on proper root cause analysis, if we are to see a resolution to the issues we value so highly.

Even more derisory are the bold gestures of a Chancellor when he says in his budget speech '*I* have given £x million to single parents/pensioners/the unemployed' as though he were some philanthropic (and anachronistically paternalistic) industrialist doling out largesse from his hard-earned profits. All politicians should be reminded, at every available opportunity, that the money they take off us only to redistribute to us (and no doubt leaking value like a sieve in the process) is not their money and in no way signifies their philanthropy or that of their party's policies. Moreover, we need to add that they should take as little as necessary and use it as wisely as possible. When public spending is absorbing an ever-increasing and significant share of GDP the value motive should always be invoked as a salutary reminder.

So what recommendation might we have for any budding, value-driven politician? A very simple one. Understand the absolute simplicity of added value. All voters are intelligent enough to know that one £ more spent on sweeping the streets is one £ less available for drugs on the NHS. This is not rocket science. Resist the temptation to talk about increasing 'spending' and instead focus on the output and know what you are talking about. When you pour more money into the police or the health service, tell us what we will get for that money. Bring it down to a practical level that everyone can understand. If we plan to reduce, for example, the cost of bringing cancer patients to a point of remission then say that, and then tell us how it will be measured. If there is no absolute definition of 'remission' then tell us that you have managed to get the best cancer doctors in the country to agree on a meaningful measure; one that they all subscribe to and for which they are all prepared to be held accountable. How simple do these messages have to be to convince the voting public?

Some politicians also need to break the increasingly vicious and pernicious cycle of spin. Spin is not only anathema and antithetical to the value motive, the two tend to be directly but inversely related. The less value delivered by a government the more they have to spin. Suggesting tough and challenging performance targets in a vain attempt to win votes ('tough on crime and tough on the causes of crime'), without bothering to engage those on the ground who have to deliver, is bound to set up a downward spiral. Those who were not engaged are not committed and they fight the new system rather than support it. Therefore the targets are never achieved and the spin doctors have to bury them and produce new ones. The vicious cycle starts all over again. It will take a very bold politician to break this cycle but then isn't that precisely the sort of leadership we all ultimately crave? As a populace we don't mind taking our medicine, almost regardless of how strong and unpalatable it is, as long as we are convinced and fully accept that we need treatment. It would also help if the medicine had only been prescribed after a full and proper diagnosis of the ailment had taken place and we all were aware of the likely side effects.

What we do not want is more legislation. Previous legislation did not stop Enron, WorldCom or Parmalat (to name but the biggest, highest profile cases). Trying to legislate for value misses the whole point of the value motive, and, as anyone having to adhere to Sarbox will tell you, increases business costs significantly. It is the innate value motivation of the citizenry that has to be given its full and natural voice if we are to keep producing the sort of society we want. More legislation also falls foul of some of life's most unavoidable Catch-22s. If you legislate for corporate governance to improve (Sarbanes-Oxley) you have a chance, just a chance, that some of the already law-abiding, corporate 'governors' will stay on the right side of the law. But then the legislation was not really intended for those who were already law abiding. It was designed for the crooks and the cheats who will do whatever they can to take as much money out of a business by whatever means they can. There is plenty of evidence that legislation does not alter the attitudes or behaviours of crooks and cheats; except to find other, more devious, routes around the law. Those who are determined to jump the lights will not be deterred by adding more lights. Introducing legislation for those who are not inclined to be law abiding just creates more work for the police, lawyers and fraud squads and that could be sapping as much value as it creates (think of the costs of failed fraud cases).

Perhaps the politicians who are genuinely interested in reducing corruption (assuming they are not personally involved in such activity) should utilize the most powerful instrument of law known to man, the community. If the theory of probability and the performance curve (see Chapter 5) are fundamental truths about the makeup of society (i.e. transgressors form a very small minority) then we are fortunate that the vast majority of citizens are extremely law abiding and abhor those who are not. What better way to attack some of society's gravest ills than to mobilize these forces against them? Where are the annual reports demanded of companies that tell us everything we need to know about their value rather than their profits and losses and balance sheets? Where are the human capital reports that at least suggest that the company is doing everything it can to get the best value out of its people? But there is no need to cajole or coerce these companies. What we want is just a continuous stream of value information.

Are chocolate manufacturers (or most other modern food manufacturers for that matter) helping to overcome an obesity problem, which is reaching epidemic proportions, while they are making their profits? Pepsico and other food companies have been having discussions with the UK's Food Standards Agency over the proposals for 'signpost labelling', which tells consumers how much fat, salt and sugar goes into a product (see http://www.food.gov.uk/news/newsarchive/2006/jun/boardupdate) and we should ask what Pepsico's real motives are here. If society starts to really value this information then customers will have to start voting with their feet and their pockets. Equally, if fair trade organizations can convince us that they offer a viable alternative to profit-only organizations, by increasing competition and thereby giving more value in the longer term, then maybe more customers will vote for them. What politicians can do is put in place mechanisms and procedures that aim to ensure that proper recognition is given to those who are genuinely following the value motive, in both spirit and intent.

This is a simple recommendation but that does not automatically make it a naïve one. It is readily accepted that this represents a complete paradigm shift. Maybe that sounds like an oxymoron, how can we have a *simple* paradigm shift? Perhaps a more pertinent question would be how could we *not* have a simple paradigm shift? Where is the evidence in history that there has ever been such a development as a complex paradigm shift? The big paradigm shifts, independent travel (the advent of cars and mass transport), mass communication and computerization might all produce complex shifts in society but the simple essence of each one of those has been captured in no more than two words. More importantly, the vast majority of people are capable of understanding and using them all. Compare this to some of the supposed paradigm shifts that were meant to have happened in the business community. The paradigm shift from conventional accounting to balanced scorecards; from conventional to lean manufacturing; from quality control to quality assurance. How does anyone explain to a production line worker what a strategy alignment map is? All that has been achieved is a very patchy recognition that some of these represent real changes and very little common agreement as to what they really mean. More importantly, any results that may have been achieved from all of these supposed shifts often seem to be illusory.

THE FIRST, SECOND AND THIRD SECTORS HAVE TO BECOME ONE

One such paradigm shift was meant to be the third way. One version of this equates to some form of modern social democracy. To the simple economist it is somewhere between the pendulum swings of capitalism and socialism. We are unlikely to ever see a clear definition or description of what the third way might actually look like but, to those of us who can see the obvious weaknesses in both capitalism and socialism, the notion that there might be a hybrid third way has an immediate appeal; even without any discussion of practicalities. Well, maybe, just maybe, the value motive is and always has been the third way. Maybe it was always a case of waiting for its time to come. It has been staring us in the face for a long time but it has not been articulated as a coherent, socio-economic–political philosophy. We have all been happy to talk about value for money but not the totality of value with all of its implications and ramifications.

One recent development that puts this whole debate in a different light are several recent studies suggesting that western societies are no happier than they were in the 1950s. A visit to the Happiness Foundation (yes, such an organization really exists) tells us that, on their World Database of Happiness, Mexico scores higher (using a life satisfaction rating of 0 to 10) than the USA (and the UK). Perhaps pointing this out to those Mexicans trying to cross the border into the USA could be the best possible weapon the border patrols will ever have to deter illegal immigrants? There is definitely a discernible undercurrent in western society, and probably eastern societies as well, that the direction in which we are all heading may not be the best direction. Whether we pursue a third or even a fourth way there is a growing appetite for an alternative. Whatever alternative we choose though, it has to be one clear way. So the next key recommendation is to rid ourselves of our existing and increasingly outmoded false dichotomies.

If we start asking organizations to report, for example, on how well they utilize and capitalize on their human capital let us not see this as just another adjunct to existing corporate reporting regulations. Any organization should have a responsibility to do so because they are all commanding society's scarce resources and should be as accountable for them as possible. We want competition because competition is good. If an NHS hospital adds less value than a commercial hospital then we want more commercial hospitals and the legal entity we deal with is irrelevant in value terms (even if the law has to change to cope with that). Those wedded to the 'NHS ethos' will find it difficult to justify calling it ethical if patients suffer, in comparative terms.

Equally, fair trade organizations will have to convince us that fair trade not only has short-term goals but a longer-term goal of better, more valuable trade. If they cannot do that then the next best thing is to ensure that any 'lazy' coffee farmer (hypothetically) is not being supported by an otherwise laudable enterprise. Fair trade has to mean the best use of human capital as much as any commercial organization. The first challenge for these other sectors, therefore, is to be willing to use a universally acceptable common language of value.

The motivation levels in these sectors can be just as powerful, if not more so, than in those where profit is the key driver. Nevertheless, there needs to be a clear distinction made between arguments stemming from emotions and from those delivered with passion. Emotional arguments are those where the facts, evidence or sheer logic do not support the contention. In a Roffey Park (a UK management college) brochure of summer 2006 advertising its services, under the heading of 'research@roffeypark – Recognising the value of difference', it declares that 'There is a moral case for diversity since it is a good thing in itself.' Now, apart from the fact that defining the key terms in this sentence would be philosophically challenging, whether everyone would agree that there is indeed a self-evident, moral case for diversity is highly questionable. The brochure continues by asserting that 'There is also a business case', although it makes no attempt to actually present either of these cases for us. If we genuinely believe that, say, diversity means more women should have the opportunity of entering senior management then let us see the a priori case for this. Let us also see the a posteriori evidence and conclusions from those women who are in management already. Once we are clear that there is a substantial case let us argue it with all of the passion we can muster. Relying on unfounded arguments and assumptions will certainly not help the cause. This is all assuming, of course, that those who manage these other sector organizations have a fundamental belief in the principle of meritocracy.

Some organizations appear to encapsulate the best of both profit and value. The Grameen Bank (www.grameen-info.org) seems to be run on commercial lines but provides a high value service helping people to help themselves out of a spiral of poverty. In the more conventional charity field Oxfam was one of the pioneers of charity retailing to provide significant funds for putting towards their good causes. Both of these organizations might have their detractors but the value proposition from both seems crystal clear. They are only doing what they declared they have set out to do. So these other sectors, if they want to offer a different alternative, might actually make a stronger argument if they offered a fresh and improved method of organizational management. One that could even be adopted or adapted by the commercial sector. If they did, they might not leave themselves open to the sort of public reaction suggested by a survey carried out by think-tank nfp-Synergy (*The Times*, 20th June 2006), which declared that 'more than 80% of people think paying charity chief executives £60,000 a year is excessive ... (they) settled on £46,000 as an acceptable reward for running a charity with an income of between £10 million and £25 million'.

We have to ask ourselves what was influencing the attitudes of the people who took part in this survey? Do they believe that anyone working for a charity should be doing so at a lower salary than the market rate for their skills would suggest? Do those who work for charities have to follow a different set of rules and, if so, why? If market rates do not determine salaries, what set of rules would? Or are the people who answered the survey just reacting emotionally and plucking an arbitrary figure out of the air? Within the criteria and parameters set by a charity's value statement there is nothing wrong with it trying to attract as many donations as possible. If this is one of its goals then why should they not pay whatever they have to get the best chief executive, and by 'best' we mean someone who can create the largest funds possible? Charities have to compete for funds and therefore it makes sense that they should compete equally in the labour market for those who they think will do the best job for them. Having said that, if this survey is accurately revealing a public perception that different criteria should be applied to charitable organizations, then charities would do well to listen to them and start convincing prospective donors of the value of an 'expensive' CEO.

It is not just charities that have to think about how they are managed though. Precisely the same argument would apply to the chief executives, or any other managers, in any public sector or not-for-profit organization; especially when one views them from a value standpoint. Perhaps a more pertinent question therefore, that the survey team should have been asking, is not what should the CEOs be paid but why should management be paid at all? One would think that people who work for a charity are so committed they should not need much management. For example, one organization, Suma, which is a commercial concern but run along cooperative lines (http://www.suma.co.uk/aboutus. html), is a £20m, 120 employee, 100% employee-owned workers' cooperative which is a wholesaler of health foods and whole foods. Yet it describes itself as 'at heart, a political statement that workers can successfully manage their own businesses without an owner/manager elite'.

Whether we subscribe to these same values or not perhaps we should at least see if we can learn anything from their attempts at managing without managers. This should be of interest to any organization, particularly commercial concerns that have done everything in their power in recent decades to minimize the size and cost of management (some would say without much success). There is plenty to read on Suma's website but under the heading 'Working at Suma' they show that it '. . . is quite unlike other businesses. All our workers must be more self-motivated and take more initiative. SUMA departmental coordinators do not have an overseer role in the normal sense. Workers support each other in highly flexible teams.' The simple, obvious idea here is that if everyone owns an organization and shares its values, two of the main purposes of management (to control and obtain a certain performance level) become redundant. Anyone interested enough to read further will find this has not all been easy going but it is, nevertheless, a very interesting organization trying to produce a very different organizational design template for the future.

Suma is not alone in rethinking management. All sectors can learn from each other. Some of the more recent generation of industrial philanthropists are now being referred to as 'venture philanthropists' because they 'want to see returns on their "investment" and bring the discipline of business to their giving' (*Sunday Times*, 15th January 2006). Sir Tom Hunter, entrepreneur and founder of the retailer Sports Division, remarked that 'up to 5% of any donation made by the Hunter Foundation is spent on assessing (evaluating) the impact of donations'. Then, in case anyone might get the wrong impression about his motives, he adds that 'we want to see that our money has made a difference' and 'I am still committed to wealth creation – I have not turned into Mother Teresa'. Despite Tom Hunter wanting to maintain his capitalist credentials, probably because they are a genuine source of great pride to him, he obviously sees no real distinction to be made between making money and spending it wisely. He does not want to see anything wasted; the simplest test ever for anyone who professes to already following the value motive. If we all share his motivation then perhaps we should start to reconsider some organizations in this light.

VALUE SPECIAL CASES AND DEAD LOSSES

Having defined value earlier as outputs per £ it is now time to question, at last, whether some outputs are worth having at all. We are not going to get embroiled in trying to distinguish between 'good' and 'bad' outputs because that would be a point-less exercise. However, there are some outputs that we would all agree we would happily do without if we could. An obvious example would be litigation. No one would suggest that lawyers do not add value for their clients but the best value they can add is to save them ever going to court. Divorce lawyers can only agree a split of a fixed amount of assets. This is a zero sum game, one spouse's gain is the other spouse's loss. Society's goal is surely to have as little contractual wrangling as possible and arbitration to solve whatever disputes arise. This begs the obvious question whether law firms see it this way. Similarly, marriage guidance counselling services obviously help many couples through diffi-cult times but perhaps their goal should be resolving the root causes of marital disharmony and these go much further back and much deeper than after-the-event counselling.

In other words, the goal of some organizations is to put themselves out of business. These are difficult special cases because trying to get employees of such organizations motivated, to give of their best, means asking them to put themselves out of a job. The starkest examples of this type of organization are those who deal with complaints, whether it is a citizens' advice bureau or an ombudsman's office. The ultimate test of their value would be no complaints. Yet if you put it to such organizations that this should be part of their declared value statement it tends to elicit pained expressions and quizzical looks.

Other special cases are those organizations where the only benefit they bring is to a very narrow or vested interest. The most obvious examples would be public relations, lobbying or advertising agencies. There is nothing inherently non-value about any of these but asking them to justify their existence in value, rather than in profit terms or in terms of satisfying narrow vested interests, can be quite problematic for them. Take the example we used earlier of BP trying to promote a greener image. If this better image results in more drivers pulling into a BP garage to fill up, then the PR agency has helped BP to increase profits. But where is the added value to society if BP is actually no greener, in real terms, than its competitors? Conversely, if BP develops greener, more ecologically beneficial fuels, but consumers don't care because all they want is to drive their car, regardless of its environmental impact, then again where is the benefit? The added value for the PR agency would be to achieve both ends at once. They could also add value to society by convincing drivers to walk more, but it is unlikely that an oil company would see this as one of their goals. Which brings us back to tobacco companies.

We looked earlier at the tobacco company that set out, as part of its CSR agenda, to reduce the amount of young people smoking. If their goal really was to bring this to zero there would be a high probability that they would eventually put themselves out of business; assuming most smokers start young. We should keep asking these simple questions of such companies, not because of an ethical agenda, but from a management standpoint. How well can an organization be managed when it sends conflicting signals to its customers, its employees and its shareholders?

It is amazing how little attention we pay to this aspect of organizations. The UK's Royal Mail, until recently the official monopoly provider of public postal delivery services and one of the biggest employers in the world, has finally started to show some profits after having soaked up public subsidies for years. This profit is touted by Royal Mail's management as an indicator of how well they are managing the business. Yet, from a customer's perspective, the same management team has increased the cost of postage; reduced the number of deliveries per day; been less specific about collection times on post boxes; has chosen to deliver more mail by road rather than rail (for cost saving purposes, regardless of the environmental impact); reneged on an earlier decision to limit the amount of junk mail we all receive;

offered cars as an incentive to get workers to come to work; suggested giving the same workers free shares when Royal Mail is privatized (despite the same workers' unions having resisted productivity improvements through automation for many years) and is now introducing pricing by size of letter as well as by weight (presumably to increase average revenue per item although that is not their declared intention). It would be very difficult for anyone in Royal Mail's management to express any of this in added value terms but it is about time someone in government at least asked the question. The Royal Mail also provides us with a perfect example of how not to reconcile employee behaviours with the strategic goals of the organization. In 2006 they suspended one of their own postmen for telling his customers how they could stop receiving junk mail, because this would reduce their revenue.

Many Royal Mail customers will feel that the value of the service they are getting is diminishing. Customers are not stupid and already apply their own value criteria to areas where no profit is made. Charities are now under much more pressure than they ever used to be to show what percentage of the money they collect actually ends up in the hands of the causes they purport to serve. Common sense and human nature will encourage any donor to put their money where it is seen to be used to best advantage. The 2004 tsunami appeal brought on itself some very adverse publicity when it was discovered that some of the charities involved were not able to actually spend all of the money they had collected. This would have largely been solved by making sure that those who donated through the Disaster Emergency Fund ticked a box indicating they were happy for their donation to be used wherever the DEF deemed it worthwhile. These are all simple, obvious management failings that should never have arisen but they still do. The value motive and the disciplined questioning that goes with it will reduce such aberrations significantly.

The final group of special cases we might look at would be quangos and NGOs – organizations with no real accountability as they sit on the periphery. Inevitably they try to influence from a distance but to what extent do they even try to add value and do they accept any responsibility and accountability? Most UN bodies fall into this category. Take the International Labour Organization, which attempts to provide decent work in countries where there are abuses of child labour and even slavery. However committed these UN officials undoubtedly are, it is only their value, or lack of it, on which we should base our judgements. Their output is not to write reports or produce surveys but to reduce the incidence of child labour.

Where an organization has even fewer distinct outputs than this (take the BBC or any broadcasting organization), we need to ask even more searching questions and force them to declare what they value. High quality drama or soap operas? Top notch documentaries or cheap game shows? If we take away the customer's normal mechanism for making their choices known, that is having a choice whether to spend their money on a licence fee or pay-per-view satellite programmes, then such organizations have an even more pressing need to declare what their value is going to be. How about actual versus planned viewing figures for every £1000 spent on production? Regardless of the range and type of organizations that we might consider from a value perspective, should there be any fundamental difference between the way they are managed? This brings us around to one of the sorest points of all – management education itself.

VALUE MANAGEMENT EDUCATION

According to the sort of statistics beloved by business schools from around the world, getting an MBA increases your salary by anything up to about 60%. It is pointless bothering to challenge the veracity of this statistic because even if it were true it does not actually tell us what the business schools want it to tell us. It may well be true that the difference between someone's salary before they do their MBA and what they manage to earn afterwards shows a significant increase, but there are two pieces of information missing in this equation. First, it does not tell us that gaining the MBA *caused* the huge increase. Second, it does not tell us whether the organizations that pay the extra salaries get better outputs or value from their newly qualified MBAs. Certainly Enron's talent management programme, replete with young and thrusting, MBA-qualified managers, could hardly be called a success.

Henry Mintzberg, in his book *Managers not MBAs* (FT Prentice Hall, 2004), argues that putting very young and inexperienced people through an MBA does not teach them the real management skills that make the difference. Those skills and the crucial experiences that reinforce them can only be learned in the crucible of day-to-day operational management. There is not much new in this supposedly iconoclastic view though. The late Peter Drucker (*The Times*, 19th January 2006) roundly condemned Harvard Business School which he said 'combines the worst of German academic arrogance with bad American theological habits'. For his pains Drucker was, not surprisingly, left off the syllabus of some business schools. The suggestion in this article was that the main reason Drucker was not in many schools' curricula was that his work crossed too many boundaries for the sort of silo course teaching methods used on MBA programmes. It is the disjointed and disconnected nature of this amalgam of academic disciplines that is probably the biggest weakness, not just on MBA programmes, but in management education generally. How many managers have been on the 'finance for non-financial managers course' and why has there never been a counter-balancing course called 'non-finance matters for financial managers'? No wonder accountants are still using methods of double entry bookkeeping invented over 500 years ago because we still think everything revolves around them.

There is a definite lack of synthesis in management thinking and therefore management education. Hence we see organizations going for 'lean' (not even lean production) when it is crystal clear that they are not aware of all the other elements involved in Toyota's original, holistic philosophy of kaizen. You also see organizations that try to skip several steps in their evolutionary journey of organizational maturity. So the NHS is now trying to become lean when it is obvious that many of their doctors do not want 'production line' thinking to infiltrate what they see as the preserve of high quality professionals (see Chapter 4). In effect, any organization trying to follow a particular management model, especially if it is only a partial model rather than a holistic one, risks alienating its own managers who will always subscribe to their own mental models.

This is one of the most obvious failings in current management education, the whole concept that management needs a model, be it total quality management, business re-engineering, balanced scorecards or CSR. The models have been so overemphasized that they have displaced the ultimate goal, value creation, as the focus of management thinking. They have allowed managers who say 'here is our scorecard' off the hook. We should be asking them to show us the value of what they are doing not the techniques they employ. Toyota became the leading automotive company in the world, after starting at a severe disadvantage, by becoming obsessed with value not by drawing performance scorecards. If managers want to beat a path to any door then it should be towards the doors where the methodologies have clearly demonstrated their superiority. Just as we should not waste our time trying to distinguish between profit and not-for-profit organizations, we should not be comparing balanced scorecards with European Quality Awards. The whole notion of management 'models' misses the point; value is unique to a particular

organization and its customer base, because it is a unique reconciliation of differing values. Models are OK as guides but they
are increasingly being used as a complete modus operandi and
this encourages blind adherence rather than intelligent, mature
and adaptive thinking.

It might be because we have seen a plethora of 'new' management theories over the last half-century (although the old
adage that there is nothing new under the sun is a salutary
reminder) that there has been a belief that all of this amounts to
huge organizational change. We have therefore seen many so-
called change management programmes trying to engender a
greater customer focus (whatever that means) or a more responsive organization, or some similarly nebulous inexactitude, but
has there ever been a need for real fundamental change? After
all, there is plenty of evidence that people and their values do
not fundamentally change throughout their lives. Anyone interested in reading the history of Toyota will see that the principles
that underpinned the organization in 1937 are still those which
guide it today. To all outward appearances it has changed in many
ways, especially being in an industry that has to constantly change
technology and vehicle design. But the values and behaviours that
create the value from engineering, technology and design have
been the same all along.

Western management education has completely misread the
philosophy of continuous improvement (and all that implies) as
necessitating continuous change when it means quite the opposite. It means progress based on a consistency that many western
organizations have failed to establish, and are unlikely to, when
the average tenure of a FTSE 100 CEO is less than five years
(*The Times*, 2nd July 2005 – "Top bosses last only 4½ years
on average"). The corporations that reacted to Champy and
Hammer's exhortations to re-engineer (*Re-engineering the Corporation*, 1996) had probably already moved onto another management fad by the time the authors admitted that most re-engineering

projects did not actually deliver value. Those who subscribe to balanced business scorecards should also note that Kaplan and Norton would attest to the fact that many scorecards do not deliver value either.

In summary, whatever reasons lie behind the inexorable growth in business schools, management theories, models and the qualifications they produce, we have found ourselves in the 21st century in a position where there is no consensus on what the key ingredients of organizational success are. That in itself is a serious indictment but not as serious as a much simpler fact, which is that there is not even a consensus on what a universal criterion of success might look like. Where is the common definition of value? Alternative organizational forms and entities have only served to confuse this debate. Perhaps we should dust off a relatively old 'new' management concept, that of 'world class' (where you just had to add your own words such as engineering, manufacturing etc.), and restate it very simply as that which can be seen to be focused on creating maximum value. This is not a relative term though. When we say the pursuit of maximum value we have to mean it, if it is ever to qualify for the title of truly world class. So what auditing methodology would be required to convince us that this title had really been earned?

AUDITING THE VALUE MOTIVE

It is high time those of us interested in value challenged accounting conventions and the auditing methods they have spawned. There are considerable problems with current methods of accounting and financial control:

- they often treat people as overheads rather than as a source of value;

- they have no way of indicating the difference between an organization that manages its people well and those that do not;
- they tend to be more concerned with controlling costs rather than unleashing value;
- they are generally working on historical figures rather than accurate predictors of future performance;
- the performance measures used are often pure activities and disconnected from the value chain;
- they subscribe to a fallacious concept of intangibles and then compound the crime by failing to measure them;
- they purport to check that financial and control systems are working but have no methodology for auditing human systems.

Whatever motive drives an organization, all shareholders and prospective investors, financial and investment analysts, governments, customers and employees will have an interest in anything that tells them how well the organization is doing. Not just in terms of last year's financials but future longer-term prospects. Will its management methods of today stand the test of time in an increasingly uncertain and competitive world? If Norton was disappointed with progress in this area up to 2001 he would not receive any reassurance that things are getting any better in 2006 if he looks at the UK DTI's (Department for Trade and Industry) Value Added Scoreboard which defines value added simply as sales less the cost of bought-in goods and services, takes a historical perspective and uses simplistic correlations instead of trying to establish causation.

Auditing authorities are increasingly tasked with trying to provide real insights into the value of organizations but their technology is just not up to the job. No one who subscribes to the notion of intangible assets has found a satisfactory way of measuring them, especially those relating to human capital (knowledge, creativity, innovation, initiative, judgement). Is this because intangibles are, by definition, difficult to measure or is it because the concept of intangibles is just plain wrong? If we look at some of the latest thinking in the accounting and investment community (*Accounting for Investment Analysts – An International Perspective*, updated for IFRS2005 by Kenneth M. Lee, 3rd edition, 2004 BG Consulting Group Ltd, London) the word 'human' does not even appear in the index. Moreover, intangible assets are defined as 'an asset with no physical presence'. He continues by observing that 'Typically such assets pose difficulties for accountants and analysts. These mainly arise because it is very difficult to measure value.' Yet he admits 'the capitalisation of intangibles is a highly relevant issue when analysing financial statements . . . Intangibles have become increasingly important for valuing companies as physical assets become less important.' So here we have an admission that the disease exists with no hint of a cure.

What such observers are saying is that organizations are organic. They grow and mutate and looking at share price or price/earning ratios does not offer any insights into the workings of the organism itself. Understanding the nature of the organism is key to explaining the vast discrepancies between book values and market capitalization or market value. Share prices in many industries are volatile, to say the least, and can swing in either direction for the flimsiest of reasons (an analyst recommends 'sell') on a daily basis. If the Dow Jones or the FTSE is at an all-time high or low does this tell us anything meaningful about the long-term, value-creating potential of these businesses? Organic value comes largely from the quality of the people and how they are organized; the human systems and processes, the culture and the esprit de corps that some organizations seem able to cultivate. Value is not a quick win or an easy target. By its very nature it demands organizational leadership that will stick with it through thick and thin. It also requires managing the people side of the business in a very different way.

A NEW MANAGEMENT DISCIPLINE – VALUING THE HUMAN CONTRIBUTION

Of all the management disciplines currently available to an organization the biggest, most serious and most glaring omission is a
failure to produce a credible discipline to measure and manage
the value of people. Very rarely, if ever, is people management
seen as a competitive differentiator. One supermarket may manage
its supply chain, logistics, purchasing or marketing better than
another but do any of them set out with the specific strategic
goal of managing their people better than their competitors?
People issues are often intractable and unpredictable so dealing
with them is difficult and is usually left until last or even avoided
altogether, if at all possible. Large corporations think they can
just build any people problems into their P&L. They try to just
pay for whatever employee relations they want. Unfortunately,
this short-sighted approach has been seen to fail time and time
again. Esso (now Exxon) negotiated their famous Fawley agreement (for the Fawley refinery near Southampton, UK) as far back
as 1960. At the time it was hailed as a landmark agreement and
ended up as the worst of all worlds; high wages, poor productivity, low motivation and the constant threat of industrial action.
Because labour costs were a fraction of total costs in the oil
industry managers thought they did not have to manage it. They
thought they could buy it off. Management can no longer just
factor in people costs; a lesson that organizations such as GM and
Ford still have to learn. It is not people costs that they have to
manage well but people value.

We might have hoped that the proliferation of MBAs would
have heralded a new enlightenment but recent examples prove
otherwise. British Airways, apart from playing a 'dirty tricks'
campaign (which it lost) with its upstart rival Virgin, has shown
just how entrenched outmoded management attitudes are. It
also reveals the extent to which we have not developed effective

methods for resolving some of the most intractable people problems in long-established businesses. Three successive major industrial relations disputes in successive years (2003 to 2005) under chief executive Rod Eddington brought about no fundamentally different attitude from management to employee relations. Rod Eddington was fêted, as he retired, for turning around BA's fortunes and bringing it back to profitability. Many business pundits praised him and he is still highly respected. The figures speak for themselves. Comparative turnover for 2004/2005 was £8.9bn and £7.8bn respectively, with profits of £5m and £415m. The profit increase was primarily the result of huge staff cuts from 65640 to 45000. While some observers might argue it took strong management to see the staff cuts through, it is still just the oldest and most obvious trick in the book for executives who are struggling to produce a profit. So this could hardly be described as new or enlightened thinking. We need not dwell here either on what these figures tell us about Rod Eddington's predecessors who managed to get themselves into such an over-manned situation in the first place. Good industrial relations is not just about keeping the planes flying but getting more value out of every employee. BA and many other large corporations have still not learnt this simple lesson.

Usually, any explicit attempts to manage people are managed and disseminated under the auspices of the policies, initiatives and programmes of the HR department. A function that has never developed a sufficiently rigorous set of disciplines to manage people for greatest value. Just ask the HR team what value they add and you will never receive a convincing answer. This is because conventional HR theory is born out of the same silo, management mentality and management education system. It subscribes wholeheartedly to the concept of intangibles and therefore regards any attempt at linking all human activity to value, through a clear value chain, as unworkable. Worse still, often the worst PC (politically correct) 'police' reside in the HR team with their personal agendas of the glass ceiling or ageism, so they do not even try and they see no reason why the glass ceiling should not be more of a priority than profit maximization. Instead it tells its board to trust its use of 'best HR practice'.

Boards of directors who employ such HR people get everything they deserve. They have generally, either through complicity or complacency, happily left the HR team to it, knowing that employees will at least feel that someone is on their side and looking after their interests; and that saves them having to do that personally. They abdicate their leadership role of declaring and delivering a vision. HR becomes a buffer between the cold imperatives of senior management and the need to maintain commitment in the workforce. Really caring about your employees is hard work, so all of this militates against sound people management. Profit-making managers want a money-making formula, they do not seek out strategic human resource challenges. Some even think technology is king and will do everything for them. Hence call centre growth and outsourcing that replaces people in the equation whenever and wherever technology allows.

In these circumstances HR departments have managed to make themselves irrelevant to the pursuit of value, which is why they are so rarely a credible or loud voice in the boardroom. Yet there still remains the huge challenge, as Kenneth Lee openly admits, of somehow managing the things that organizations cannot show easily on a P&L or balance sheet. What is called for is not a revised HR team but a complete shift in management thinking. The value motive requires a different management discipline. A totally joined-up, holistic and systemic discipline. When companies are being taken over and restructured there needs to be someone who has the expertise to see where the value of the human contribution fits. They have to spot leaks in value from employees who do not share the values of their new employer. They have to stand up to bean counters who see people as overheads and convince them of the need to distinguish between those who do add value and those that do not. This is an emerging management discipline in its own right. Let us call it human value management, for want of a better title. So what will distinguish it from all others?

Well, for a start, it is not a single discipline. It is complete and holistic. This means marketing, operations, finance, sales, production, IT and R&D all have to reshape themselves around it. For example, the IT teams who always scoff at the ignorance of their management colleagues, those unable to specify exactly what they want from their new IT systems, will have to wipe the smug, knowing smiles off their faces. The IT team's value cannot be judged by the quality of their IT systems but by the same value outputs as everyone else. Suggesting any of these functions is an island and managed well, in its own right, will be seen as the nonsense it has always been under the rule of the value motive. In one worst case scenario a large pharmaceutical company runs its IT operation as a completely separate division from the rest of the organization. What signals does that send about joined-up thinking, competing cultures and value? Value means working together, we all know that, but human value management will have to be a very clever discipline that makes people want to work together towards the common goal of value.

The very first step in that discipline, declaring the value statement (see Chapter 2), is not only intended to make all department heads see very clearly what value means for them personally but also to give them an opportunity to openly challenge it. It is the fudging of value objectives that stores up internal conflicts and rivalries for future battles. Effective line managers can only do so much on their own. Human value management is ensuring his or her efforts complement everyone else's. One line manager cannot vouch for the cooperation of all members of other departments. They have no say in this matter yet still have to rely on others if they are to create value. In effect, human value management is doing everything that a line manager cannot do, on their own, to get the best value out of people. This means that all managers have to adopt the same rules of the game, follow the same system, embody the same principles. This is not an objective, sterile discipline, it has to be rooted in the values of the people who work in the organization. Admittedly, principles, almost by definition, are difficult to stick to and no one sticks to their own principles 100% but at least they guide our behaviour in a very consistent, unshakeable fashion. Having principles that mean something, and continually trying to work more closely to them, provides a very solid foundation on which to build great value.

Let us never forget though that probably the most natural, evolutionary, human motivation of all will always be personal survival, which means, first and foremost, looking after one's own interests. Fortunately this is very closely followed by a desire to look after the interests of others, because we all know that is also in our own best interests. With value, both sets of interests are simultaneously integrated and reinforcing. With profit only the first predominates and the second becomes a desirable by-product, if we are lucky. But the profit motive can guarantee neither. The value motive has been staring society in the face for many years. It is now time for it to assert itself.

So, if we really want our organizations to create as much value as possible this needs to be their single, unambiguous goal. Any ambiguity, confusion or dissent will immediately reduce the probability of reaching that goal. Real value management is not for the weak willed or the half-hearted. The challenge it represents is huge and there will always be more value to be mined. As much as the ordinary citizen will want as much value for themselves, through their own earning power and the wise use of their taxes, they will not always rush, unaided, to produce as much value as they can in their own working environment. They need leadership and encouragement, not to give them the necessary motivation but to unleash that which is already latent within all of us.

Is it too naïve to expect capitalists to suddenly offer maximum value? Of course it is. Sharing knowledge, for example, inherent in the search for value, is often anathema to competing profit-driven companies. Car companies only share design costs with competitors when they have to. Our best hope is that those who do seek real value will not only set an example but will make those who adhere to the purist version of the profit motive less competitive. Our governments, who have a vested interest in creating societal value, should do everything they can to aid this transformation process and being hard on white-collar crime and the abuse of monopolies must remain at the top of their agenda.

The real, final irony in all of this of course is that the value motive should produce more profit than the profit motive; as Toyota and other value-driven organizations have already proved. So let us try singing the praises of the value motive, at the tops of our voices, together, in perfect harmony.

INDEX

absenteeism 193, 212
abuse of power 5
accountability 42
Accounting for People Taskforce 211
act of faith management
        practices 220–1
activity measures 150–3
added value 41–4, 48, 49–50, 70, 136
    definition 41, 42, 72
    as a distillation process 51–4, 148
    intangibles and 71–5
    variables 42, 48, 50–1, 72
added value measures 150–3
added value performance 171, 172
affirmative action plan 206
age discrimination 209–10
Air Touch Communications 93
alcohol consumption 98
allocation of scarce resources 1–7
altruism 79
ambition 77–8
Arthur Andersen 78
Asda 212
assessment centres 174
asset stripping 9, 44–7
Audit Commission 143–4
auditing the value motive 249–51

Baker, Gerard 231
balanced scorecard 131–2, 175, 192,
        236, 247, 249
banking 45, 228–30
    ethics of 9–10
baseline valuation 48
basic value 37–41, 60, 136, 139
BAT 99
BBC 245
Becker 132
benchmarking 173–4, 212
Bentham, Jeremy 91, 224
Berners-Lee, Tim 12
Big Issue, The 118, 119–20
Blair, Tony 83, 84
blame cultures 134, 220
blame game 185–6
Bond, Sir John 228
book values 188
BP 191–2, 204, 226, 242–3
brand 53
Branson, Sir Richard 2, 82
British Airways (BA) 57–9, 252, 253
British Medical Association 123
Browne, Lord John 226
Buffett, Warren 12
business failures 148

business re-engineering *see* re-engineering

Cadbury 185, 207
Cadbury Schweppes 97
Canon 26, 57, 92
capitalism 2, 4, 15, 16, 23, 88–91, 102, 103, 113, 226, 236
cartels 5
causality 172–3, 174–5
centralism 219
Cereal Partner World-wide (CPW) 107–8
change management 158, 248
charities 19, 105, 239–40, 244
child labour 8, 110, 245
Churchill, Winston 89, 185
Citigroup 35–6, 95
Dr Evil computer program 227
closed loop feedback system 164
Coca-Cola 80–2, 83, 84–5, 108
C2 brand 82, 84
Dasani water 82, 84, 156, 204
Common Agricultural Policy (CAP) 226
communism 2, 219
Compaq/Hewlett Packard merger 63–6
competence frameworks 174
compliance 60
continuous improvement 248–9
Co-operative Bank 9–10
cooperativism 2
corporate social responsibility (CSR) 23, 58, 106–17, 247
correlation approach 172, 175
cost/benefit analysis 70, 146
costs 42, 72
crazy frog franchise 102
creativity 43–4, 73–4
critical value 38
culture shift 158
customer engagement 159
customer intimacy 159
customer satisfaction 55, 64, 158, 159, 176
CVC 46

de Bono, Edward 136
Debenhams 46–7
decentralism 219
deconstruction 175
Dell 66
Department of Trade and Industry (DTI) 110, 211, 250
Diageo 97
discrimination
age 209–10
racial 206–7
distillation process, value as 185
diversity 205–10, 238
Dodge brothers 24
double entry bookkeeping 216–17, 247
Drucker, Peter 54, 143, 246
drugs industry 108–9
dual surgery system 121

Ebbers, Bernie 78
EBIT (earnings before interest and tax) 29
EBITDA (earnings before interest and tax, depreciation and amortization) 29
economic system, value as 85–8
Eddington, Rod 253
Edison, Thomas 95
Edwards Deming, W. 143
employee attitudes 53–4
employee performance curve 178–81, 197–8
employee performance management 178–85
employee satisfaction 176
employee–customer–profit chain theory 176–8, 220
Enron 29, 78, 106, 184, 231, 234, 246
entrepreneur 5, 148
environmentalism 23
Esso 252
Ethical Trading Initiative 111
ethics 8, 97, 98, 111, 113, 114
banking 9–10
ethnic diversity 206–7

Ethnic Minority Employment Task
    Force 206
European Commission 3
European Foundation for Quality
    Management (EFQM)
    business excellence model 134–6
    management 110, 192, 210
European Quality awards 247
European Union 3, 110, 209
    Competition Commission 14, 88
evaluation 161–5
exploitation 5
externalities 67
Exxon 252
ExxonMobil 191

fair trade 113, 114–16, 235, 238
feedback sheet 151, 152
Fielden, Dr Jonathan 121, 123
Financial Services Authority 35
Fiorina, Carly 65–6
flexibility 219–20
Food Standards Agency (UK) 235
Ford, Bill 25
Ford, Henry 24–5, 36
Ford Motor Company 24–6, 27, 28,
    35, 57, 73, 169, 211, 217, 252
FTSE 100 Index 177
full time equivalent (FTV) 171–2

Gates, Bill 11–16, 118
Gates Foundation, Bill and Melinda 12,
    13, 14
GE 54, 179
General Mills 107–8
General Motors (GM) 27, 28, 35, 169,
    211, 217, 218, 252
Ghosn, Carlos 209
globalization 22–3
Goldman Sachs 93, 94, 95, 96
Google 15
Grameen Bank 239
Grandmet 97
greed 5, 48
Green, Stephen 227–8
Green Book 146

Gregory, Alan 45
GSK 83

Hanson, Lord 44
Happiness Foundation 237
Harvard Business School 246
healthcare 6, 108–9, 154–6
    resources 224–5
    systems 83–4, 121–4
Hewitt, Patricia 83, 84
Hewlett, Bill 65
Hewlett, Walter 63, 65, 66
Hewlett-Packard 67
    Compaq merger 63–6
holistic value management 185–7
Honda 217
hospitals, inspection 143
hours of work 128
House of Commons Public Accounts
    Committee 144
HSBC 227, 228
human asset accounting (HAA) 215
human asset valuation (HAV) 215
Human Capital Index (HCI) 172
human capital management
    (HCM) 210–14, 220, 221,
    222
human capital measurement 189,
    216–22
human resources departments 253–4
human resources scorecards 132
human rights 23, 113
human value management 255–6
Hunter, Sir Tom 241
Hunter Foundation 241
Huselid 132

industrial relations disputes 253
inspection, government philosophy
    of 143–4
intangible assets 250–1
intangibles 33, 43, 71–5, 188
    measuring and managing 156–61
    people 187–92
integrity 54
Intel 226

intellectual capital 216
International Labour Organization 245
internet 12
Internet Explorer 15
intrinsic value 37–8
invisible hand 93
Islam 92–3
IT systems 255

Japanization 27
JJB 110, 111
John Lewis Partnership 212–13

kaizen 247
Kaplan, Robert 131, 134, 249
Kelloggs 41
Kershaw, Nigel 118
key performance indicators (KPIs) 128–9
key ratio 172
Kross, Katie 108
kyosei 26

Lawrence, Stephen 208
Lay, Kenneth 78
Leadership Trust 224
leadership, value motive as 223–31
lean organizations 247
lean production techniques 173, 175
lean systems 124
Lee, Kenneth 254
Lev, Baruch 188
Lewis, John 215
Lewis, Spedan 213
Lexus 73
litigation 242
Logie-Baird, John 95

Macpherson Report 208
management by objectives (MBO) 143
management information system (MIS) 128, 129, 132, 143, 194, 197
management philosophy 219

Marck Sharpe Dohme 107
market price 5
Marks & Spencer's 177–8
mass production 24, 25
Matako, John 45
maximum value 249
MBAs 246, 252
McMahon, Ian 97
Mead, Scott 93, 94, 95, 96
measurables 33
Merck, George 107
merger and acquisitions 45, 63–6
meritocracy 238
Merril Lynch 46
Metropolitan Police 208
Microsoft 118, 226
    Media Player 14
    Office 12, 13
    Windows 12, 13, 31
    Xbox 13, 15
Microsoft Paradox 11–17, 96
Mintzberg, Henry 246
misanthropy 96
mission statement 54–6, 57
monopolies 11–13
moral value of equal rights 205
motivation 2
motive, power of 77–9
multiplier effect 147, 148
must-haves 38
MySpace 15

National Audit Office 143
National Centre for Popular Music 21–2, 147
National Health Services (NHS) 6, 83, 84, 108–9, 122–4, 222, 224–5, 233, 247
    ethos 237
National Institute of Drug Abuse 109
Nestlé SA 107
Netcare UK 123
Netscape 15
networks 149
nfp-Synergy 239

Nike 112–13
Nissan 209
non-critical value 38–9
non-for-profit, definition 17
non-governmental organizations
    (NGOs) 245
non-profit, definition 17
non-profit sectors 5
non-profit-making organizations 17
normal distribution curve 178–81
Norton, David 131, 132, 134, 249,
    250
not-for-profit organizations 49, 117
not-for-value organization 21, 117

Office for National Statistics
    (ONS) 145
organic foods 112
organic values 251
organization 186–7
Oxfam 239

paradigm shift 235–6
Parker, Sir Peter 4
Parmalat 29, 106, 234
people challenge 227
people management 167–71, 219
    failure in 194–5
    style 219
people measurement box 193–22
people value, measurement of 171–5
Pepsico 235
performance bands, predetermined
    196
performance curve 234
performance measurement
    vs activity and added value
        measures 150–3
    employee 178–85
    purpose of 153–6
    theory vs practice 142–50
personal capital 215–16
personal values 91, 92
Peters, Tom 135
philanthropy 4, 11, 12, 15, 16
Philpott, John 144, 145, 151

police force inspection 143
politically correct agenda 70, 71
post-rationalization 175
price/earning ratios 251
private equity buy-out 46
private equity partnerships 45
probability, theory of 234
production line techniques, surgery
    and 121–2, 123
profit and loss accounting 216
profit, definition 4, 7–8, 18
profit motive 1–7
programme of change 158–9
public enquiries 186
public relations 242–3
public sector 120–6, 222
public service 105, 122
public spending 232
public statement, value in 54–62

quality 42, 72
quangos 245
quantity of output 42, 72
quasi-markets 5, 6

RAC 212
racial discrimination 206–7
racism 208–9
rape conviction rate 199–204
rate tarts 230
Real Player 14
real value management 256
re-engineering 48, 66, 93, 94, 158,
    247–9
refocusing 158
regional development agency 149,
    150
Reid, John 186
reputation 53
return on investment (ROI)
    human capital 171
    for intangibles 159–61
revenue 42, 72
Rockefeller, John 225
Roosevelt, Teddy 225
root cause analysis 174

Rowe, Dr Mike 208
Royal Mail 243–4

Saratoga Institute 171
Sarbanes-Oxley Act 89, 189, 231, 234
scapegoats 185–6
school inspection 143
scorecard 130–4, 210, 220
  balanced 131–2, 175, 192, 236, 247, 249
  human resources 132
Sears 176–7
Securities and Exchange Commission (US) 231
share prices 251
Shell 190–1, 222
Sheppard, Lord Allen 97
signpost labelling 235
skewed curve 199
Skype 15
Smith, Adam 3–4, 48, 88, 93
Smith, David 124
smoking 98–9
social change 118
social enterprise 23, 97, 117–20, 125
Social Enterprise Alliance 117
Social Enterprise Coalition 117, 118
social justice 93
social mission 117
social purpose 118
socialism 102, 236
spin 233–4
Sports Division 241
staff turnover 193, 212
Standard & Poor's 217
Standard Oil 225
standards 39
statistics, failures in 172
Stelzer, Irwin 225, 226
strategic objectives 117
strategy maps 134
Suma 240–1
Sun Microsystems 14

Sunday Times 100 Best Companies to Work 177
Sunderland, John 97, 207
supply chain management 110, 173
surplus 8–9, 16, 19–20
sweatshops 187–8
synergies 46
systems 85–8

talent management programme 185
talking shop 149
tangibles 74
taxation 69, 102, 121
Taylorism 24
Teresa, Mother 2
Tesco 53, 111, 112, 116
Texas Pacific 46
Thatcherism 105
third sector 104, 105–6, 109
'third way' 103, 104, 236–7
3 box system 136–42
  added value activities 139–40
  must-have activity 137–9
  nice-to-have activities 140–2
title capital 215
tobacco industry 98–9
total quality management 247
Toyota Motor Corporation 24, 25, 28, 35, 57, 92, 133, 169, 217, 218, 221, 222, 247, 248, 257
  Global Vision 2010 26–7
traffic light systems 86–7, 125, 221
triangulation 145
triple bottom line 106–17
Trotsky, Leon 113
Trump, Donald 2
turf wars 220

Ulrich 132
underperformers 195
unemployment 45, 118
unethical employment practices 110
unions 24
United Nations 245
unmeasurables 33

Value Added Scoreboard 250
value
    definition of 29–34, 34–7, 59–60,
        102
    politician's definition of 231–6
value agenda 62–4
value for money 47
value management education 245–9
value needs 70
value organizations 19
value statement 20, 56–62, 255
    for commercial company 63–8
    definition 56
    for a public sector organization
        68–71
value to society 12
value words 32–3
VAT registration 148
venture philanthropists 241

Virgin group 82, 83, 252
vision 57
vitality curve 179
Vodafone 93–4, 95

Wal-Mart 111, 212
Watt, James 79
Watts, Sir Philip 190
Weill, Sandy 36, 95
Welch, Jack 54, 179
whistleblowers 78
wine industry 2–3
World Database of Happiness 237
WorldCom 29, 78, 106, 234
Wyatt, Watson 172

Xbox (Microsoft) 13, 15

Yaquby, Sheikh Nizam 92

Index compiled by Annette Musker